TEXTUAL SOURCES FOR THE STUDY OF RELIGION
edited by John R. Hinnells

Hinduism

TEXTUAL SOURCES FOR THE STUDY OF RELIGION

Judaism ed. P. S. Alexander
Zoroastrianism ed. Mary Boyce
Sikhism ed. W. H. McLeod
Islam ed. A. Rippin and J. Knappert

Further titles are in preparation

TEXTUAL SOURCES FOR THE STUDY OF

Hinduism

edited and translated
by Wendy Doniger O'Flaherty

**with Daniel Gold, David Haberman
and David Shulman**

Manchester
University Press

Copyright [c] Wendy Doniger O'Flaherty 1988

Published by MANCHESTER UNIVERSITY PRESS
Oxford Road, Manchester M13 9PL

British Library cataloguing in publication data
Textual sources for the study of Hinduism. –
(Textual sources for the study of religion)
1. Hinduism
I. O'Flaherty, Wendy Doniger   II. Series
294.5   BL1202

ISBN 0–7190–1866–8 *hardback*
0–7190–1867–6 *paperback*

CONTENTS

9 The Tamil tradition *David Shulman*   168

GENERAL INTRODUCTION

This series is planned to meet a fundamental need in the study of religions, namely that for new, reliable translations of major texts. The first systematic attempt to provide such translations was the monumental *Sacred Books of the East* in the nineteenth century. These were pioneering volumes but, naturally, are now somewhat out of date. Since linguistic studies have advanced and more materials have come to light it is important to make some of these findings of twentieth-century scholarship available to students. Books in this series are written by specialists in the respective textual traditions, so that students can work on the secure foundation of authoritative translations of major literary sources.

But it is not only that linguistic and textual studies have advanced in the twentieth century. There has also been a broadening of the perspective within which religions are studied. The nineteenth-century focus was largely on scriptural traditions and the 'official' theological writings of the great thinkers within each tradition. Religious studies should, obviously, include such materials; but this series also reflects more recent scholarly trends in that it is concerned with a much wider range of literature, with liturgy and legend, folklore and faith, mysticism and modern thought, political issues, poetry and popular writings. However important scriptural texts are in a number of religions, even the most authoritative writings have been interpreted and elucidated; their thoughts have been developed and adapted. Texts are part of living, changing religions, and the anthologies in this series seek to encapsulate something of the rich variety to be found in each tradition. Thus editors are concerned with the textual sources for studying daily religious life as exemplified in worship or in law as well as with tracing the great movements of thought. The translations are accompanied by generous annotation, glosses and explanations, thus providing valuable aids to understanding the especial character of each religion.

Books in this series are intended primarily for students in higher education in universities and colleges, but it is hoped that they will be of interest also for schools and for members of some, at least, of the religious communities with whose traditions they are concerned.

John R. Hinnells

FOREWORD AND ACKNOWLEDGEMENTS

This is not *the* sourcebook for the study of Hinduism; it is *a* sourcebook for the study of Hinduism, or, more precisely, *my* sourcebook for the study of Hinduism. So voluminous and varied are the texts of Hinduism that anyone who attempts to make any selection at all produces not a true image of the religious literature but rather a projection of his or her own preferences; the literature of Hinduism is a Rohrschach test for any scholar foolish enough to try to encompass it in a single volume. There is, therefore, no fair representation of the content or ideas or concepts of Hinduism in this voume; I have not aimed for the sort of distribution that Ninian Smart aimed for in his most useful *Sacred Texts of the World* (sacred narrative, doctrine, ritual, institutional expression, experience, and ethics). Inevitably, the sources (vernacular as well as Sanskritic) do reflect certain enduring Hindu preoccupations, such as the two central concepts of karma and dharma, though I made no conscious effort to select passages on these subjects.

Instead, taking the term 'sources' rather literally, I have tried to make a genuinely representative selection of genres, of the sorts of texts that one encounters in the study of Hinduism, the types of discourse in which Hinduism carries on its sacred conversations, the different forms rather than the different contents of Hinduism: Vedas, Puranas, Shastras, vernacular literatures, and so forth. And in order to give a true taste of the particular flavour of each of these genres, I have made rather longish selections from each, rather than quick commando raids to pick out the famous passage or the key concepts. I have also included several texts that give long lists (of things to do and not to do, of types of creatures, of the names of god, and so on), in part because this is a quintessentially Hindu modality of discourse, and in part because it compresses into a small text a great deal of human thought, which makes it particularly useful for a sourcebook.

These longer passages may also facilitate classroom discussion of the complexities implicit in each text and of the ways in which different genres deal with the same theme. (The bibliographies for each selection also provide useful background material for classroom discussion.) The medical Shastras, for example, deal with ethics in ways that overlap with but differ from the ethics of the Dharma Shastras, and mental health in ways that sometimes supplement and sometimes contradict the discussions of mental health in the Puranas. The Puranas deal with political science in ways that both resemble and diverge from the political science of the Artha Shastras. The Tantric texts offer explicit (even mischievous) challenges to more traditional views on marriage, death, religion, and caste. The story of the creation of the universe is told differently in the Vedas, the Brahmanas, and the Puranas, though certain basic concepts remain central to all of the variants.

Within each genre, I have picked the texts that I like best, and these have tended to be texts about women, animals, sin, food, and sacrifice; the arbitrariness of this selection was in any case inevitable, but it does have the incidental advantage of demonstrating how certain themes run like a thread through several different genres, though each genre may make an entirely different use of that theme. Thus, for example, a ferrywoman is seduced first in the Sanskrit Epic (section 3.1.1) and then in a Bengali poem (section 8.1); a sinner is saved in a Sanskrit Purana (4.2.1) and in a Tamil story (9.4). I have particularly striven to show the relationship between what might be called mainstream Hinduism and the alternative Hinduisms. Mainstream Hinduism is the Hinduism of the Sanskrit dharma texts, the Hinduism that supports caste law and orients itself in terms of the Veda; this is the Establishment that establishes the rules of the game of life in India. But it is a game that many others play by different rules, and these alternative rules are also represented in this volume: devotional Hinduism (*bhakti*) challenges many of the mainstream rules, Tantric Hinduism reverses them, and the regional and folk traditions cut the ground away from the mainstream by putting forth alternative views of those same central themes.

I have also tried to include a number of texts not so well known in the West, though I have not hesitated to use some old favourites when they were my favourites too. In this same hope of making this a truly varied, if not truly representative, selection, I asked Daniel Gold, David Haberman, and David Shulman to translate selections of texts from the vernacular languages that they know so much better than I do: Hindi, Bengali, and Tamil (and Telugu). Though it is true that Sanskrit is the language of the Vedic canon that Hindus use to define themselves, and the language of many texts that all educated Indians know, it is also true that most of Hinduism is actually *done* in the vernacular, in what A. K. Ramanujan has called the mother tongue that every Indian has, in contrast with the father tongue, Sanskrit. These necessarily brief selections in Hindi, Bengali, Tamil, and Telugu will at least make the general reader aware of the existence of whole universes of textual sources which are far too often neglected in surveys of Hinduism.

Very few of these texts, if indeed any, are known to *all* Hindus, or sacred to all Hindus; but most of them have earned a permanent place in some tradition. They are sacred texts not in the sense of canonical texts (a concept with little

meaning for a religion as pluralistic as Hinduism) but in the sense of a text regarded by a group of worshippers as a source of religious meaning. Each of these texts contains words that have been preserved, often at great cost, by someone who thought that they were essential to the religious life of the community, however small that community might be.

I have purposely steered away from mythology, as there are already at least two useful sourcebooks on this subject, my own *Hindu Myths* and J. A. B. van Buitenen's and Cornelia Dimmitt's *Classical Hindu Mythology* (see Bibliography). Similarly, I have included relatively little philosophy in this volume, since this need has been well filled by the good sourcebook by Radhakrishnan and Moore. I have tried to avoid some of the texts translated by Ainslee Embree and Stephen Hay in their *Sources of Indian Tradition* (though when I really needed a text that they used, I used it, and retranslated it). My policy of selection thus differs from that of two other, more comprehensive volumes in this series, dealing with Sikhism and Zoroastrianism, religions for which there was, on the one hand, a greater *need* for a representative selection (there being no other sourcebooks available for those traditions) and, on the other hand, a greater *possibility* of making such a selection (there being a more limited literature of sacred texts in those traditions).

What remains here is therefore an emphasis on the rituals of Hinduism, a bias in itself perhaps justifiable on the grounds that it is shared by most Hindus; Hinduism as a whole has been well characterised as orthoprax rather than orthodox: Hindus define themselves by what they do rather than by what they think. This, then, is a book less about What Hindus Believe and more about How to Be a Hindu.

A word about translation. All the texts in this volume have been newly translated, with the exception of the hymns from the *Rig Veda* that I had already translated for the Penguin Classics; I have somewhat modified them here. I have tried to be as literal as possible, and to leave nothing out, with one exception: I have omitted some of the vocatives used in the *Mahabharata* and the Puranas, space-fillers that often refer to interlocutors who play no significant role in the selected passages. Assuming that my reader knows no Sanskrit, I have tried to translate even technical terms like *atman* (which I render either as 'self' or as 'soul') and *brahman* (which I render as 'ultimate reality', in part to distinguish it from the upper-case god Brahma, the creator). And I have rendered as 'Untouchable' all of the many Sanskrit terms for people beyond the Hindu pale, including tribals (such as Nishadas), the lowest castes (such as Candalas), and general terms of caste opprobrium (such as Shvapakas, 'dog-cookers'). But I have presumed to teach the reader a very little bit of Sanskrit, and given myself the dispensation of using less than a dozen Sanskrit words, some of which are already familiar to English-speaking readers: dharma and karma, to begin with, and guru, pandit, yoga, and avatar; the names of certain groups of texts (Vedas, Brahmanas, Puranas, Shastras, Tantras) and classes of society (Brahmins, Kshatriyas, Vaishyas, and Shudras) or creatures (Gandharvas and Nagas); and a few recurrent and useful terms such as mantra and lingam. These are explained at the first usages and defined in the glossarial index. I hope and trust that the rest is in English.

I am grateful to the Department of Philosophy and Religious Studies, University of Canterbury, Christchurch, New Zealand, for giving me a place of peace, beauty, and (human) warmth in which to write this book; and especially to Colin Brown, Paul Harrison, Bob Stoothoff (and Judy, Emma, Jason, and Kiri), Bill Shepherd, Ian Catanach, Hally Cederman, Louise Holmes, Margaret Orbell, and Rachel McAlpine; and *especially* to Jim Wilson, who made it all possible and then made it all great fun. It was a great happiness for me to work on this book with three colleagues, once students, who share many of my tastes in things Indian but have their own unique ways of thinking Indologically: Daniel Gold, of the Department of Asian Studies, Cornell University; David Haberman of the Department of Religion, Williams College; and David Shulman, of the Department of Indian, Iranian, and Armenian Studies, Hebrew University, Jerusalem. Indeed, their presence in this undertaking – a vernacular triad, with me as the transcendent Sanskrit fourth – was the best part of all.

To them, and to all the other *chelas* who grow up to become colleagues – and to one in particular – I would like to dedicate this book.

1 INTRODUCTION TO THE SANSKRIT SOURCES

(Note: introductory surveys of the Hindi, Bengali, and Tamil/Telugu literatures precede each of those sections.)

This will be, I fear, the usual, stupefyingly boring survey of the Sanskrit sources, thought I hope at least to make it gratifyingly brief. Western readers, as Antoine de Saint Exupery's Little Prince pointed out, don't feel that they know something unless they can *count* it; when they want to know a literature, they want to know when it was written and how many pages are in it. The Hindus, unfortunately, did not care to supply us with this information. Most Hindu texts can be dated, with confidence, only 'some time between 1000 B.C. and A.D. 1500'. There is a ray of hope, however, that one can construct a relative chronology: we can usually tell when one text comes after another and in a sense replies to it. It is such a relative chronology that I will attempt to supply here, as concisely as possible. I will not try to summarise the contents of these various genres, since that purpose is meant to be served by the reading of the actual excerpts contained in this volume; rough summaries of this sort are also available elsewhere (see Bibliography). But perhaps it will be useful to have an idealised numerical frame in which the various separate textual pieces in the book can be fitted together in the reader's mind.

The people whom we call Hindus actually define themselves in terms of their 'textual sources': they are the people whose sacred text is the Veda. The term 'Veda' is often used in a general sense, to denote an entire body of literature, Vedic literature, that we would be inclined to call their scripture. Scripture, however, is precisely what the Veda is *not*: the Hindus took great pains not to write it down for many centuries, long after they had begun to use writing for a number of other practical purposes. They call the Veda *shruti*, 'that which is heard', both because it is a revealed, inspired text, that was 'heard' by the seers to whom the gods spoke it, and because it continued to be 'heard' that is, recited orally, by succeeding generations of Hindus. These texts were preserved orally for many centuries; and when the *Rig Veda* was finally written down, the readings of all the different manuscripts were found to have been preserved perfectly, syllable for syllable the same.

Vedic literature consists of a number of texts. First comes the *Rig Veda*, the earliest Indian text (indeed, one of the oldest texts in any Indo-European language), composed somewhere in north-west India (probably in the region of the Punjab) in around 1000 B.C. This text consists of 1,028 hymns, prayers to be used in the course of a sacrifice; it is divided into ten books, of which the first and the tenth are thought to be somewhat later than the central eight. The *Rig*

Veda is by far the most important of the Vedic texts; indeed, the term 'the Veda' is frequently used in a more specific sense, to refer to the *Rig Veda* alone. The *Sama Veda* is composed essentially of hymns taken from the *Rig Veda* (with some seventy-five additional stanzas), rearranged in order to facilitate the singing or chanting of the verses. The *Yajur Veda* is a collection of ritual formulae and explanations used by the priests in performing the Vedic sacrifice.

These three texts, intimately connected, were the original corpus of Vedic literature and are still often referred to as 'the three Vedas'. But a fourth text, the *Atharva Veda*, was composed a century or two after the first triad. This is a text of an entirely different nature; although 1,200 of its 6,000 stanzas are taken from the *Rig Veda*, the great bulk of the work is a collection of magic spells and incantations, drawing upon ancient folk materials. It was added to the three original Vedas to form the quartet known as 'the four Vedas'.

At roughly the same time as the *Atharva Veda* recension, about 900 B.C., several different priestly schools began to record and preserve their expositions of the meaning of the sacrifice, the hymns, and the prayers; this resulted in the texts called the Brahmanas, each attached to one of the Vedas: the *Aitareya* and *Kaushitaki Brahmanas* of the *Rig Veda*; the *Tandya, Shadvimsha, Chandogya*, and *Jaiminiya Brahmanas* of the *Sama Veda*; and the *Taittiriya* and *Shatapatha Brahmanas* of the *Yajur Veda*. (Another Brahmana of the *Yajur Veda*, the *Kathaka*, survives only in fragments.) These texts were followed by the *Aranyakas*, or 'forest books', which were, in turn, followed, around 700 B.C., by the Upanishads. The Upanishads supply the basis of later Hindu philosophy; they alone of the Vedic corpus are widely known and quoted by most well-educated Hindus, and their central ideas have also become a part of the spiritual arsenal of rank-and-file Hindus, while the earlier Vedic texts remain largely the special reserve stock of priests and scholars.

This, then, is *shruti*, 'heard' scripture. All the other sacred texts of Hinduism are called *smriti*, 'what is remembered', that is, what humans have thought of in response of *shruti*. The *smriti* texts were written down at an early period, but were constantly modified. Thus we are faced with what is to us a paradox: the Hindu oral tradition is fixed, the manuscript tradition fluid. All the *smriti* texts exist in many different recensions, with many variant readings, whole chapters left out or put in; and most of them exist, as well, in vernacular translations. Yet all *smriti* is regarded as rooted in the *shruti*; the text that anyone loves and knows best may be called 'the fifth Veda'. If all of Western philosophy is nothing but a footnote to Plato, it is surely true that all Indian philosophy is regarded as nothing but a commentary on the Veda.

Most obviously and directly related to the *shruti* literature is the philosophical literature of India, much of which takes the form of commentaries on the Vedas, particularly upon the Upanishads. There are traditionally said to be six main or orthodox *darshanas* ('views'), doctrines or schools of Hindu philosophy, that form three pairs, Karma Mimamsa and Uttara Mimamsa,

Sankhya and Yoga, and Vaisheshika and Nyaya. The texts of these schools developed in constant dialogue and cross-fertilisation with one another and with Buddhism; they tend to regard the same philosophical problems as central and to share many basic ideas about those problems. Yet each has its own point of view, developed in many cases through further commentaries and sub-commentaries – variations on variations on the theme of the Veda.

The school of the Purva Mimamsa ('Former Investigation'), sometimes called the Karma Mimamsa ('Ritual Investigation'), deals with the sacrificial part of the Veda; Jaimini's *Purva-Mimamsa-Sutra* is the most important text in this corpus. The Uttara Mimamsa ('Later Investigation'), also known as Vedanta ('End of the Veda'), deals with the Upanishads, and is by far the best known branch of Indian philosophy; the basic text of this corpus is the *Vedanta-Sutras* (or *Brahma-Sutras*), attributed to Badarayana; I have included in this volume selections from the commentaries of Shankara and Ramanuja upon this text.

The basic tenets of the philosophy of Sankhya, as elucidated in the *Sankhya-Karika* attributed to Ishvara Krishna, are a part of the general conceptual framework of Hinduism; they appear in the Epics and Puranas, in the *Bhagavad Gita*, and in the writings of other philosophical schools. Sanhkya recognises three kinds of evidence: perception, inference, and *shruti*. It divides the universe into spirit (*purusha*) and nature (*prakriti*), the latter further subdivided into three constituent qualities (*gunas*): goodness (*sattva*), energy (*rajas*), and darkness (*tamas*). The principal text of the Yoga system, the *Yoga-Sutra* of Patanjali, is closely related to the *Sankhya-Karika*: but to the Sankhya system, that recognises the various Hindu gods but not a single God, Yoga adds the element of the Lord (Ishvara) and a method (yoga) of attaining the isolation of the spirit by mastering the body and the mind through physical exercise and meditation.

The standard text of the Vaisheshika system is the *Vaisheshika-Sutra* of Kanada Kashyapa, which recognises nine classes of realities: four classes of atoms, plus space (*akasha*), time (*kala*), direction (*dik*), an infinity of souls (*atmans*), and mind (*manas*). Like the Sankhyas, Vaisheshikas acknowledge the Hindu gods but not a single God. Nyaya ('Logic') is closely related to Vaisheshika; both are indifferent to renunciation and favourable to the householder life. The fundamental Nyaya text is Gautama's *Nyaya-Sutra*, which discusses sixteen topics: proof, things to be proved, doubt, motive, example, conclusion, syllogisms, *reductio ad absurdum*, ascertainment, thesis, sophistical wrangling, cavilling, fallacious reasoning, futility, quibbling, and talk that is beside the point.

These philosophical texts set forth ideas that are assumed and often discussed in all other branches of Hindu literature, whether it be fiction or science. For, like the rest of Hindu sacred literature, the philosophical texts are regarded as *smriti* commentaries on *shruti*; as such, they deal with topics that are also treated in the other great branch of *smriti*, the literature of the Dharma

Shastras or textbooks of dharma, that encompasses both the Dharma Shastras proper and the two great Sanskrit Epics, the *Mahabharata* and the *Ramayana*.

The earliest of the Dharma Shastras are roughly contemporaneous with the Sanskrit epics, but they are themselves based on earlier texts that are intimately related to the Brahmanas: the sacrificial texts (Shrauta Sutras), household texts (Grihya Sutras), and dharma texts (Dharma Sutras). The Book of the Laws of Manu (*Manava-dharma-shastra*) is by far the most famous, and probably one of the oldest, of the Dharma Shastras, but it refers to others of this genre – the law books of Yajñavalkya, Narada, Brihaspati, and Vishnu, in particular – which, in turn, refer to Manu, in the chicken-and-egg phenomenon so natural to Indian texts and so exasperating to scholars who try to date those texts.

The *Mahabharata*, a book of some 100,000 verses (ten times as long as the *Iliad* and the *Odyssey* combined), was composed in north-west India over a period of several centuries; the *Ramayana*, which is shorter and more homogeneous than the *Mahabharata*, was composed in north-west India during a shorter period. People who like to count things might say that the *Mahabharata* was composed between 300 B.C. and A.D. 300, and the *Ramayana* between 200 B.C. and A.D. 200. But the glossy tidiness of these broad periods is somewhat tarnished when we realise that people continued to add new material to the Epics well into the medieval period.

Both the Dharma Shastras and the Epics mingle narrative and exposition, in a typically Indian manner; they begin with questions of dharma and use narratives to illustrate the human dilemmas that arise from the doctrinal prescriptions. But the Dharma Shastras place exposition in the foreground and devote far more space to it, illustrating doctrinal points with only occasional and relatively brief narratives. The Epics and Puranas, by contrast, place narrative in the foreground and tell much longer stories. Yet some of the Epic discussions of dharma are very long; one entire book of the *Mahabharata*, and one of the longest at that, the *Shanti Parvan*, is nothing but a didactic exposition; and the *Bhagavad Gita*, one of the central texts of Hindu doctrine, is a conversation between the hero Arjuna and the incarnate god Krishna on the eve of the great battle of the Bharatas. The Hindus regard the Epics both as great poems and as great textbooks; we may think that they are about the war of the Bharatas and the battle between Rama and Ravana, but the Hindus think that they are about dharma.

This is all the more true of the Puranas or 'ancient texts', miscellaneous compendia of myth, ritual, philosophy, history, and, always, dharma. The contents of the Puranas will be discussed and, in a limited way, demonstrated in the main body of this volume; for the moment, it might be useful to place them in the context of Indian literature as a whole. Useful, but not easy. The dating of the Epics is a precise science compared to the dating of the Puranas, which quote one another and most of the rest of Indian literature with a most cavalier lack of respect for copyright. No one even agrees as to the number of the Puranas; it is usually said that there are eighteen, though it is not always the *same* eighteen, and in any case eighteeen is a suspiciously sacred number in India (there are eighteen books of the *Mahabharata*, for instance).

But even the unruly Puranas can be corralled into rough groups which can be ranged in chronological relationship to one another. All these dates are A.D.; and all of them are based upon the often misguided conjectures of scholars; I have arranged them alphabetically to augment the false semblance of scientific efficiency: *Agni*: 850; *Bhagavata*: 950; *Bhavishya*: 500–1200; *Brahma*: 900–1350; *Brahmanda*: 350–950; *Brahmavaivarta*: 750–1550; *Brihaddharma*: 1250; *Brihannaradiya*: 750–900; *Devi*: 550–650; *Devibhagavata*: 850–1350; *Garuda*: 900; *Harivamsha*: 450; *Kalika*: 1350; *Kalki*: 1500–1700; *Kurma*: 550–850; *Linga*: 600–1000; *Mahabhagavata*: 1100; *Markandeya*: 250; *Matsya*: 250–500; *Narasimha*: 400–500; *Padma*: 750; *Samba*: 500–800; *Saura*: 950–1150; *Shiva*: 750–1350; *Skanda*: 700–1150; *Vamana*: 450–900; *Varaha*: 750; *Vayu*: 350; *Vishnu*: 450.

Finally, we encounter the mysterious Tantras, a class of Sanskrit texts dating from about the seventh century A.D. and dealing with esoteric practices aiming at the purification of the body and the control of physiological and psychological processes. The Tantras are particularly associated with techniques of yoga, the worship of the Goddess, the use of ritual diagrams (yantras and mandalas) and magic syllables (mantras). They are generally regarded as 'left-hand' or unorthodox, and many Tantra rituals do in fact involve the use of substances and actions that are diametrically opposed to the laws of caste Hinduism.

This brings us to the end of the general outline of the Sanskrit literature of Hinduism; and it brings us to the beginning of the vernacular literatures, that will be discussed individually at the beginning of the sections that deal with Hindi, Bengali, and Tamil/Telugu. I will also say a bit more about each of the genres of the Sanskrit texts at the beginning of each section. For now, enough of the overture; let the actors themselves, the texts, speak.

2 VEDAS

2.1 RITUALS

The Rig Veda itself is a liturgical text, meant to be recited in the course of various sacrificial rituals; and the Brahmanas and Aranyakas are entirely devoted to the Vedic ritual. The two elements essential to all of these rituals were the sacred fire, Agni (cognate with the Latin ignis) *and the Soma juice, a hallucinogenic liquid pressed from the Soma plant and then drunk by the priests during the sacrifice. Both Agni and Soma (together with most other important elements of the world) were also incarnate as gods, and most of the hymns of the* Rig Veda *are addressed to them.*

2.1.1. Rig Veda

2.1.1.1 Invocation of Agni

Appropriately placed at the very beginning of the Rig Veda, *this hymn invites Agni, fire, to come to the sacrifice, where he appears incarnate as the divine priest, here addressed as Angiras, the name of an ancient family of priests. As custodian of the ritual that imposes form and meaning on the chaos of life, Agni is also addressed as the guardian of the Order,* ritam, *the Vedic predecessor of the later Hindu concept of dharma.*

I pray to Agni, the household priest who is the god of the sacrifice, the one who chants and invokes and brings most treasure. Agni earned the prayers of the ancient sages, and of those of the present, too; he will bring the gods here. Through Agni one may win wealth, and growth from day to day, glorious and most abounding in heroic sons. Agni, the sacrificial ritual that you encompass on all sides – only that one goes to the gods. Agni, the priest with the sharp sight of a poet, the true and most brilliant, the god will come with the gods. Whatever good you wish to do for the one who worships you, Agni, through you, O Angiras, that comes true. To you, Agni, who shine upon darkness, we come day after day, bringing our thoughts and homage to you, the king over sacrifices, the shining guardian of the Order, growing in your own house. Be easy for us to reach, like a father to his son. Abide with us, Agni, for our happiness. (*Rig Veda* 1.1)

2.1.1.2 Hymn to the funeral fire

Agni appears here both as the cremation fire that carries the corpse to the world of the fathers, or ancestors, and as the ritual fire that carries the offerings to the world of the gods; in both aspects he is addressed as the 'knower of creatures'. The hymn expresses the belief that the dead man will be reborn according to his natural affinities, according to the way such things are arranged, or, perhaps, according to his own good works that will win him a place in heaven. Though there are a few Vedic passages that suggest the beginnings of a theory of rebirth, the Rig Veda *generally, rather vaguely, implies that the dead live in a pleasant world with their fathers, ruled by Yama, king of the dead. In the course of the funeral ritual referred to in this hymn, the limbs of a scapegoat were placed over the dead man, so that Agni would consume them and not the corpse with his violent flames, and the limbs and caul (inner membrane of the embryo) or skin of a dead cow would be used in addition to or in place of the scapegoat, while the corpse would be anointed with fat and suet. A special sacrificial drink was offered to the gods at the funeral, and a wooden cup that the dead man had used in life to make Soma offerings to the gods and the fathers ('who love Soma') would be filled with melted butter and placed at the head of the corpse. In addition, a hot oblation was given to the fathers. The final verses accompany the ritual of dousing the fire with water so thoroughly that it produces a marsh where water-plants, 'cool' plants, and frogs may thrive. Thus new life sprouts at the end of the funeral.*

[To Agni:] Do not burn him entirely, Agni, or engulf him in your flames. Do not consume his skin or his flesh. When you have cooked him perfectly, O knower of creatures, only then send him forth to the fathers. When you cook him perfectly, O knower of creatures, then give him over to the fathers. When he goes on the path that leads away the vital breath, then he will be led by the will of the gods. [To the dead man:] May your eye go to the sun, your vital breath to the wind. Go to the sky or to earth, as is your nature; or go to the waters, if that is your fate. Take root in the plants with your limbs.

[To the funeral fire:] The goat is your share; burn him with your heat. Let your brilliant light and flame burn him. With your gentle forms, O knower of creatures, carry this man to the world of those who have done good deeds. Set him free again to go to the fathers, Agni, when he has been offered as an oblation in you and wanders with the sacrificial drink. Let him reach his own descendants, dressing himself in a life-span. O knower of creatures, let him join with a body.

[To the dead man:] Whatever the black bird has pecked out of you, or the ant, the snake, or even a beast of prey, may Agni who eats all things make it whole, and Soma who has entered the Brahmins. Gird yourself with the limbs of the cow as an armour against Agni, and cover yourself with fat and suet, so that he will not embrace you with his impetuous heat in his passionate desire to burn you up.

[To the funeral fire:] O Agni, do not overturn this cup, that is dear to the gods and to those who love Soma, fit for the gods to drink from, a cup in which the immortal gods carouse.

I send the flesh-eating fire far away. Let him go to those whose king is Yama, carrying away all impurities. But let that other (form of fire), the knower of creatures, come here and carry the oblation to the gods, since he knows the way in advance.

[To the dead man:] The flesh-eating fire has entered your house, though he sees there the other, the knower of creatures; I take that god away to the sacrifice of the fathers. Let him carry the heated drink to the farthest dwelling-place.

[To the funeral fire:] Agni who carries away the corpse, who gives sacrifice to the fathers who are strengthened by truth – let him proclaim the oblation to the gods and to the fathers.

[To the new fire:] Joyously would we put you in place, joyously would we kindle you. Joyously carry the joyous fathers here to eat the oblation. Now, Agni, quench and revive the very one you have burnt up. Let water plants grow in this place. O cool one, bringer of coolness; O fresh one, bringer of freshness; unite with the female frog. Delight and inspire this Agni. (*Rig Veda* 10.16)

2.1.1.3 The horse sacrifice
The horse sacrifice was the most elaborate of all Vedic sacrifices, performed by a

great king to establish his supremacy and to ensure the prosperity and fertility of his kingdom. Though it was seldom performed even in ancient times, it remained the most important paradigm both for sacrifice and for kingship throughout Hindu literature. This hymn, strikingly concrete in its detail, describes the ancient Indian horse sacrifice, beginning with the ceremonial procession of the horse with the goat, leading to the actual slaughter. It then dwells upon the material instruments of the sacrifice which are to accompany the horse to heaven; it refers to balls, that may be the balls of rice that the wives of the king give to the stallion (as in 2.1.2.2.1 below); they may also be balls of flesh. A goat appears as the supplementary offering at the horse sacrifice, as he is at the funeral sacrifice of a human. In addition to the real goat, the stallion is associated with several mythological animals: the two bay stallions that are the horses of Indra, king of the gods; the two roan mares that are the horses of the Maruts, gods of the storm; and the donkey that belongs to the Ashvins, twin gods, themselves half horse.

Four main priests officiated at the sacrifice. The invoker (the Hotri) summoned the gods and offered the oblations; the officiant (Adhvaryu) would be responsible for the physical implements of the sacrifice; the overseer (also called the Brahman) would perform restorations for any ritual errors or personal misdeeds; the cantor (Udgatri) would sing the verses. The slaughterer (Shamitri, literally the 'quieter') would kill the animal and the carver (Kshatri) would dismember him. A more general sort of priest is called the Ritvig, the sacrificial priest. The cry of 'Vashat!' (or, in some ceremonies, 'Svaha!') is made to catch the attention of the gods when an offering is made; it is roughly equivalent to 'Amen!'

The horse is addressed as 'you' intermittently throughout the hymn, but the poet also addresses the priests, the congregation of mourners, and several gods. Mitra is 'the friend,' often closely linked with Varuna, the god of the waters and of the moral order; Aryaman the Active is a minor god of war; Indra is the king of the gods and the god of rain; the Ribhus are the artists of the gods; the Maruts are the gods of the storm; Pushan is the god of journeys and the god who nourishes the embryo; Tvashtri is the artisan and architect of the gods. Aditi, the goddess of infinity and creation, is invoked in the final general wish for expiation as well as for the specific cleansing of the sin of killing the horse – a wish that pervades the entire hymn.

[To the gods:] Mitra, Varuna, Aryaman the Active, Indra the ruler of the Ribhus, and the Maruts – let them not fail to heed us when we proclaim in the assembly the heroic deeds of the racehorse who was born of the gods. When they lead the firmly grasped offering in front of the horse that is covered with cloths and heirlooms, the dappled goat goes bleating straight to the dear dwelling of Indra and Pushan. This goat for all the gods is led forward with the racehorse as the share for Pushan. When they lead forth the welcome offering with the charger, Tvashtri urges him on to great fame. When, as the ritual law ordains, the men circle three times, leading the horse that is to be the oblation on the path to the gods, the goat who is the share for Pushan goes first, announcing the sacrifice to the gods.

[To the priests:] The invoker, the officiant, the overseer, the fire-kindler, the holder of the pressing-stones, the cantor, the sacrificial priest – fill your bellies with this well-prepared, well-sacrificed sacrifice. The hewers of the sacrificial stake and those who carry it, and those who carve the knob for the horse's sacrificial stake, and those who gather together the things to cook the charger – let their approval encourage us.

The horse with his smooth back went forth into the fields of the gods, just when I made my prayer. The inspired sages exult in him. We have made him a welcome companion at the banquet of the gods.

[To the horse:] The charger's rope and halter, the reins and bridle on the head, and even the grass that has been held up to the mouth – let all that stay with you even among the gods. Whatever of the horse's flesh the fly has eaten, or whatever stays stuck to the stake or the axe, or to the hands or nails of the slaughterer – let all of that stay with you even among the gods. Whatever food remains in the stomach, sending forth gas, or whatever smell there is from the raw flesh – let the slaughterers make that well done; let them cook the sacrificial animal until he is perfectly cooked. Whatever runs off your body when it has been placed on the spit and roasted by the fire, let it not lie there in the earth or on the grass, but let it be given to the gods who long for it.

[To the priests:] Those (priests) who see that the racehorse is cooked, who say, 'It smells good! Take it away!', and who wait for the doling out of the flesh of the charger – let their approval encourage us. The testing fork for the cauldron that cooks the flesh, the pots for pouring the broth, the cover of the bowls to keep it warm, the hooks, the dishes – all these attend the horse.

[To the horse:] The place where the horse walks, where he rests, where he rolls, and the fetters on the horse's feet, and what he has drunk and the fodder he has eaten – let all of that stay with you even among the gods. Let not the fire that reeks of smoke darken you, nor the red-hot cauldron split into pieces.

The gods receive the horse who has been sacrificed, worshipped, consecrated, and sanctified with the cry of 'Vashat!' The cloth that they spread beneath the horse, the upper covering, the golden trappings on him, the halter and the fetters on his feet – let these things that are his own bind the horse among the gods.

[To the horse:] If someone riding you has struck you too hard with heel or whip when you shied, I make all these things well again for you with prayer, as they do with the ladle for the oblation in sacrifices.

[To the priests:] The axe cuts through the thirty-four ribs of the racehorse who is the companion of the gods. Keep the limbs undamaged and place them in the proper pattern. Cut them apart, calling out piece by piece. One (priest) is the slaughterer of the horse of Tvashtri; two (priests) restrain him. This is the rule.

[To the horse:] As many of your limbs as I set out, according to the rules, so many balls I offer into the fire. Let not your dear soul burn you as you go away. Let not the axe do lasting harm to your body. Let no greedy, clumsy slaughterer hack in the wrong place and damage your limbs with his knife. You do not really die through this, nor are you harmed. You go to the gods on paths pleasant to go on. The two bay stallions, the two roan mares are now your chariot mates. The racehorse has been set in the donkey's yoke.

[To the gods:] Let this racehorse bring us good cattle and good horses, male children and all nourishing wealth. Let Aditi make us free from sin. Let the horse with our offerings achieve sovereign power for us. (*Rig Veda* 1.162)

2.1.2 Brahmanas

2.1.2.1 The offering into the fire (Agnihotra)

2.1.2.1.1 The creation of fire, the eater

The principal gods in this, as in most Brahmana rituals and myths, are Prajapati, 'lord of progeny' or 'lord of creatures', the Vedic god of creation, and Speech, a feminine noun in Sanskrit, a goddess in the Rig Veda. This passage is typical in its use of verbal etymologies – most of them different from what philologists believe to be the actual derivations of the words; in its interest in Speech as a creative force; and in its concern with food and death, and the relationship between food and death. Like most of the Brahmanas, its underlying aim is to determine a way not to die. In this episode, the author puns on the idea that Prajapati loses his power of speech (as he will lose other powers in the course of creation) because he becomes literally speechless with terror.

Truly, Prajapati alone existed here in the beginning. He thought, 'How can I bring forth creatures?' He exhausted himself and produced heat. He gave birth to Agni, fire, from his mouth. Since he created him from his mouth, therefore Agni is an eater of food. And whoever knows that Agni is an eater of food in this way, he himself becomes an eater of food. Thus he gave birth to him first of the gods; since '*agni*' is the same as '*agri*' ('first'), he is called Agni. As soon as he was born, he went in front; and people say of anyone who goes in front, 'He goes first.' This is why Agni is called Agni.

Then Prajapati thought, 'I have given birth to this Agni, this eater of food, from my own self. But there is no food here but me, whom he would surely not eat.' Now, at that time the earth was quite bald; there were no plants or trees. This was what was on his mind.

Then Agni turned toward Prajapati with a wide-open mouth, and as Prajapati became frightened, the female who was his greatness went away from him. For Speech is his own greatness, and Speech left him. He wished to make an offering into his own self. He rubbed (his hands), and because he rubbed them, they have no hair on them. And there he found the offering of clarified butter or the offering of milk – both of them are essentially milk.

But this offering did not satisfy Prajapati, for it had become mixed with hairs. He poured it out (into the fire, Agni) and said, 'Suck this and burn it' (*osha dhaya*). The plants arose from it, and therefore they are called plants (*oshadhayas*). He rubbed (his hands) a second time, and there he found another offering of clarified butter or of milk – both of them are essentially milk.

This offering satisfied him. But he was in doubt, wondering, 'Shall I offer it or not?' His own greatness (i.e. Speech) said to him, 'Offer it!' Prajapati realised, 'What is my own (*sva*) has spoken (*aha*)', and he made the offering. And therefore one says 'Svaha!' when making an offering. From that there arose the (sun) who heats and the (wind) who blows. And Agni turned away from him.

Thus, by making an offering, Prajapati gave birth to himself and saved himself from Agni, from Death, who was about to eat him. And whoever knows about this and offers the Agnihotra oblation, he gives birth to himself in his progeny, just as Prajapati gave birth to himself. And in this very same way, he saves himself from Agni, from Death, when he is about to eat him.

For when he dies, and they place him on the fire, then he is born out of the fire, and then the fire consumes only his body. And just as he is born from his father or from his mother, in that very way he is born from the fire. But whoever does not offer the Agnihotra oblation, he *never* comes to life again. And that is why the Agnihotra *must* be offered. (*Shatapatha Brahmana* 2.2.4.1–8)

2.1.2.1.2 The origins of death and the fire-altar

This text describes a ritual that the gods performed once, in the beginning, and that men now perform in imitation of them. It offers a remarkable twist on the concept (immortalised by Mircea Eliade), that by repeating the ritual that the gods did in illo tempore, *one achieves what the gods achieved. Since, at the crucial point in this story, the gods are doing the ritual* wrong, *the people who nowadays still copy them at this inadequate stage are also doing it wrong, and will fail, as the gods failed, to become immortal.*

These rituals depend on analogies or connections (bandhus) on many levels: between the ritual done then and the ritual done now; between the priests and the gods; between the sounds of words and the things that they designate; between parts of the body and parts of the universe; and between divisions of time (particularly ritual time, and most particularly liminal, transitional periods) and divisions of things. There were three seasons (spring, summer, and autumn) at this period in Indian literature, and hence three seasonal rituals (performed every four months). Later literature designated six seasons (spring, summer, rains, autumn, winter, and the 'cool' season).

The most important mythological analogy or connection in this passage is the underlying assertion that the god of creation, Prajapati, is also the god of death, Yama. The corresponding analogy of the ritual is that of the fire altar, that is built of bricks made specifically in proportion to the exact height of the sacrificer, so that the altar becomes an exact analogue of the sacrificer's body. Since the fire-altar is the central concern of this text, the word 'fire' here connotes both the general knowledge and ritual of the fire and the more specific knowledge and ritual of the

*building of the fire-altar. And the word 'karma' here means both action (in
contrast with thought) and the most important of all actions: ritual action.*

*Later, in the Upanishads, karma takes on its third meaning: the cumulative
effect of good and bad actions that determine rebirth. Indeed, one may see in this
passage a very early foreshadowing of the doctrine of rebirth, but probably this is
still rebirth in some extraterrestrial Vedic world, not yet the rebirth on earth that is
the innovation of the Upanishads.*

It is Death who is really the Year. For the Year is the one who wears away the
life-span of mortals by means of day and night, so that they die; therefore the
year is Death. And if someone knows that Death is the Year, the Year does not
wear away his life-span by means of day and night before old age, and so he
lives out a full life-span.

And he is really the Ender. For he is the one who goes to the end of the
life-span of mortals by means of day and night, so that they die; therefore he is
the Ender. And if someone knows that Death, the Year, is the Ender, the
Ender does not go to the end of his life-span by means of day and night before
old age, and so he lives out a full life-span.

The gods were afraid of this Ender, Death, the Year, who is Prajapati; they
thought, 'Let him not go to the end of our life-spans by means of day and
night.' They performed these sacrificial rituals – the Agnihotra, the new moon
and full moon sacrifices, the seasonal four-month offerings, the animal
sacrifice, and the Soma sacrifice. But when they sacrificed with these sacrificial
rituals they did not attain immortality.

Then they built a fire-altar. They laid down an indeterminate number of
enclosing stones, and an indeterminate number of bricks with special formulas
and an indeterminate number of bricks that fill the space – just as even now
some people lay down the altar, saying. 'This is how the gods did it.' But they
did not attain immortality.

They went on singing praises and exhausting themselves, for they wanted
very much to achieve immortality. Then Prajapati said to them, 'You are not
laying down all my forms; either you overdo it or you leave something out.
That is why you do not become immortal.' They said, 'Tell us yourself, then,
how we can lay down all your forms.'

He said, 'Lay down three hundred and sixty enclosing stones, three hundred
and sixty bricks with special formulas, plus thirty-six more; and lay down ten
thousand and eight hundred bricks that fill the space; and then you will be
laying down all my forms, and you will become immortal.' And so the gods laid
them down in just that way, and so they became immortal.

Death said to the gods, 'All men will become immortal in precisely this way,
and then what share will be mine?' They said, 'From now on, no one else will
become immortal together with the body. But as soon as you have taken (the
body as) your share, then, after separating from his body, he will become
immortal – if he is someone who has achieved immortality through knowledge
or through action (karma).' Now, when they said, 'through knowledge or

through action,' they meant by 'knowledge' the knowledge of the fire(-altar), and by 'action' the ritual of the fire(-altar). And those who have this knowledge, or who do this ritual, they come to life again when they have died, and as soon as they come to life again they come to immortal life. But those who do not have this knowledge or who do not do this ritual, when they die they come to life again, but they become the food of this (Death) again and again. (*Shatapatha Brahmana* 10.4.3.1–10)

2.1.2.1.3. Prajapati dismembered and remembered

Falling apart and coming back together again is seen in Vedic literature as the problem of creation. The most common verb designating creation in the Brahmanas, srij, *means literally to emit; it refers to the emitting of a child from the body of a woman, of physical substances (tears, phlegm, urine, blood, and so forth) from any human body, of speech from the mouth, of dreams from the mind, and of the universe from Prajapati. When too much has been emitted, the creator is weakened and must be re-charged.*

In particular, things fall apart at their junctures or liminal points, joints; 'parvan' means both the joint of a human body (knee, elbow, and so forth) and the juncture or liminal moment of transition between one time period and another. The two junctures central to the ritual in this passage are the twilights, dawn and sunset, as well as the junctures of the full moon and the new moon, and the beginnings of the seasons, all of which must be ritually joined.

*The problem of falling apart in the act of creation is then analogised to the ever-present fear that the sacrifice itself will fall apart or go wrong in some way, which makes necessary complex restorations (*prayashcitti*) both for possible flaws in the performance of the sacrifice and for more general flaws in the life of the sacrificer.*

When Prajapati had emitted from himself his created beings, his joints were loosened. Now, Prajapati himself is really the year, and so his joints are the two junctures of day and night, the full moon and the new moon, and the beginnings of the seasons. With his loosened joints he was unable to get himself together, and so the gods drew him together by means of these sacrificial offerings: with the Agnihotra oblation into the fire they drew together the joint that is the two junctures of day and night; with the full-moon offering and the new-moon offering they drew together the joint that is the full moon and the new moon; and with the three offerings that are given every four months they drew together the joint that is the beginning of the seasons.

With his joints drawn together, he went forth to eat this food, the food that is for Prajapati to eat. Whoever knows this and begins to fast at that very moment, he draws together the joints of Prajapati that are that moment, and Prajapati helps him. Whoever knows this and begins to fast becomes truly an eater of food. Therefore he should begin to fast at that precise moment. (*Shatapatha Brahmana* 1.6.3.35–7)

2.1.2.2. The horse sacrifice

This text describes the horse sacrifice in great detail; I have selected from it a few key moments containing elements that are basic to Hindu thinking about all rituals. The first excerpt makes explicit the sexual symbolism; the next describes the preliminary killing of a dog, at the beginning of the ceremony, after the stallion has wandered for a year; then comes the killing of the stallion. There follows a ritual in which the king's wives pantomimed copulation with the dead horse, to the accompaniment of obscene verses that were already a source of embarrassment to the author of this text, who prescribes a restoration of clean, 'perfumed' speech at the end, to purify the vital breath that may have been driven out by the dirty talk that has gone before. The next passage tries to account for the obscenity with an elaborate, and strikingly cynical, political analogy between the horse's copulation with the queen and the king's use of his people. The horse is then dismembered – as was Prajapati, of whom the horse is another form. Finally, a restoration is prescribed in case anything goes wrong – in the life that the sacrifice is meant to restore, or in the sacrifice itself; or even in case everything goes right.

2.1.2.2.1. Seed as rice

The seed in this passage is physically present in the form of rice and symbolises the gold that is given to the priests. Through the identification of the horse, Prajapati, and the sacrificer, the seed that is placed in 'him' through the surrogate of rice is simultaneously placed in the priests, in the horse, in Prajapati, and in the sacrificer himself.

The priest cooks the priests' rice; this is really seed that he makes. Whatever clarified butter is left over, he uses to smear a rope. For clarified butter is brilliance, and the horse is of the nature of Prajapati, and so he furnishes Prajapati with abundant brilliance.

But the horse is still unpurified and unfit to be sacrificed. The rope is made of *darbha* grass, and *darbha* grasses are a means of purification; thus he purifies the horse and immolates one that is purified and fit to be sacrificed.

Now, when the horse was being immolated, his seed went out of him and became shining gold. Thus when (the sacrificer) gives shining gold (to the priests) he furnishes (the horse) with abundant seed.

Prajapati emitted the sacrifice. His greatness went out of him and entered the great sacrificial priests. Together with the great sacrificial priests he sought it, and together with the great sacrificial priests he found it. And when the great sacrificial priests eat the priests' rice, the sacrificer obtains for himself the greatness of the sacrifice. He gives shining gold in (the form of) the priests' rice, for rice is seed, and seed is gold, and thus by means of what is really seed he places seed in him. It is a hundred-weight of gold, for a man's life-span is a hundred years, and a man has a hundred powers. Thus he places long life, power, and virility in himself. (*Shatapatha Brahmana* 13.1.1.1–4)

2.1.2.2.2 Killing the dog

Four-eyed dogs, either supernatural animals or dogs with round marks above each eye, guard the portals of Yama's kingdom of hell. But the term catur-aksha *may also designate four* dice, *indicating the winning throw at the beginning of the agonistic sacrifice. Varuna is invoked as guardian of the moral order.*

(They lead the horse and dog to a pool located to the south of the sacrificial ground. When the dog can no longer touch bottom in the water, the officiating priest) hands over the four-eyed dog, saying, 'Varuna assails the one who would kill the horse'. He (the son of a prostitute) kills the four-eyed dog while saying the formula, 'Off with the mortal! Off with the dog!' Truly the dog is evil, one's fraternal enemy. Thus he slays his evil, his fraternal enemy. The club (used for the killing) is made of Sidhraka wood. Thus (the priest) accomplishes (*sadhayati*) every ritual for (the sacrificer).

The son of a whore kills (the dog). The gods have put sorrow into the whore. Thus he kills sorrow by means of sorrow. They say that evil seeks to grasp him who offers the horse sacrifice. He throws the dog beneath the feet of the horse. The horse that belongs to Prajapati has a thunderbolt. Thus by a thunderbolt he tramples down evil, the fraternal enemy. (*Taittiriya Brahmana* 3.8.4.2)

2.1.2.2.3 Killing the horse

The sacrificial animal is said to be 'quieted', by the priest known as the 'quieter' (the Shamitri or slaughterer); similarly, 'quietus' used to be a word for death, in English. This is a euphemism for the killing of the horse through the gentle means of suffocation, supposedly with his acquiescence. Euphemistic words for 'mother' or 'lady' are also used to designate the various queens who participate in this obscene ritual; and euphemisms obscure the speech made by one queen to another, perhaps complaining that she is not being brought to the stallion.

When the gods went upwards, they did not know the world of heaven, but the horse knew it; they go upwards with a horse in order to know the world of heaven. A cloth, an upper cloth, and gold is what they spread out for the horse, as they do for no other sacrificial animal, and on that they 'quiet' him. Thus they set him apart from all other sacrificial animals.

They kill this sacrificial animal when they 'quiet' him. As the priest 'quiets' him he says, 'Svaha to the breath! Svaha to the outward breath! Svaha to the inward breath!' and he offers the oblations. Thus he places the vital breaths within him, and thus the sacrifice is made with him as if he were a living sacrificial beast.

He leads up the (king's) wives, saying, 'Mother, Little Mother, Dear Little Mother!' 'No one is leading me!' (says one woman). Thus he summons them, and thus he makes them fit for the sacrifice. Saying, 'We call on you, (Indra), leader of the hosts of the hosts', the wives walk around (the horse) and thus make amends to him; and they also make amends to him by fanning him. They walk around him three times, for there are three worlds; and they fan him with these worlds. They walk around him three times more, which makes six; for there are six seasons; and they fan him with the seasons.

But the vital breaths go out of those who perform the fanning in the sacrifice. Nine times they walk about him, for there are nine vital breaths; thus they place the vital breaths in themselves, and the vital breaths do not go out of them. (They say,) 'I will urge the one who places the embryo'; 'You urge the one who places the embryo.' Now, the embryo means progeny and animals; thus she places progeny and animals in herself. (*Shatapatha Brahmana* 13.2.8.1–4)

2.1.2.2.4 The mockery of the women

This text merely refers to a series of insults by quoting the first words; a more complete version of some of the insults is given in the next text translated in this series, 2.1.2.2.5. Thus, the implication of the metaphor of the deer in the field seems to be that the farmer is unhappy about the loss of his crops, not happy that he has accidentally fed an animal. In this text, the response is simply a repetition of the verse itself; but when it is glossed in 2.1.2.2.5, the response is a parallel situation: the husband is sorry that his wife has been defiled, not glad that she has cuckolded him with a richer man. (The full text appears in the Vajasaneyi Samhita.*) The passage closes with a Rig Vedic verse (4.39.6) to Dadhikravan, a magical horse; as it contains the phrase, 'May he make our mouths sweet-smelling and prolong our lives', it serves to expiate the obscenity of the preceding passage. This obscenity, that will be immediately apparent to the English-speaking reader, was equally apparent to the ancient Indians. Though this part of the horse sacrifice is often referred to nervously in later Sanskrit texts, and remains a paradigm for many later myths, it is never (to my knowledge) quoted in full, nor has it ever been translated into English in its entirety. The present translation is thus intended to make explicit an important episode in Indian religious history that is often talked about by people (Hindus and Westerners) who literally do not know what it is that they are talking about.*

A cloth, an upper cloth, and gold is what they spread out for the horse, and on that they 'quiet' him. When the sacrificial animals have been 'quieted', the (king's) wives come up with water for washing the feet – four wives, and a maiden as the fifth, and four hundred women attendants. When the water for washing the feet is ready, they make the chief queen (Mahishi) lie down next to the horse, and they cover the two of them up with the upper cloth as they say the verse, 'Let the two of us cover ourselves in the world of heaven', for the world of heaven is where they 'quiet' the sacrificial animal. Then they draw out the penis of the horse and place it in the vagina of the chief queen, while she says, 'May the vigorous virile male, the layer of seed, lay the seed'; this she says for sexual intercourse.

While they are lying there, the sacrificer insults the horse by saying, 'Lift up her thighs and put it in her rectum.' No one insults (the sacrificer) back, lest there should be someone to act as a rival against the sacrificer.

The officiant (Adhvaryu) then insults the maiden: 'Hey, maiden, hey, maiden, the little female bird . . .' and she insults him back: 'Hey, officiant, hey, officiant, that little bird. . . .'

And then the overseer (Brahman) insults the chief queen: 'Hey, chief queen, hey, chief queen, your mother and father climb to the top of a tree. . . .' She has as her attendants a hundred daughters of kings; they insult the overseer in return: 'Hey, overseer, hey, overseer, your mother and your father play in the top of a tree. . . .'

Then the cantor (Udgatri) insults the king's favourite wife: 'Hey, favourite, hey, favourite, wife, raise her up erect. . . .' She has as her attendants a hundred royal women; they insult the cantor in return: 'Hey, cantor, hey, cantor, raise *him* up erect. . . .'

Then the invoker (Hotri) insults the rejected wife: 'Hey, rejected wife, hey, rejected wife, when inside her tight crack. . . .' She has as her attendants a hundred daughters of bards and village headmen; they insult the invoker in return: 'Hey, invoker, hey, invoker, when the gods see that miserable penis. . . .'

Then the carver (Kshatri) insults the fourth wife: 'Hey, fourth wife, hey, fourth wife, when the deer eats the barley, (the farmer) does not hope to nourish the animal. . . .' She has as her attendants a hundred daughters of carvers and charioteers; they insult the carver in return: 'Hey, carver, hey, carver, when the deer eats the barley, (the farmer) does not hope to nourish the animal. . . .'

These insulting speeches are for all kinds of attainment, for through the horse sacrifice all desires are achieved. Thinking, 'With all kinds of speech we will achieve all kinds of desires', they make the chief queen get up. Then the women walk back the way they came, and the others utter at the end a sweet-smelling verse, the verse that begins, 'I praise Dadhikravan.'

For the life-span and the gods go out of those who speak impure speech in the sacrifice. Thus they purify their speech to keep the gods from going out of the sacrifice. (*Shatapatha Brahmana* 13.5.2.1–10)

2.1.2.2.5 The king copulates with the people

'The little female bird rocks back and forth making the sound "ahalag" as he thrusts the penis into the slit, making the sound "nigalgal", and the vulva swallows it up.' Now, that bird is really the people, for the people rock back and forth at the thrust of the royal power. And the slit is the people, and the penis is the royal power, which presses against the people; and so the one who has royal power is hurtful to the people.

'Your mother and father climb to the top of a tree; saying, "I desire to have you," your father passes his fist back and forth in the slit.' Now, the mother is this (earth), and the father is that (sky); by means of these two (the priest) causes (the king) to go to the world of heaven. The top of the royal power is glory, and thus he causes him to attain the pinnacle of royal power, glory. The slit is the people, and the fist is royal power, which presses against the people;

and so the one who has royal power is hurtful to the people.

'When the deer eats the barley, (the farmer) does not hope to nourish the animal; when the low-born woman becomes the mistress of a noble man, (her husband) does not hope to get rich on that nourishment.' Now, the barley is the people, and the deer is the royal power; thus he makes the people food for the royal power, and so the one who has royal power eats the people. And so the king does not raise animals; and so one does not anoint as king the son of a woman born of the people.

But the vital breaths go out of those who speak impure speech in the sacrifice. And so they utter at the end a sweet-smelling verse, the verse that begins, 'I praise Dadhikravan.' Thus they purify (their) speech, and the vital breaths do not go out of them. (*Shatapatha Brahmana* 13.2.9.6–9)

2.1.2.2.6 Dismembering the horse

Prajapati's eye swelled up (*ashvayat*); then it fell out. From that, the horse (*ashva*) was born. Because of the swelling, the horse is called a horse. By means of the horse sacrifice, the gods put that eye back in place; and whoever sacrifices with the horse sacrifice makes Prajapati whole, and he himself becomes whole. Indeed, this is the restoration for everything; it is the cure for everything. By means of this, the gods crossed over every evil; by means of this they even crossed over the evil of killing a Brahmin. And whoever sacrifices with the horse sacrifice crosses over every evil, even the killing of a Brahmin.

It was the left eye of Prajapati that swelled up; that is why they cut into pieces the left side of the horse, though they use the right side of other sacrificial animals. There is a mat made of reeds. For the horse had the waters as his womb, and the reeds are born in the waters; thus one unites him with the womb from which he was born. The chant they use is the four-fold chant. For a bee wounded the horse's thigh, and by means of the four-fold chant they restored him; thus they use the four-fold chant for the sake of the wholeness of the horse. The last day is an overnight ritual using all of the chants; for the overnight ritual that uses all of the chants is everything, and the horse sacrifice is everything; through it, one obtains everything and keeps everything. (*Shatapatha Brahmana* 13.3.1.1–4)

2.1.2.2.7 The restorations

This text invokes Vayu as the god who transforms the seed within the womb, who breathes life into the embryo, and Agni as the digestive fire within the bellies of all creatures. The penultimate part of this ritual may also be performed not as part of the horse sacrifice but merely by itself, to find lost objects.

Now for the restorations. If the horse should mount a mare, (the priest) should make an oblation of milk to the wind (Vayu); for the wind is the one who transforms the seed; the wind is the vital breath, and the vital breath is what transforms the seed. Thus he puts seed (back) into (the horse) by means of seed.

And if the horse should become lame, he should make an offering of rice and milk to Pushan, for Pushan rules over domestic animals; thus he satisfies the one who owns domestic animals, who rules over domestic animals, and so the horse becomes healthy.

And if the horse should be sick but not lame, he should make an offering to the fire within-all-men, the offering of a cake on twelve bricks, on earth-bricks; for this (earth) is the fire within-all-men; thus he satisfies this earth, and so the horse becomes healthy.

And if the horse's eye should become injured or diseased, he should make an offering of rice and milk to the sun, Surya; for the sun is the eye of creatures; when he rises, everything here moves; thus he puts an eye (back) into (the horse) by means of an eye. And he uses an offering of rice and milk (*caru*) because it is by means of the eye that the self moves (*carati*).

And if the horse should die in water, he should make an offering of rice and milk with barley to Varuna, for Varuna seizes the one who dies in water; thus he satisfies the god who seizes (the horse). And when that god is satisfied with him, he allows him to slaughter another (horse), and so he slaughters one that has been approved by that god. And he uses an offering made of barley because barley is of the nature of Varuna.

And if the horse should get lost, he should make a sacrificial offering of three oblations: an offering of a cake on one brick for heaven and earth, an offering of milk for the wind, and an offering of rice and milk for the sun. For whatever is lost is lost between heaven and earth; and the wind blows upon it, and the sun warms it; nothing is ever lost beyond the realm of these gods. And even by itself, this ritual finds what has been lost; whatever other thing of his is lost, let him sacrifice with this ritual, and he will surely find it.

And if enemies should get the horse, or if the horse should die other than in water, they should bring another horse and consecrate it by sprinkling it with water; this is the restoration for that. (*Shatapatha Brahmana* 13.3.8.1–6)

2.1.2.3 The human sacrifice of Shunahshepa

This story involves a chain of substitutions made possible by the analogies between the original and the surrogate. First a living child, whose name, Rohita, means 'Red deer', is given in return for a prayer and a promise. Then that child is substituted for the usual sacrificial animal; and then another child is substituted for that child, a Brahmin or priest for a Kshatriya or member of the royal and martial class. This substitute child, Shunahshepa, is himself a kind of substitute: he and his brothers are named after dogs, not persons. Shunahshepa also stands in, liminally, for his older and younger brothers. And in the sacrifice, the Soma plant (accompanied by Vedic verses) is substituted for the human victim. Finally, after being substituted for the son of the king, Shunahshepa finally substitutes for the eldest son of a royal sage.

The intermixture of castes in this myth is complex. Shunahshepa's name and those of his brothers are the names of Untouchables, not Brahmins. But the text explicitly identifies Ajigarta as a Brahmin seer and Shunahshepa himself as a Brahmin. Later, Shunahshepa accuses his cruel father of acting like a Shudra when he is willing to sacrifice his own son; Shudras are the lowest of the four classes of Indian society, the slaves, ranked below the three classes of twice-born men, members of the Aryan community (Brahmins, Kshatriyas, and Vaishyas, or the common people). Thus Shunahshepa's father, Ajigarta, is a Brahmin who acts like a Shudra or Untouchable (and gives his sons Untouchable names); later, the ungenerous sons of the king are cursed to become transformed into Dasyus or 'slaves', the non-Aryan people of India, beyond the Hindu pale.

But as these people are brought lower by their evil deeds, to the point where the bottom of the Aryan world shades off into the dark world of the non-Aryans, so Shunahshepa rises by his virtues to the point where the top two classes, Brahmin and Kshatriya, begin to blur. In renaming Shunahshepa, Vishvamitra has confirmed Shunahshepa's Brahmin nature; but then, when he is to be made king, Shunahshepa asks how he can become the son of a Kshatriya. Vishvamitra himself, though a Vedic priest, is actually a royal sage (rajarshi); he was born a king, and his sons are descendants of Kushika and Gathin, two great kings, but through his deeds he became a sage. As Vishvamitra is both a king and a sage, Shunahshepa (now called Devarata) inherits from him both royal power and sacred knowledge.

The tale begins with a reference to the three debts that every man has: he owes sacrifices to the gods, a son (to make the funeral offerings) to the fathers or ancestors, and the study of the Vedas to the sages. It also contains a very early reference to the doctrine of the four Ages, or Yugas, of steadily decreasing length and quality, named after four throws of the dice. The first is the Krita Yuga, the winning throw of four, the Golden Age; the second and third are the Age of the Trey and the age of the Deuce; and the last, the present age, is the throw of one, the Kali Yuga or Dark Age.

Harishcandra Vaidhasa, the descendant of Ikshvaku, was the son of a king; he had a hundred wives, but none of them bore him a son. (The sages) Parvata and Narada lived in his house; he asked Narada, 'People who understand and those who do not understand, both of them desire a son. What does one get by means of a son? Tell me that, Narada.' When Narada was asked this question in one verse, he answered in ten:

'If a father sees the face of his son born alive, he repays a debt through him and achieves immortality. As many joys as there are in the earth for creatures who have vital breath, as many as there are in fire, and as many as there are in water, greater than this is the joy that a father has in a son. Fathers have always crossed over the deep darkness by means of a son, for a son gives a father comfort and carries him across; the self is born from the self. What use is dirt or the black antelope skin (of the ascetic)? What use are beards and asceticism? "Seek a son, O Brahmins"; that is what people keep saying. Food is breath and clothing is protection; gold is beauty and cattle are marriage; a wife is a friend and a daughter is misery. But a son is a light in the highest heaven.

'The father enters his wife; he becomes an embryo inside her, who is now his mother. In her he becomes new again and is born in the tenth month. And so the wife is called wife (*jaya*) because he is born (*jayate*) again in her. This is the potency; the potency infuses the seed. The gods and the seers together brought great glory to her; the gods said to men, "This is your mother again. There is no heavenly world for a man who has no son." All the beasts know this, and therefore a son mounts his mother or his sister. This is the broad path, easy to use, on which those who have sons travel without sorrow. The beasts and birds look at it, and therefore they have intercourse even with their mother.' This is what (Narada) told (Harishcandra).

Then (Narada) said to (Harishcandra), 'Seek help from Varuna, the king; say to him, "Let a son be born to me, and I will sacrifice him to you."' '' 'Yes,' said (Harishcandra). He went to Varuna, the king, and said, 'Let a son be born to me, and I will sacrifice him to you.' 'Yes,' said (Varuna). A son was born to (Harishcandra), named Rohita. (Varuna) said to (Harishcandra), 'A son has been born to you; sacrifice him to me.' (Harishcandra) said, 'When the sacrificial beast becomes over ten days old, he becomes fit for sacrifice. Let him become over ten days old, and then I will sacrifice to you.' 'Yes,' said (Varuna). (Rohita) became over ten days old. (Varuna) said to (Harishcandra), 'He has become over ten days old; sacrifice him to me.' (Harishcandra) said, 'Just when the teeth of the sacrificial beast appear, that is when he becomes fit for sacrifice. Let his teeth appear, and then I will sacrifice to you.' 'Yes,' said (Varuna).

(Rohita's) teeth appeared. (Varuna) said to (Harishcandra), 'His teeth have appeared; sacrifice him to me.' (Harishcandra) said, 'When the teeth of the sacrificial beast fall out, he becomes fit for sacrifice. Let his teeth fall out, and then I will sacrifice to you.' 'Yes,' said (Varuna). (Rohita's) teeth fell out. (Varuna) said to (Harishcandra), 'His teeth have fallen out; sacrifice him to me.' (Harishcandra) said, 'Just when the teeth of the sacrificial beast appear again, that is when he becomes fit for sacrifice. Let his teeth appear again, and then I will sacrifice him to you.' 'Yes,' said (Varuna). (Rohita's) teeth appeared again. (Varuna) said to (Harishcandra), 'His teeth have appeared again; sacrifice him to me.' (Harishcandra) said, 'When the Kshatriya is able to bear arms, he becomes fit for sacrifice. Let him win his arms, and then I will sacrifice to you.' 'Yes,' said (Varuna). (Rohita) won his arms. (Varuna) said to (Harishcandra), 'He has won his arms; sacrifice him to me.'

'Yes,' said (Harishcandra), and then he spoke to his son: 'My dear son, this one gave you to me. Come, let me sacrifice you to him.' 'No,' said (Rohita), and he took up his bow and went to the wilderness, and for a year he wandered in the wilderness. Then Varuna seized (Harishcandra), the descendant of Ikshvaku, (with disease), and so his belly swelled up.

When Rohita heard about this, he came back from the wilderness to the village. Indra took a human form and went to him and said, 'Various kinds of good fortune belong to one who exhausts himself – so we have heard, Rohita. Evil dwells among men in a crowd; Indra himself is the friend of the wanderer.

Wander.' Thinking to himself, 'This Brahmin told me to wander,' (Rohita) wandered in the wilderness for a second year. He came back from the wilderness to the village.

Indra took a human form and went to him and said, 'The legs of the wanderer flower, and his body grows and bears fruit. All his evils fall asleep, slain by his exhaustion on the journey. Wander.' Thinking to himself, 'This Brahmin told me to wander,' (Rohita) wandered in the wilderness for a third year. He came back from the wilderness to the village. Indra took a human form and went to him and said, 'The lot of the man who sits, sits; of the man who stands up, it stands up; the lot of the man who lies down, lies down; and of the man who moves forth as he wanders, it moves forth. Wander.' Thinking to himself, 'This Brahmin told me to wander,' (Rohita) wandered in the wilderness for a fourth year.

He came back from the wilderness to the village. Indra took a human form and went to him and said, 'The man who lies down becomes the Dark Age, and when he gets up he is the Age of the Deuce. Standing upright, he is the Age of the Trey, but he becomes the Golden Age when he wanders. Wander.' Thinking to himself, 'This Brahmin told me to wander,' (Rohita) wandered in the wilderness for a fifth year.

He came back from the wilderness to the village. Indra took a human form and went to him and said, 'Wandering, one finds honey; wandering, the sweet Udumbara fruit. Look at the superiority of the sun, who never gets tired of wandering. Wander.' Thinking to himself, 'This Brahmin told me to wander,' (Rohita) wandered in the wilderness for a sixth year.

In the wilderness, he came upon Ajigarta Sauyavasi, a seer, who was overcome with hunger. He had three sons: Shunahpucha, Shunahshepa, and Shunolangula ('Dog-arse', 'Dog-prick', and 'Dog-tail'). (Rohita) said to (Ajigarta), 'Seer, I will give you a hundred (cows); I want to ransom myself by means of one of these (sons).' The father held back his eldest son and said, 'Not this one.' 'Not this one,' said the mother, speaking of the youngest. But they agreed upon the middle son, Shunahshepa. (Rohita) give (Ajigarta) a hundred (cows), took the boy, and went back from the wilderness to the village.

He came to his father and said, 'My dear father, come, let me ransom myself with this one.' (Harishchandra) went up to Varuna, the king, and said, 'Let me sacrifice this one to you.' 'Yes,' said Varuna; 'a Brahmin is more than a Kshatriya.' (Varuna) proclaimed to (Harishchandra) the sacrificial ritual of the consecration of a king. And on the occasion of the anointing, (Harishchandra) took (Shunahshepa) for the human sacrificial beast.

Vishvamitra was his invoker, Jamadagni his officiant, Vasishtha his overseer, and Ayasya his cantor. When (Shunahshepa) had been brought forward, they could not find anyone to tie him down. Ajigarta Sauyavasi said, 'Give me another hundred and I will tie him down.' They gave him another hundred (cows), and he tied him down. But when (Shunahshepa) had been brought forward, tied down, and carried around the fire, they could not find anyone to slaughter him. Ajigarta Sauyavasi said, 'Give me another hundred and I will slaughter him.' They gave him another hundred, and he stepped forward, whetting his knife.

Then Shunahshepa realised, 'They are going to slaughter me as if I were not a human being. Come, I will ask the gods for help.' He sought help from Prajapati first among the gods, with the verse that begins, 'Now who, which one of the immortals . . .?' (*Rig Veda* 1.24.1). Prajapati said to him, 'Agni is the nearest of the gods. Seek help from him.' He sought help from Agni with the verse that begins, 'Agni, first of the immortals . . .' (*Rig Veda* 1.24.2). Agni said to him, 'Savitri is the one in charge of Soma pressings. Seek help from him.' He sought help from Savitri with the three verses that begin, 'You, Savitri, the god . . .' (1.24.3–5). Savitri said to him, 'You were tied down for Varuna, the king. Seek help from him.' He sought help from Varuna, the king, with the next thirty-one verses (1.24.6–25 and 1.25.1–11). Varuna said to him, 'Agni is the one who is the mouth of the gods, the best friend. Praise him and we will set you free.' He praised Agni with the next twenty-two verses (1.26.1–10; 1.27.1–12). Agni said to him, 'Praise the All-gods, and we will set you free.' He praised the All-gods with the verse, 'We bow to the big ones; we bow to the small ones' (1.27.13).

The All-gods said to him, 'Indra is the one who is the mightiest of the gods, the most powerful, the strongest, the best, the best at bringing people across trouble. Praise him, and then we will set you free.' He praised Indra with the hymn that begins, 'O true one, the drinkers of Soma . . .' (1.29) and with the (first) fifteen verses of the hymn that follows it (1.30.1–15). When Indra had been praised with those verses he was satisfied, and he gave (Shunahshepa) a chariot made of gold. Then Shunahshepa went back to him with the verse that begins, 'Indra forever . . .' (1.30.16), and Indra said to him, 'Praise the Ashvins, and then we will set you free.' He praised the Ashvins with the following three verses (1.30.17–19). The Ashvins said to him, 'Praise Ushas, the dawn, and then we will set you free.' He praised Ushas with the following three verses (1.30.20–22). At each verse that he recited, one rope fell away (from Shunahshepa) and the belly of (Harishcandra) the descendant of Ikshvaku became smaller; and when the last verse was recited, the (last) rope fell away, and (Harishcandra) the descendant of Ikshvaku was free of disease.

The priests said to (Shunahshepa), 'Now you tell us how to perform this ritual today.' Then Shunahshepa had a vision of the rapid Soma pressing, and he pressed the Soma with four verses (1.28.5–8); and he put it into the wooden bowl while reciting (1.28.9); and he took hold of it and made the offering while reciting (1.28.1–4). Then he led (Harishcandra) the descendant of Ikshvaku to the final purifying bath, reciting (4.1.4–5), and caused him to worship the upper fire into which oblations are offered, while saying the verse, 'Shunahshepa was tied down for a thousand . . .' (5.2.7).

Then Shunahshepa sat down on Vishvamitra's lap. Ajigarta Sauyavasi said, 'Seer, give me back my son.' 'No,' said Vishvamitra, 'the gods have given him to me.' And (Shunahshepa) became known as Devarata ('given [*rata*] by the gods [*devas*]'), the son of Vishvamitra. His descendants are the Kapileyas and the Babhravas.

Ajigarta Sauyavasi said (to Shunahshepa), 'Come here; let us invite you. By birth, you are the son of Ajigarta, a descendant of Angiras, a famous sage. O seer, do not depart from the line of your grandfathers; come back to me.' Shunahshepa said, 'They all saw you with the butchering knife in your hand, something that has never happened even among Shudras. You chose three hundred cows over me, O descendant of the sage Angiras.' Ajigarta Sauyavasi said, 'My dear boy, this great evil action that I committed pains me. I would like to make amends to you for that. Please accept a thousand cows.' Shunahshepa said, 'He who has once committed an evil act would commit another one. You have not given up your Shudra ways; what you have done cannot be mended and restored.' At the word, 'restored', Vishvamitra joined in and said, 'Sauyavasi was truly horrible as he stood there, ready to commit the slaughter, holding the butchering knife. Do not be his son; become my son.'

Shunahshepa said (to Vishvamitra), 'O son of a king, tell us how I who am a descendant of Angiras can become your son.' Vishvamitra said, 'You would be the oldest of my sons; your offspring would be the highest. Accept my divine inheritance; with this I invite you.' Shunahshepa said, 'Tell (your other sons) to agree to my friendship and my good fortune, so that I may become your son, O bull of the Bharatas.' Vishvamitra announced to his sons: 'Madhuchandas, Rishabha, Renu, and Ashtaka, listen, and all your brothers: grant him the status of the eldest son.'

Now, Vishvamitra had a hundred sons, fifty of them older than Madhuchandas and fifty younger. The older ones did not think this was a good idea. (Vishvamitra) cursed them: 'Your offspring will inherit the ends (of the earth).' They are the Andhras, Pundras, Shabaras, Pulindas, and Mutibas who live in large numbers beyond the borders (of the sacred land of India, Aryavarta); most of the Dasyus are the descendants of Vishvamitra. But Madhuchandas and the other fifty said, 'We accept what our father has agreed to. All of us place you (Shunahshepa) in front of us; we stand after you.' Then Vishvamitra was pleased, and he praised his sons: 'My sons, you will have cattle and heroic sons, since by agreeing to my will you have made me a man with heroic sons. With the heroic Devarata in front to lead you, you, my sons, the descendants of king Gathin, will all become prosperous. This is the truth I tell you. This is your hero, Devarata; follow him, O descendants of king Kushika. As his inheritance from me, he shall have you and the knowledge that we know.' The sons of Vishvamitra all agreed to this happily, all of them together; the descendants of king Gathin made Devarata the ruler and the eldest. The sage Devarata received both inheritances, the right to rule over the Jahnus and the divine knowledge of the descendants of Gathin.

This is the story of Shunahshepa, told in hundreds of verses called Gathas in addition to verses from the *Rig Veda*. The invoker tells this story to the king after the king has been anointed. (The invoker) tells it while seated on a golden cushion, and (the officiant) says the responses while seated on a golden cushion. Gold is glory, and so (the invoker) makes (the king) prosper in glory. 'Om' is the response to a verse from the *Rig Veda*; 'Yes' is the response to a Gatha verse. For 'Om' has to do with the gods, and 'Yes' has to do with men. In this way, by means of what has to do with the gods and what has to do with men, (the narrator) sets (the king) free from evil and from sin. Therefore a victorious king should have this story of Shunahshepa recited, even when he is not sacrificing, and then not the slightest bit of sin will be left in him. He should give a thousand (cows) to the one who tells the story, and a hundred to the one who makes the responses, and the two (gold) cushions and a white mule-chariot to the invoker (in addition to the thousand cows). And those who wish for sons should also tell the story, and they will get sons; yes, they will get sons. (*Aitareya Brahmana* 7.13–18)

2.1.3 Upanishads: meditation on the sacrificial horse
The Upanishads are philosophical speculations on the prayers and rituals of the Rig Veda; *each Upanishad, like each Brahmana, is attached to a particular Veda. This text, which belongs to the* Shatapatha Brahmana *of the* White Yajur Veda *(the text that describes the horse sacrifice), is a meditation on the horse sacrifice.*

The horse is here linked with the Gandharvas (cognate with 'centaur'), demigods connected with horses and fertility, the male consorts of the celestial nymphs (Apsarases). And in addition to his associations with Prajapati and Death, inherited from the Brahmanas, the horse is like the cosmic Person, himself a form of Prajapati: the horse creates the hymns (the Rig Veda), *the formulas (the* Yajur Veda), *and the chants (the* Sama Veda), *in a manner that parallels their creation from the dismemberment of the cosmic Person (see below, 2.2.1.1). Other connections with human sacrifice are also quite clear: the horse is allowed to grow for a year, just as Shunahshepa is allowed to grow older before he is sacrificed. The stallion was set free to wander for a year before he was sacrificed; Shunahshepa duplicated this wandering when he went into the wilderness to avoid his own sacrifice.*

Om! The dawn is the head of the sacrificial horse. The sun is his eye, the wind his breath, the fire within-all-men his open mouth. The year is the body of the sacrificial horse. The sky is his back, the middle realm of space his stomach, the earth his underbelly; the quarters of the sky are his sides, the intermediate quarters his ribs; the seasons are his limbs, the junctures between the months and the fortnights his joints; day and night are his feet, the stars are his bones, and the clouds are his flesh. The food in his stomach is the sands, and the rivers are his entrails; his liver and lungs are the mountains, and the plants and trees are the hairs on his body. The east is his forehand, and the setting sun is his hindquarters. When he yawns, then there is lightning; when he shakes himself, it thunders; and when he urinates, it rains. Speech is his whinny.

The day is the golden bowl in front of the horse; its womb is in the eastern ocean. The night is the golden bowl behind the horse; its womb is in the western ocean. These two bowls arose on both sides of the horse. He becomes a charger and carries the gods; he becomes a racehorse and carries the Gandharvas; he becomes a running horse and carries the demons; he becomes a stallion and carries men. The sea is his kinsman; the sea is his womb.

In the beginning, there was nothing at all here. This world was enveloped by death, by hunger, for truly hunger is death. Then (death) thought to himself: 'I wish I had a body.' He moved about, praising, and water came out of him as he was praising. 'Water (*kam*) came out of me while I was praising (*arcatas*),' he thought; and this is why brightness is called brightness (*arka*). Whoever knows this reason why brightness is called brightness always has water. For the waters are brightness.

The froth of the waters became solid; it became the earth. He became exhausted on this (earth); and from him, exhausted and heated, came out a heat that became fire. He divided himself into three parts. (Fire was one third); the sun was one third; and air was one third. Thus the vital breath is divided into three parts. The eastern quarter is his head; the north-east and south-east are his shoulders; the western quarter is his tail; the north-west and south-west are his thighs; the south and north are his flanks; the sky is his back; the middle realm of space is his stomach. This (earth) is his chest. He stands firm in the waters; whoever knows this stands firm wherever he goes.

He desired, 'I wish that a second body were produced for me.' He, who was hunger, death, caused speech to copulate with mind. The seed that was there became the year; for there had not been a year before that. (Death) bore (the year) for as long a time as a year, and after that he emitted him. As soon as (the year) was born, (death) opened his mouth wide to eat him. (The year) made the sound, 'Bhan!' (a cry of terror, but also the root of a verb that means 'to speak'), and that became speech.

(Death) thought to himself, 'If I kill him, I will make just a little food for myself, less (than if I let him live and grow).' With that speech, with that body, he emitted this whole world, whatever exists – the hymns, the formulas, the chants, the metres, the sacrifices, the creatures, the animals. And whatever he emitted, he started to eat. Indeed, he eats (*atti*) everything; that is why Aditi (the infinite) is called Aditi. And whoever knows why Aditi is called Aditi becomes an eater of everything; everything becomes his food.

He desired, 'Let me sacrifice more, with a greater sacrifice.' He exhausted himself, and he generated heat in himself, and out of him as he was exhausted and heated came glory and virility. Now, glory and virility are the vital breaths; and so when the vital breaths had gone out of him, his body began to swell. His mind was in his body.

He desired, 'I wish this body were fit for sacrifice. I wish that I could have it for my own body.' And it became a horse (*ashva*) because it had swelled (*ashvat*). 'It has become fit for sacrifice (*medhyam*),' he thought, and that is why the horse sacrifice is called the Ashva-medha. Whoever knows him in this way really knows the horse sacrifice.

He thought about him but did not confine him. After a year, he sacrificed him to himself, and assigned (other) sacrificial animals to the (other) gods. Therefore when men sacrifice to Prajapati they call it a sacrifice to all the gods.

The (sun) who heats is really the horse sacrifice, and the year is its body. This (earthly) fire is brightness, and the worlds are its body. They are two, the (solar) brightness and the (earthly fire of the) horse sacrifice; but they are also a single god, death.

He (who knows this) conquers repeated death; death does not get him; he becomes one of these gods. (*Brihadaranyaka Upanishad* 1.1.1–2; 1.2.1–7)

2.2 MYTHS

2.2.1 *Rig Veda*

2.2.1.1 The dismemberment of the cosmic Person

In this famous hymn, called the Purushasukta *or the 'Hymn of Man', the gods create the world by dismembering the cosmic giant, Purusha, the primeval male or Person, who is the victim in a Vedic sacrifice. This sacrifice creates the whole universe, including the four classes of ancient Indian society (the* varnas). *The 'sacrifice' designates both the ritual and the victim killed in the ritual; moreover, the Person is both the victim that the gods sacrificed and the divinity to whom the sacrifice was dedicated; that is, he is both the subject and the object of the sacrifice. These are typical Vedic paradoxes that we will encounter again in other texts. The sacrifice creates the sacrifice; so, too, Purusha creates Viraj, the active female creative principle, and Viraj creates Purusha. In later Sankhya philosophy, where Purusha is regarded as spirit, Viraj is replaced as the consort of Purusha by Prakriti, or material nature.*

The Person has a thousand heads, a thousand eyes, a thousand feet. He pervaded the earth on all sides and extended beyond it as far as ten fingers. It is the Person who is all this, whatever has been and whatever is to be. He is the ruler of immortality, when he grows beyond everything through food. Such is his greatness, and the Person is yet more than this. All creatures are a quarter of him; three quarters are what is immortal in heaven. With three quarters the Person rose upwards, and one quarter of him still remains here. From this (quarter on earth) he spread out in all directions, into that which eats and that which does not eat. From him Viraj was born, and from Viraj came the Person. When he was born, he ranged beyond the earth behind and before.

When the gods performed the sacrifice with the Person as the offering, spring was the clarified butter, summer the fuel, autumn the oblation. They anointed the Person, the sacrifice born at the beginning, upon the sacred grass. With him the gods, perfected beings, and sages sacrificed. From that sacrifice in which everything was offered, the melted fat was collected, and he made it into those beasts who live in the air, in the forest, and in villages. From that sacrifice in which everything was offered, the verses and chants were born, the metres were born from it, and from it the formulas were born. Horses were born from it, and those other animals that have two rows of teeth; cows were born from it, and from it goats and sheep were born.

When they divided the Person, into how many parts did they apportion him? What do they call his mouth, his two arms and thighs and feet? His mouth became the Brahmin; his arms were made into the Kshatriya (warrior); his thighs the Vaishyas (the people); and from his feet the Shudras (servants) were born. The moon was born from his mind; from his eye the sun was born. Indra and Agni came from his mouth, and from his vital breath the Wind was born. From his navel the middle realm of space arose; from his head the sky evolved. From his two feet came the earth, and the quarters of the sky from his ear. Thus they set the worlds in order.

There were seven enclosing-sticks for him and thrice seven fuel-sticks, when the gods, performing the sacrifice, bound the Person as the sacrificial beast. With the sacrifice the gods sacrificed to the sacrifice. These were the first dharmas. These very powers reached the dome of the sky where dwell the perfected beings, the ancient gods. (*Rig Veda* 10.90)

2.2.1.2 The three strides of Vishnu

Vishnu seems prominent in the Rig Veda *only through Hindu hindsight. This hymn, the only one addressed to Vishnu alone, is the basis of the later myth of the dwarf avatar who takes three steps to win the world from the demons. But the propping apart of heaven and earth, measuring out and establishing the three worlds for all creatures to dwell in, is a central Vedic cosmogonic act, usually attributed not to Vishnu but to more important Vedic gods like Indra or Varuna.*

Let me now sing the heroic deeds of Vishnu, who has measured apart the realms of earth, who propped up the upper dwelling-place, striding far as he stepped forth three times. They praise for his heroic deeds Vishnu who lurks in the mountains, wandering like a ferocious wild beast, in whose three wide strides all creatures dwell. Let this song of inspiration go forth to Vishnu, the wide-striding bull who lives in the mountains, who alone with but three steps measured apart this long, far-reaching dwelling-place. In his three footprints, inexhaustibly full of honey, people rejoice in the sacrificial drink. Alone, he supports threefold the earth and the sky and all creatures. Would that I might reach his dear place of refuge, where men who love the gods rejoice. For there one draws close to the wide-striding Vishnu; there, in his highest footstep, is the fountain of honey. We wish to go to your dwelling-places, where there are untiring, many-horned cattle. There the highest footstep of the wide-stepping bull shines brightly down. (*Rig Veda* 1.154)

2.2.1.3 Rudra

Only three hymns are addressed to Rudra in the Rig Veda, *but even there the rich ambivalence of his character lays the basis for the development of his descendant, the Hindu god Shiva. This hymn invokes Rudra on behalf of Manu, the primeval ancestor of mankind, who performed the first sacrifice by mortals for immortals. It calls upon Rudra's servants and children, the Maruts, gods of the storm, and begs for protection from the killing of men and the killing of cattle.*

We bring these thoughts to the mighty Rudra, the god with braided hair, who rules over heroes, so that it will be well with our two-footed and four-footed creatures, and in this village all will flourish unharmed. Have mercy on us, Rudra, and give us life-force. We wish to bow low in service to you who rule over heroes. Whatever happiness and health Manu the father won by sacrifice, we wish to gain that with you to lead us forth. We wish to gain your kindness, Rudra, through sacrifice to the gods, for you are generous. O ruler over heroes, come to our families with kindness. Let us offer the oblation to you with our heroes free from injury.

We call down for help the dreaded Rudra who completes the sacrifice, the sage who flies. Let him repel far from us the anger of the gods; it is his kindness that we choose to have. Tawny boar of the sky, dreaded form with braided hair, we call you down and we bow low. Holding in his hand the healing medicines that we long for, let him grant us protection, shelter, refuge. These words are spoken for Rudra, the father of the Maruts, words sweeter than sweet, to strengthen him. And grant us, O immortal, the food for mortals.

Have mercy on us, and on our children and grandchildren. Do not slaughter the great one among us or the small one among us, nor the growing or the grown. Rudra, do not kill our father or our mother, nor harm the bodies dear to us. Do not harm us in our children or grandchildren, nor in our life-span, nor in our cows or our horses. Rudra, do not in fury slaughter our heroes. With oblations we call you here for ever.

I have driven these praises to you as the herdsman drives his cattle. Grant us kindness, father of the Maruts, for your kindness brings blessings most merciful, and so it is your help that we choose to have. Keep far away from us your cow-killing and man-killing power, O ruler of heroes. Have mercy on us and speak for us, O god, and grant us double protection. Seeking help, we have spoken in homage to him. Let Rudra with the Maruts hear our call. Let Mitra, Varuna, Aditi, the goddess of the river Sindhu, Earth and Sky grant this to us. (*Rig Veda* 1.114)

2.2.2 Brahmanas: the creation of gods and demons

The arbitrary nature of the distinction between gods and demons, both sons of Prajapati, is emphasised by the circular logic of this myth: Prajapati makes the demons evil because they are evil, and he creates them out of darkness, but he then makes their substance into night. The text challenges traditional statements that the gods conquered the demons in fair combat, maintaining that, instead, Prajapati corrupted them.

Prajapati was born to live for a thousand years. Just as one might see in the distance the far shore of a river, so he saw the far shore of his own life. He desired progeny, and so he sang hymns and exhausted himself, and he placed the power to produce progeny in himself. From his mouth he created the gods, and when the gods were created they entered the sky (*divam*); and this is why the gods are gods (*devas*), because when they were created they entered the sky. And there was daylight (*diva*) for him when he had created them, and this is why the gods are gods, because there was daylight for him when he had created them.

Then with his downward breath he created the demons; when they were created they entered this earth, and there was darkness for him when he had created them. Then he knew that he had created evil, since darkness appeared to him when he had created them. Then he pierced them with evil, and it was because of this that they were overcome.

Therefore it is said, 'The battle between gods and demons did not happen as it is told in the narratives and histories, for Prajapati pierced them with evil and it was because of this that they were overcome.' And so the sage has said, 'You have not fought with anyone for a single day, nor do you have any enemy, O bountiful Indra. Your battles which they tell about are all magic illusion; you fought no enemy today, nor in the past' (*Rig Veda* 10.54.2).

The daylight which had appeared for him when he had created the gods he made into day; and the darkness which had appeared for him when he had created the demons he made into night. And they are day and night. (*Shatapatha Brahmana* 11.1.6.6–11)

2.2.3 Upanishads

2.2.3.1 Indra and the demons

This text gives two different but related explanations for the origin of heresy, both of which expand upon the theme of the preceding text, the corruption of the demons by the gods. In the first episode, Brihaspati, the household priest of the gods, takes the form of Shukra, the household priest of the demons, in order to teach the demons a wrong doctrine. In the course of this corruption, he actually cites scripture: he quotes from the Katha Upanishad *(2.4), in which the boy Naciketas goes to the world of the dead and questions the god of death. In the second episode, the creator himself – Brahma has already come to replace Prajapati in this role – teaches Shukra a wrong doctrine.*

Brihaspati became Shukra, and for the safety of Indra and the destruction of the demons he emitted this ignorance, in which what is auspicious is said to be inauspicious, and what is inauspicious is said to be auspicious. (This doctrine) says, 'You should study the dharma that destroys the Vedas and the Shastras.' Therefore you should not study this doctrine. It is false. It is like a barren women whose fruit is limited to mere sexual pleasure. You should shun it as you would shun a woman who has fallen from her virtue. For it has been said: "The two are radically opposed to one another and far apart: ignorance, and what is known as knowledge. I think that Naciketas longs for wisdom, and you are not swung back and forth by many desires." The one who knows the two of them together, ignorance and knowledge, crosses over death by means of ignorance and attains immortality by means of knowledge. But those who are internally clothed in ignorance, thinking that they are themselves firm in their learning, they wander about being beaten, deluded, like blind men led by a blind man.'

The gods and the demons went to Brahma because they desired the Self. They bowed to him and said, 'Sir, we desire the Self. Please tell us.' He thought for a long time and then decided, 'These demons have a different sort of a self,' and so he spoke to them about a different self; and so they were deluded and go on living on that, with great attachment to the body, rejecting the raft of salvation and praising what is false. They see what is untrue as true, as in the magic that Indra spreads with his net. And so what is set forth in the Vedas is true; wise men go on living on that, on what is said in the Vedas; and so a Brahmin should not study what is non-Vedic. That is the meaning (of this story). (*Maitri Upanishad* 7.9–10)

2.2.3.2 Satyakama and the animals

This text challenges several traditional hierarchies. It begins by disregarding the supremacy of the father over the mother (and the necessity for the woman to be chaste, let alone married). In order to be initiated as a student, the boy needs to tell his teacher his patronymic, or the name of his father's ritual ancestor. This is normally used as the second name, after the boy's given name (here, Satyakama); but occasionally, as here, a boy's second name would be derived from the name of his mother. The text ends by casting a cynical glance at the relationship between teachers and pupils: the teacher does nothing for his pupil, but the pupil gives him full credit.

Once upon a time, Satyakama Jabala said to his mother, Jabala, 'Madam, I want to live the life of a chaste student. What line of male sages (*gotra*) am I descended from?' She said to him, 'I don't know, dear, what line of male sages you are descended from. When I was young I moved around a lot, as I was working, and I got you. And so I don't know what line of male sages you are descended from. But my name is Jabala; and your name is Satyakama ('lover of truth'). So why don't you say that you are Satyakama Jabala?'

(Satyakama) went to Gautama the son of Haridrumata and said, 'Sir, I wish to live the life of a chaste student. I wish to study with you.' (Gautama) said to (Satyakama), 'What line of male sages are you descended from, my dear?' (Satyakama) said, 'I don't know, sir, what line of male sages I am descended from. I asked my mother, and she answered me: "When I was young I moved around a lot, as I was working, and I got you. And so I don't know what line of male sages you are descended from. But my name is Jabala; and your name is Satyakama ('lover of truth')." So I say that I am Satyakama Jabala, sir.'

(Gautama) said to (Satyakama), 'No one who was not a Brahmin would be able to say that. Bring the fuel, my dear; I will intitiate you. You have not deviated from the truth.' He initiated him and then he singled out four hundred lean, weak cows, and he said, 'Look after these, my dear.' As (Satyakama) was driving them away, he said, 'I will not return until there are a thousand.' He lived away for a number of years. When they reached a thousand, the bull spoke to him: 'Satyakama!' 'Sir,' he replied. 'My dear, we have reached a thousand. Bring us to your teacher's house. And let me tell you one of the four feet of the ultimate reality (*brahman*).' 'Tell me, sir.' 'One sixteenth is the east, one sixteenth the west, one sixteenth the south, and one sixteenth the north. My dear, this is the foot of the ultimate reality, consisting of four sixteenths, that is called the Clear. Whoever knows this and worships the quarter of ultimate reality, consisting of four sixteenths, that is called the Clear becomes clear in this world and wins clear worlds. Fire will tell you (another) foot.'

The next morning, he drove the cows on. Where they arrived at evening, there he built a fire, penned up the cows, put fuel on, and set down to the west of the fire, facing east. The fire spoke to him: 'Satyakama!' 'Sir,' he replied. 'My dear, let me tell you one of the four feet of the ultimate reality.' 'Tell me, sir.' 'One sixteenth is the earth, one sixteenth the middle realm of space, one sixteenth the sky, and one sixteenth the ocean. My dear, this is the foot of the ultimate reality, consisting of four sixteenths, that is called the Endless. Whoever knows this and worships the quarter of ultimate reality, consisting of four sixteenths, that is called the Endless becomes endless in this world and wins endless worlds. A swan will tell you (another) foot.'

The next morning, he drove the cows on. Where they arrived at evening, there he built a fire, penned up the cows, put fuel on, and sat down to the west of the fire, facing east. A swan flew up to him and addressed him: 'Satyakama!' 'Sir,' he replied. 'My dear, let me tell you one of the four feet of the ultimate reality.' 'Tell me, sir.' 'One sixteenth is the fire, one sixteenth the sun, one sixteenth the moon, and one sixteeth lightning. My dear, this is the foot of the ultimate reality, consisting of four sixteenths, that is called the Luminous. Whoever knows this and worships the quarter of ultimate reality, consisting of four sixteenths, that is called the Luminous becomes luminous in this world and wins luminous worlds. A cormorant will tell you (another) foot.'

The next morning, he drove the cows on. Where they arrived at evening, there he built a fire, penned up the cows, put fuel on, and sat down to the west of the fire, facing east. A cormorant flew up to him and addressed him: 'Satyakama!' 'Sir,' he replied. 'My dear, let me tell you one of the four feet of the ultimate reality.' 'Tell me, sir.' 'One sixteenth is the breath, one sixteenth the eye, one sixteenth the ear, and one sixteenth the mind. My dear, this is the foot of the ultimate reality, consisting of four sixteenths, that is called the

Supported. Whoever knows this and worships the quarter of ultimate reality, consisting of four sixteenths, that is called the Supported becomes supported in this world and wins supported worlds.'

He reached the home of his teacher. The teacher said to him, 'Satyakama!' 'Sir,' he replied. 'My dear, you shine like one who knows the ultimate reality. Who has taught you?' 'Others than men,' he replied; 'but, sir, I would like you to tell me. For I have heard from people like you, sir, that the knowledge learnt from a teacher helps one best to achieve his goals.' He told this to him and left nothing out; he left nothing out at all. (*Chandogya Upanishad* 4.4–9)

2.3 PHILOSOPHY

2.3.1 *Rig Veda*: creation

This short, linguistically straightforward hymn, known, from its first word, as the 'Nasadiya' or 'There was not' hymn, has provoked hundreds of complex commentaries among Indian theologians and Western scholars. For it raises unanswerable questions, piling up paradoxes. It tells of creation by means of the heat (tapas) *that is generated by ritual activity and by the physical mortification of the body, as well as creation by sexual means: one verse employs chiasmus to contrast male seed-placers, giving-forth, above, with female powers, impulse, below. The hymn refers to several sorts of 'connections', metaphoric bonds and more literal bonds, measuring cords by which the poets delimit – and hence create – the elements.*

There was neither non-existence nor existence then; there was neither the realm of space nor the sky which is beyond. What stirred? Where? In whose protection? Was there water, bottomlessly deep? There was neither death nor immortality then. There was no distinguishing sign of night nor of day. That one breathed, windless, by its own impulse. Other than that there was nothing beyond. Darkness was hidden by darkness in the beginning; with no distinguishing sign, all this was water. The life force that was covered with emptiness, that one arose through the power of heat.

Desire came upon that one in the beginning; that was the first seed of mind. Poets seeking in their heart with wisdom found the bond of existence in non-existence. Their cord was extended across. Was there below? Was there above? There were seed-placers; there were powers. There was impulse beneath; there was giving-forth above.

Who really knows? Who will here proclaim it? Whence was it produced? Whence is this creation? The gods came afterwards, with the creation of this universe. Who then knows whence it has arisen? Whence this creation has arisen – perhaps it formed itself, or perhaps it did not – the one who looks down on it, in the highest heaven, only he knows – or perhaps he does not know. (*Rig Veda* 10.129)

2.3.2 Upanishads

2.3.2.1 The self

The Upanishads say much about the self or soul (atman), *the individual self that is also the universal Self, identified with the ultimate reality* (brahman). *But the soul can never be described, merely analogised; whatever you say it is like, it is not really that: 'Not thus, not thus* (neti, neti)'. *This passage speaks of the origin of the Self.*

At that time, all of this (world) was undifferentiated. By means of name and form it became differentiated – 'This has this name; this has this form.' And even now people say, 'This is his name; this is his form,' distinguishing by means of name and form. He entered in here, right up to the tips of his fingernails, as a razor is hidden in a razor sheath, or as fire is inside firewood. People do not see him, for (whatever they see) is incomplete. Whenever one breaths, he becomes breath; whenever one speaks, he is speech; seeing, he is the eye; hearing, the ear; thinking, the mind. These are just the names for his acts. Whoever worships one (aspect) or another does not understand, for he is incomplete in any one or another. Rather, one should worship with the thought, 'This is the Self', for all of these become one in that. That by which one can follow the footprints of this All, that is the Self, through which this All is known, just as one might track down and find something by a footprint. Whoever knows this finds fame and praise. (*Brihadaranyaka Upanishad* 1.4.7)

2.3.2.2 The ultimate reality and the two birds

This passage represents another attempt to describe, in metaphor, the relationship between the individual soul and the ultimate reality. It also begins to endow that ultimate reality with specific characteristics that are more theistic than pantheistic, to identify it with the god Rudra, and to address him. The unborn Person to which the passage refers is Purusha, the male, spirit; the female is Prakriti, nature, who, according to Sankhya philosophy, consists of the three qualities (gunas): *darkness* (tamas, *that is black*), *energy* (rajas, *that is red*), *and goodness* (sattva, *that is white*). *Each soul is another unborn spirit that becomes involved with Prakriti during each incarnation and leaves her at each death. The passage quotes* Rig Veda *1.164.20, a famous verse about two birds; the one who does not eat is the ultimate reality; the other, the one who does eat, is the individual soul.*

The One who has no colour himself but distributes many colours in his secret purpose, by the various uses of his power (*shakti*), the One into whom the whole world dissolves, as he is its end and its beginning – he is god. Let him give us clear minds! It is he who is fire, he who is the sun; he who is the wind, and he who is the moon. He is what is pure; he is Brahma. He is the waters; he is Prajapati.

You are woman; you are man. You are the boy and also the girl. You are an old man stumbling with his cane. As soon as you are born, you face in every direction. You are the dark blue bird and the green bird with red eyes. The lightning is your child. You are the seasons and the seas. You have no beginning, but you exist with power, from which all creatures are born.

The one unborn Person takes his pleasure in lying with the one unborn female, who is red, white, and black, and produces many creatures like herself. Another unborn person takes his pleasure from her and then leaves her.

'Two birds, friends joined together, clutch the same tree. One of them eats the sweet fruit; the other looks on but does not eat.' On that one tree one person grieves for his impotence; he is deluded and depressed. But when he sees the other, the Lord who takes pleasure in his own greatness, (the first) becomes free from sorrow.

The undying syllable of the hymn (the *Rig Veda*) is the final abode where all gods have taken their seat. What can one who does not know this do with the hymn? Only those who know it sit together here. The sacred chants, the sacrifices, the ceremonies, the laws, the past, the future, and what the Vedas declare – the one who uses Illusion projects the whole world out of this (ultimate reality) and confines the other one in it by means of Illusion. So you should realise that Nature is Illusion, and that the great lord is the one who uses Illusion. This whole universe is pervaded by creatures that are parts of him. (*Shvetashvatara Upanishad* 4.1–10)

2.3.2.3 Rebirth

This is the first explicit discussion of the doctrine of rebirth in Indian literature, though, as we have seen, there are tantalising precursors of such a doctrine in the Brahmanas and even in the Rig Veda. For a later, fuller expansion of the theory in the Puranas and medical texts, see below, 5.2.2 and 5.5.1–3.

Shvetaketu the descendant of Aruna went to the assembly of the Panchala (kings). Pravahana Jaibali said to him, 'Young man, has your father taught you?' 'Yes, sir, he has.' 'Do you know where created beings go from here?' 'No, sir.' 'Do you know how they come back again?' 'No, sir.' 'Do you know about the separation between the two paths, the path of the gods and the path of the fathers?' 'No, sir.' 'Do you know how the world (of heaven) over there does not get filled up?' 'No, sir.' 'Do you know how, in the fifth oblation, water comes to have a human voice?' 'No, sir.' 'Then why did you say that you had been taught? How could someone who didn't know these things say that he had been taught?'

Quite upset, he went to his father's place and said to him, 'Sir, you said, "I have taught you," but in fact you *didn't* teach me. Some man of the ruling class asked me five questions, and I wasn't able to answer a single one of them.' (His father) said, 'As you have told them to me, I don't know a single one of them. If I had known them, how would I not have told you?'

Then Gautama (the father of Shvetaketu) went to the king's place, and when he arrived he was received with honour. The next morning, he went to the assembly hall and (the king) said to him, 'Gautama, sir, choose anything you want of human wealth.' 'Your majesty,' answered (Gautama), 'human wealth is for you. But tell me just what you said to the young man.' (The king) was troubled and commanded him, 'Wait a while.' Then (the king) said to (Gautama), 'What you are asking me, Gautama, is knowledge that has never gone to Brahmins before you. And that is why, among all people, only the Kshatriyas have had the power to rule.' But then he told him:

'The world (of heaven) over there, Gautama, is a sacrificial fire. The sun is its fuel, the rays of the sun are its smoke, the day is its flame, the moon its coals, the stars its sparks. Into this fire the gods make an offering of faith, and from that oblation king Soma is born.

'The rain cloud, Gautama, is a sacrificial fire. The wind is its fuel, the mist its smoke, lightning its flame, the thunderbolt its coals, and the roar of the thunder its sparks. Into this fire the gods make an offering of king Soma, and from that oblation rain is born.

'The earth, Gautama, is a sacrificial fire. The year is its fuel, space its smoke, night its flame, the four directions its coals, the four intermediate directions its sparks. Into this fire the gods make an offering of rain, and from that oblation food is born.

'Man, Gautama, is a sacrificial fire. Speech is his fuel, breath his smoke, the tongue his flame, the eye his coals, the ear his sparks. Into this fire the gods make an offering of food, and from that oblation semen is born.

'Woman, Gautama, is a sacrificial fire. The vagina is her fuel, foreplay her smoke, the womb her flame, the penetration her coals, and the orgasm her sparks. Into this fire the gods make an offering of semen, and from that oblation the embryo is born.

'Thus in the fifth oblation, water comes to have a human voice. When the embryo has lain inside there for ten months or nine months, or however long, covered with the membrane, then he is born. When he is born, he lives as long as his allotted life-span. When he has died, they carry him to the appointed place and put him in the fire, for that is where he came from, what he was born from.

'Those who know this, and those who worship in the forest, concentrating on faith and asceticism, they are born into the flame, and from the flame into the day, and from the day into the fortnight of the waxing moon, and from the fortnight of the waxing moon into the six months during which the sun moves north; from these months, into the year; from the year into the sun; from the sun into the moon; from the moon into lightning. There a Person who is not human leads them to the ultimate reality. This is the path that the gods go on.

'But those who worship in the village, concentrating on sacrifices and good works and charity, they are born into the smoke, and from the smoke into the night, and from the night into the other fortnight, and from the other fortnight into the six months when the sun moves south. They do not reach the year. From these months they go to the world of the fathers, and from the world of the fathers to space, and from space to the moon. That is king Soma. That is the food of the gods. The gods eat that.

'When they have dwelt there for as long as there is a remnant (of their merit), then they return along that very same road that they came along, back into space; but from space they go to wind, and when one has become wind he becomes smoke, and when he has become smoke he becomes mist; when he has become mist, he becomes a cloud, and when he has become a cloud, he rains. These are then born here as rice, barley, plants, trees, sesame plants, and beans. It is difficult to move forth out of this condition; for only if someone eats him as food and then emits him as semen, he becomes that creature's semen and is born.

'And so those who behave nicely here will, in general, find a nice womb, the womb of a Brahmin or the womb of a Kshatriya or the womb of a Vaishya. But those whose behaviour here is stinking will, in general, find a stinking womb, the womb of a dog or the womb of a pig or the womb of an Untouchable. Then they become those tiny creatures who go by neither one of these two paths but are constantly returning. "Be born and die" – that is the third condition. And because of that, the world (of heaven) over there is not filled up. And one should try to protect oneself from that. There is a verse about this: "One who steals gold, or drinks wine, or sleeps with his teacher's wife, or kills a Brahmin – these four fall, along with the fifth, (any person who is) their companion." But whoever knows these five fires is not smeared with evil, not even if he is the companion of these people. He becomes pure, purified, and wins a world of merit, if he knows this, if he really knows this.' (*Chandogya Upanishad* 5.3–10)

2.3.2.4 The Person in the eye and in sleep

This passage describes a kind of internal intercourse between the universal Soul and the individual soul – here in the form of the wife of Indra – resulting in the 'emission' of speech but also in the 'emission' of dreams. The mind churns the body as fire is born of the churning of two firesticks, one male and one female. Cosmic reality becomes manifest with three quarters below and a transcendent fourth, just as the Person in the hymn of cosmic dismemberment (see above, 2.2.1.1) has one quarter below and three quarters above.

This Person who is in one's sight, dwelling in the right eye, is Indra; and his wife dwells in the left eye. The two of them come together and unite in the hollow inside the heart, and the vital seed of the two of them becomes a lump (*pinda*) of blood there. The channel that serves as the artery for the two of them is one, but it is divided into two; it extends from the heart right up to (each) eye, and is fixed there. The mind stirs up the fire of the body, and that (fire) impels the wind; the wind then moves through the chest and produces a soft murmur. Out of the fire born of this churning there appears in the heart something that is smaller than the smallest atom; but it becomes doubled in the throat, and tripled in the tongue; and when it comes out they call it a magic alphabet.

When (this Person) sees, he does not see death, nor disease, nor unhappiness. For when he sees he sees this All, and he obtains this All, altogether. The one who sees with the eye; who moves about in dreams; who is fast asleep;

and who is beyond the one who is fast asleep – this is the four-fold division (of states of consciousness), and the fourth is greater (than all the rest). For the ultimate reality moves with one foot in the first three, but he moves with three feet in the fourth. And the great Self has a dual nature, for the sake of experiencing both the true and the false; yes, the great Self has a dual nature. (*Maitri Upanishad* 7.11b.1–8)

2.3.2.5 The self in sleep
The following two passages offer two related explanations of the self in sleep and of the more general relationship between consciousness and the physical world.

2.3.2.5.1 The wandering king
When this person has fallen asleep, the person who is made of his consciousness takes to himself the consciousness by means of the consciousness of the senses (or vital breaths), and he rests in the space that is inside the heart. And when he withdraws (the senses) in that way, then the person is what we call asleep. Then the breath is withdrawn, and the voice is withdrawn, and the eye is withdrawn, and the ear is withdrawn, and the mind is withdrawn.

When he moves about in his dream, these worlds are his. Then he seems to become a great king; then he seems to become a great Brahmin; then he seems to move up or to move down. And as a great king take his people with him and moves about wherever he wishes in his own country, even so this one here, taking the senses with him, moves about wherever he wishes in his own body.

And when someone falls sound asleep and knows no one at all, having crept out from the heart into the pericardium, through the 72,000 channels called 'dikes' (*hita*) that surround it, he rests in the pericardium. And as a young prince or a great king or a great Brahmin might go to the very peak of ecstasy and rest there, even so (the sleeper) rests.

As a spider emits his thread, as tiny sparks come out of a fire, even so from this Self come all senses, all worlds, all gods, all beings. Its secret name is 'the real of the real'. The vital senses are indeed what is real; and he is what is real about them. (*Brihadaranyaka Upanishad* 2.1.17–20)

2.3.2.5.2 The chariot-maker
The individual person has two states: the state in this world, and the state in the other world; and there is a third, liminal state, the state of dreaming. When one remains in this liminal state he sees both states – this world and the other world. Now, whatever approach there is to the state in the other world, by taking that approach one sees both the evils (of this world) and the ecstasies (of that world). When he dreams, he takes the elementary matter of this all-encompassing world, and he himself takes it apart, and he himself builds it up, and by his own brightness, by his own light, he dreams. For the individual person becomes his own light in this state.

There are no chariots there, no harnessings, no roads; but he emits chariots, harnessings, and roads. There are no ecstasies, joys, or delights there; but he emits ecstasies, joys, and delights. There are no ponds, lotus pools, or flowing streams there, but he emits ponds, lotus pools, and flowing streams. For he is the maker.

And there are verses about this:

Striking down with sleep what belongs to the body, he who does not dream looks down upon those that dream. Taking up the bright seed, he goes back to his place; he is the golden person, the one swan. Guarding the low nest with his breath, the immortal one wanders about outside the nest. The immortal one goes wherever he wishes; he is the golden person, the one swan. Moving up and down inside the dream, he makes many forms, for he is a god. Now he seems to take pleasure in women, now he laughs, or sees terrifying things. People see his pleasure, but no one at all sees him. And that is why people say, 'Don't wake him up suddenly.' For it is hard to find a cure for the one who does not come back.

Now, some people say, 'This (dream state) is just his waking state, for whatever things he sees when he is awake, he sees them too when he dreams.' (But this is not so, for) here (in his dream) the person himself becomes his own source of light. . . .

As a big fish moves along both banks of a river, the eastern side and the western side, even so this person moves along both of these states, the state of dreaming and the state of being awake. (*Brihadaranyaka Upanishad* 4.3.9–14, 18)

2.3.3 Vedanta

Later Indian philosophy developed primarily through interpretations of scripture – of the Vedas and the Upanishads; hence the main school of philosophy is known as Vedanta, 'the end of the Veda'. Both Shankara and Ramanuja, two of India's greatest philosophers, wrote extensive commentaries on the Bhagavad Gita *and the* Brahma Sutras *(or Vedanta Sutras), and both frequently invoked the Upanishads in formulating their own arguments. One can get some idea of the ways in which their two approaches are both related and distinct (Shankara's philosophy being known as Non-dualism, or Advaita, and Ramanuja's as Qualified Non-dualism, or Vishishta-Advaita), by comparing their interpretations of the problem of the self in sleep, based upon the two passages from the* Brihadaranyaka Upanishad *translated above.*

2.3.3.1 Shankara dreams

(An opponent) might argue thus: It is agreed that the world created in our waking state, that is created by the highest consciousness, is the form of the real (*tathyarupa*), and so the world created in our dreaming state must also be real. There is a passage of scripture about this: 'Now, some people say, "This (dream state) is just (the same as) his waking state", for whatever things he sees when he is awake, he sees them too when he dreams' (*Brihadaranyaka*

Upanishad 4.3.14; above, 2.3.2.5.2) Thus the text tells us that the same logic applies to the state of dreaming and the state of waking. And so the world created in the liminal state (of dreaming) is real.

To this argument (the author of the *Vedanta Sutras*) says: 'But (the world created in dreams) is mere illusion, because its own form is not revealed with any totality' (3.2.3).

The word 'but' indicates that he rejects the opponent's argument. What the opponent says – that the world created in the liminal state (of dreaming) partakes of the highest reality – is not true. The world created in the liminal state is pure illusion, and there is not so much as a smell of reality in it.

'Why?' (an opponent might ask).

'Because its own form is not revealed with any totality' (says the author of the *Vedanta Sutras*). That is, because a dream does not reveal its form with the totality that is characteristic of things that partake of the highest reality.

Now, what is meant by 'totality' here?

It is the agreement of place, time, and cause, and the fact that no contradiction or falsification can be brought against it.

Is it not the case that all of these characteristics of real things – place, time, cause, and absence of contradiction – occur in a dream?

No. First, as regards place: There is no place in a dream for anything like a chariot. For a thing like a chariot could find no space within the constricted place of the human body.

Granted. But (the dreamer) will see the dream from a vantage point outside of his body. For one does perceive (in a dream) that things are separated from oneself by space. Scripture demonstrates that the dream is seen from outside the body: 'The immortal one wanders about outside the nest; the immortal one goes wherever he wishes' (*Brihadaranyaka Upanishad* 4.3.12; above, 2.3.2.5.2) And this distinction between standing still and moving about would not be relevant if the (dreaming) creature did not actually go out.

No, is the reply. It is not possible for the dreaming creature to travel the distance of a hundred leagues and return again in a mere moment. And sometimes someone tells about a dream in which he didn't come back at all: 'Lying in bed last night in the land of the Kurus, I fell asleep, and in my dream I went to the land of the Panchalas, and then, while I was still there, I woke up.' Now, if he had really gone out of his own country, he would have awakened in the land of the Panchalas; but in fact he awakened in the land of the Kurus; from this one realises, 'He did not really go there.' And the body by means of which he thinks he has gone to another place – other people standing beside him see that body lying right there in his bed. And he does not see the places that he sees in his dream as they really are; but if he actually ran around seeing them, he would perceive them as they really are when he sees them when he is awake. Indeed, scripture shows us that the dream is inside the body, in the passage that begins, 'When he moves about in his dream' and ends, 'he moves about wherever he wishes, in his own body.' (*Brihadaranyaka Upanishad*

2.1.18; above, 2.3.2.5.1) And so, lest there be a contradiction both of scripture and of reason, the scriptural passage about going outside the nest must be taken in a metaphorical sense: 'The immortal one wanders about *as if* he were outside the nest.' For someone who, even while he is dwelling inside his body, makes no use of it could be said to be outside of his body, as it were. This being so, the distinction between standing still and moving about must be understood as merely deceptive.

Now, when it comes to the question of time: there is a contradiction of time in a dream. A person dreaming in the land of Bharata (India) at night thinks that it is daytime; or sometimes a person experiences many masses of years in a dream that lasts only for a moment.

And as for causation: There are neither the usual causes for thought nor the usual causes for action in a dream. For, since the organs of perception are withdrawn in sleep, the dreamer does not have the eyes and so forth to perceive something like a chariot. And where could he get, in a mere blink of the eye, the ability – let alone the wood – to make something like a chariot?

And, finally, when it comes to non-contradiction: the chariots and so forth that are seen in a dream are contradicted by the waking state. And even in the dream itself such contradictions are easy to find, as can be demonstrated by the discrepancies between the beginning and end of a dream: 'This is a chariot,' you may sometimes decide in a dream; but then in a moment it becomes a man, and so you decide, 'This is a man'; but in a moment it is a tree. And scripture itself clearly states that the chariots and so forth in a dream do not exist: 'There are no chariots there, no harnessings, no roads.' (*Brihadaranyaka Upanishad* 4.3.10; above, 2.3.2.5.2) Therefore what is seen in a dream is mere illusion.

Then, since it is mere illusion, is there no smell of reality at all in a dream?

No, is the reply. (For then the author of the *Vedanta Sutras* goes on to say:)

'But scripture also says that a dream is a sign (of the future; a pointer, shower, manifester), and those who know say this too' (3.2.4).

For a dream is a sign of good and bad things that will happen. So scripture says, 'When a man engaged in actions for the sake of something he desires sees a woman in his dreams, then he may know from that vision in his dream that he will achieve success' (*Chandogya Upanishad* 5.2.9). And, 'If he sees a black man with black teeth, that man will kill him' – from dreams such as these, he may learn that he is not going to live long; this is what scripture says. And the people who know how to study dreams say, 'Riding on an elephant and so forth in a dream is lucky, but riding on a donkey is unlucky.' And they also believe that certain dreams that are caused by spells or gods or drugs also have the smell of reality. Here, too, the thing of which the dream is a sign may be real, but the sign itself, the sight of the woman and so forth, is false, since it is contradicted (by the waking state); this is my opinion. Therefore the statement that the dream is merely illusion is upheld. . . .

When scripture says, 'The dreamer emits from himself chariots and so forth, for he is the maker,' it is said merely because he is the cause (of their creation), but not because the dreamer actually emits the chariots and so forth right before one's eyes. He is said to be the cause in the sense that he is the one who makes the good and bad deeds that become the cause of the visions of bliss and terror that are the cause of the images of the chariots and so forth. . . .

Thus the world of the liminal (dream) state is not truly real in the same sense that the world of the creation that consists of the sky and so forth is real; this is what has been established.

However. There is no transcendent reality even in the creation that consists of the sky and so forth. For as it was established above (*Vedanta Sutras* 2.1.14), the entire expanse of the phenomenal world is mere illusion. The phenomenal world consisting of the sky and so forth has a distinct and stable form only until one sees that its very self is the ultimate reality. But the phenomenal world that arises out of the liminal state (of dreams) is contradicted every day. Therefore the sense in which the liminal world is a mere illusion must be understood as different (from the sense in which the waking world is a mere illusion). (Commentary on *Vedanta Sutras* 3.2.2–4)

2.3.3.2 Ramanuja dreams

The opponent may falsely argue thus:

Perceptions of an elephant and so forth in a dream are not real, but they are the cause of the knowledge of real things, auspicious and inauspicious (that are portended by the dream). In the same way, scripture is unreal, because it is based upon ignorance, but it is the cause of the knowledge of the real thing that is its object, namely, ultimate reality. Is there any reason why this can be contradicted?

Yes. For it is not true that the perceptions in a dream are unreal. It is only the objects that are contradicted (by the perceptions of the waking state), not the perceptions. For no one ever decides, 'The perception that I experienced when I was dreaming does not actually exist here.' But one does decide that there is a contradiction, which one understands thus: 'The vision exists, but the objects of the vision do not exist.' And the illusory perception that arises out of a magician's spells, drugs, and so forth, is also real, as it is the cause of pleasure and fear. In this case, too, there is no contradiction of the perception. And the misperception of something like a serpent in something like a rope, arising out of something like a flaw in the senses or in the object of the senses, this, too, is real, the cause of things like fear. Real, too, is the belief that a man has been bitten, arising out of the proximity of a snake, even when he has not been bitten. Real, too, is the belief in the poison of apprehension, which may actually cause death. So, too, the reflected image of something like a face in something like water becomes a real thing, the cause of a definite opinion about the face, that is a real thing. Because all of these states of consciousness have a definite origin and are the causes of actual effects, they are real.

If you say, 'But in the absence of any elephant or such a thing, how could the ideas about them be real?', I say, No (the ideas about them *are* real). For it is a rule that the mere connection between the object of the senses and the sensation that it causes is a sufficient basis for ideas about it. The reflection of the object is thus precisely a sufficient basis for its perception. And there is in fact such a reflection in this case, as the result of some flaw (in the object or in the senses). As the object is contradicted, it is regarded as unreal; but the *belief* in the object is not contradicted, and so it is said to be real. . . .

Those who know the Veda believe that all perception has as its object what is real; it is known from scripture and Shastras that everything is the very nature of everything else. The creator began his work by thinking, 'Let me become many,' and each single element was divided into three parts (the three qualities of matter – darkness, energy, and goodness). This is what the scripture says; and so each thing is perceived before one's eyes as having a triple cause. The red colour in fire is from elemental fire, the white from the waters, and the black from the earth; this is the triple form of fire. Thus scripture demonstrates that everything is combined with everything else. In the *Vishnu Purana* the beginning of creation is described thus: 'The separate elements, possessing various powers, could not create progeny without combining together, without mingling entirely. Having come together in union with one another, mixing with each other, all of them, beginning with the great element and ending with the essentially differentiated atomic particles, formed an egg' (*Vishnu Purana* 1.2.50–2; cf. below, 4.1.1). The author of this (*Vedanta*) *Sutra* also declares that the elements have three forms (*Vedanta Sutra* 3.1.3).

And scripture says that when there is no Soma available, one may use the Putika plant; for those who understand logic know that there are some qualities of the Soma plant (in the Putika plant). And when there is no rice available, one can use Nivara grains, because they have the quality of rice. One thing is similar to another when one thing contains one part of the substance of the other thing. And the scripture says that the quality of something like silver exists in something like a shell. The distinction between such things as silver and shells is simply the result of the preponderance (of silver in one and shell in the other). It is evident that things like shells resemble things like silver; therefore the existence of one in the other is established simply because it is self-evident.

Sometimes, if there is a defect in the eye or something of that sort, the part that is silver is apprehended, but without the part that is shell; then a man who wants silver will react to it. But when the defect (in the eye) is removed, and the part that is shell is apprehended, he turns back from it. Hence the perception of silver in a shell is true. So, too, the relationship between a perception that contradicts another, and the perception that is contradicted by it, becomes apparent as the result of the preponderance (of one quality over another): the preponderance of shell is grasped either in part or in its totality. The discriminations that are made in practical everyday life do not, therefore, depend upon a distinction between an object of perception that is false and one that is true, but merely upon the fact that everything is a part of the nature of everything else.

And in a dream, the Lord emits objects of the senses of such a sort that are perceived only by each individual person, according to the good or evil qualities of living creatures, and that last only for a particular time. This is what scripture says about dreams: 'There are no chariots there, no harnessings, . . . for he is the maker' (*Brihadaranyaka Upanishad* 4.3.10; above, 2.3.2.5.2). Even if these things do not exist now in such a way that they may be experienced by another person in their totality, nevertheless the Lord emits objects of the senses of such a sort that they may be perceived only by that particular person. 'For *He* is the maker': the meaning is that such a sort of making comes from Him who has such a marvellous power that what he imagines is real.

The *Katha Upanishad* (2.5.8) says, 'He who is awake in those who dream, the Person who fashions desire after desire, he is the bright seed, he is the ultimate reality, he is what is called immortal. All worlds are contained in That, and no one goes beyond That.' And the author of this (*Vedanta*) *Sutra*, too, speaks of the world created in the liminal state (3.2.1) and of sons and so forth when there is no mother (3.2.2); then he suggests that the individual soul (*jiva*) emits the objects seen in dreams, but that the world created in dreams is mere illusion, because its own form is not revealed in any totality (3.2.3). But he says, finally, that the creation of the dream world does not come merely from the imagination of the individual soul. For, though the soul has the power to make what it imagines real, a power which is part of its own nature, nevertheless, as long as it is in the state of the world of rebirth (*samsara*), its own form – including that power – is not manifest in its totality. And so this creation (of the objects in the dream world) is a marvel that arises as a result of the Lord's power to create objects that are to be experienced by each individual person.

When the *Katha Upanishad* (5.8) says, 'All worlds are contained in That, and no one goes beyond That,' it is clear that the highest Self, the Creator, is to be understood. The person lying on his bed in his own bedroom sees in his dreams things such as going in his very own body to another country and being anointed king and having his head cut off and so forth, experiences that arise as the fruits of his merits and demerits, and this happens through the creation of another body that exactly resembles the body lying on the bed. . . .

Thus it has been proven that all perception is true. The flaws in other opinions have been discussed at length by various other philosophers; knowing this, no trouble has been taken here in that regard. And indeed, what need is there for a long proof? The authorities are one's own eyes, inference, and scripture. For those who acknowledge the highest ultimate reality who has the power to make what he imagines real, who is known from scripture, who is omniscient, free from even the merest smell of any flaw, and who is a mass of good qualities that cannot be counted – for them, what cannot be achieved?

What cannot be proven? The Lord, the highest ultimate reality, created the entire universe to be enjoyed according to the qualities of virtue or vice of the individual souls; he made certain objects to be perceived in common by everyone, bringing the experience of happiness or unhappiness to all without regard for the fruits of their actions; and he made other objects to be experienced only by this or that individual person, and lasting only for a limited period of time. Thus the distinction between experiences that are contradicted (like dreams) and those that are contradicting (like waking life) is a distinction between objects of the senses that are experienced by everyone and those that are not. Thus everything is consistent. (*Shribhashya* 1.1.1)

2.3.3.2 Illusion: the man who built a house of air

The Yogavasishtha *is a Sanskrit text composed in Kashmir around the tenth century A.D., under considerable Buddhist influence. It deals with the cardinal topics of creation, doomsday, and the nature of the universe and is a popular source of Hindu self-understanding. It interweaves theoretical, philosophical discussions with rather surreal narratives, like the following abstract parable.*

Once upon a time there was a husky man made by a machine of illusion. He was a fool, with the feeble wits of a child, and he was exclusively concealed within his own idiocy. He was born one day, alone, and he remained right there, in an empty place. He was like the net-pattern that you see in space when your eyes are closed, or like a mirage that you see in a desert. There was no one there other than him; he was all that there was there. Whatever else there appeared to be there was a reflection of him, but that fool could not see it.

Then he got the idea of expanding his wealth, and he firmly resolved, 'I belong to empty space; I am empty space; empty space is mine. I will protect space; I will establish space firmly; and I myself will assiduously protect my cherished possession.' When he had made this decision, he made a house to protect empty space. Inside this house, he marked out an area and said, 'Now I have protected this empty space.' And he took pleasure in that space in the house.

But in the course of time, that house of his was destroyed, as a little wave in the water is destroyed by a wind in the season of autumn. 'Oh my! My little house-space, you have been destroyed! Oh my! Where did you go in just a moment? Oh, oh! You have been shattered!' – this is how he mourned for that space. And when he had mourned a hundred times in this way, that fool built a well to protect his empty space, and he became obsessed with his well-space. But then, in time, the well, too, was destroyed, and when the well-space was gone he sank into grief; and when he had finished lamenting his well-space, immediately he made a pot, and he became obsessed with the pot-space through the illusion of his pleasure in it. But in time the pot, too, was destroyed; whatever part of the sky that unfortunate creature took, that too was destroyed. When he finished lamenting his pot-space, he made a bowl to protect his empty space, and he became obsessed with the bowl-space. In time, the bowl, too, was destroyed, as darkness is destroyed by blazing light; and he grieved for that bowl-space.

When he finished grieving for the bowl-space, he built a great palace with four halls, all made of space, in order to protect his empty space. Time swallowed it up, too, and destroyed it as a wind destroys a withered leaf; and he became obsessed with mourning for it, too. And when he had finished mourning for his palace with four halls, he built a great granary in the form of a cloud, to protect his empty space, and he became obsessed with the space in that. But time quickly carried it away, too, as if it had been a cloud, and he was tortured by his grief for his lost granary.

Thus time, whose essence never changes, outstripped his house, four-halled palace, pot, bowl, and granary. And thus he remained, powerless in his cave in a corner of the sky, coming and going in his own mind from one impenetrable house to another, from one misery, one cloud, to another cloud that had become a source of misery, deluded by the confusion between what had gone and what had never come. (*Yogavashishtha* 6.1.112.16–35)

3 EPICS

The two great Sanskrit epics of Hinduism are the Mahabharata *and the* Ramayana. *Both have been translated into many of the vernaculars of India (Hindu, Tamil, Bengali, and so forth) and have become a part of the heritage of all Hindus, whether they know the Sanskrit text or the vernacular version.*

3.1 MAHABHARATA

The central story of the Mahabharata *is the tale of the internecine, apocalyptic battle between two sets of cousins descended from king Bharata: the Pandavas and the Kauravas. Upon this skeleton the* Mahabharata *weaves 100,000 verses of Sanskrit incorporating many loosely related myths, philosophies, and rituals.*

3.1.1 The birth of the Epic heroes
King Vicitravirya died childless; his mother, Satyavati, is concerned that the line will die out, and so she consults Bhishma, Vicitravirya's half-brother, who was born by the same father, but to another mother, and hence is the stepson of Satyavati. The ensuing arguments and acts reveal certain underlying Hindu assumptions about the nature of human birth. The woman was regarded as the field in which the man sows his seed; it was a man's duty to have a son, to satisfy the requirements of the triple goal of human life (trivarga): *dharma, profit* (artha), *and pleasure* (kama) *(to which later texts added a fourth goal,* moksha, *release).*

If a misfortune such as death, illness, a curse, or impotence prevented a man from begetting a son upon his wife, he was legally allowed (indeed, expected) to resort to the institution of Levirate marriage, by which a brother (usually a younger brother, though here an older brother) was required to beget a son upon his brother's wife.

Satyavati and Bhishma therefore decide to find someone else to impregnate the two queens, who are named Ambika and Ambalika, 'Little Mother' and 'Dear Little Mother'. (It is interesting to note that these are the names by which the queens in the horse sacrifice are summoned in another story of surrogates – the horse substituting for the king; see above, 2.1.2.2.3). The stratagem that they agree upon involves yet another son of Satyavati, the sage Vyasa, the author of the Mahabharata *and also an important actor in it. But Vyasa is not attractive to the queens; apparently some of the fishy smell that his mother, Satyavati, lost (through the favour of her lover, Parashara) still hangs about Vyasa himself. As they resist him, he curses them: Ambalika gives birth to a pale son (Pandu, father of the Pandavas, the heroes of the* Mahabharata) *and Ambika (also called Kausalya) gives birth to a blind son, Dhritarashtra, the blind father of the Kauravas, the enemies of the sons of Pandu.*

Bhishma said, 'Mother, listen and I will tell you a sure way by which the Bharata dynasty can be continued and its lineage increased: invite some Brahmin who has good qualities, and pay him, and let him beget progeny in the fields of Vicitravirya.'

Satyavati smiled in embarrassment and answered Bhishma with a trembling voice: 'Great-armed descendant of Bharata, since you have spoken the truth to me, and because I trust you, and for the continuation of our dynasty, I will speak out. And you will not be able to contradict me, such is our present emergency. You yourself are the dharma in our family; you are truth and the ultimate resort. So listen to what I say, and do it at once, for it is for your benefit and is concerned with dharma and profit. But do not reveal what is told to you in intimate confidence.

'Once upon a time, there was a king that you have heard of by the name of Vasu; a female fish in whom he placed his seed conceived me in her belly. A fisherman who understood dharma fished my mother out of the water; he took me to his home and made me his daughter. My father, who followed his dharma, had a ferry-boat, and one day when I had just become a woman, I went in that boat. Then the great seer, the wise Parashara, the best of those who uphold dharma, came to the ferry-boat wishing to cross the Yamuna river. As he was being carried across the Yamuna, the great sage approached me, tormented by lust, and said many sweet things to me to win me over. I was afraid that he would curse me, but I was also afraid of my father; however, as he promised me boons that are not easy to get, I could not bear to refuse him. I was a young girl; he overpowered me with his virility and had his will of me right there in the boat – but first he had covered the whole area with darkness. For he had seen the great seers standing on the far shore, sitting on the bank of the

Yamuna like shining fires, and the young sun was shining in the East, breaking open the sky so that it seemed to be dressed in garments of copper. And so, as soon as I said the word, the powerful Parashara, who had a firm grip on the truth, emitted a fog on the island and on the water of the Yamuna.

'Now, I used to have a powerful and disgusting smell of fish about me; the sage took it away and gave me this pleasant smell. And then the sage said to me, "When you have given birth to my child on an island of this river, you will become an intact virgin again." Then the wise ascetic, who was thoroughly satisfied, gave me back my virginity; for when I had seen the controlled virility of that noble man, I was so amazed that I swooned, and I gave myself to him. Vasishtha assembled the Brahmins, Yajnavalkya and the others, and they all performed my marriage ceremony and then went back where they had come from. And then, right on that island, the noble Parashara, in ecstasy, begat a son in me, a virgin.

'That son born of a virgin was the great seer and great yogi begotten by Parashara, known as the Man of the Island. And because he used his ascetic power to divide (vyasya) the four Vedas, the seer became known in the world as Vyasa. And because he was dark, he became known as Krishna. He speaks the truth and is an ascetic intent upon serenity, a man who has burnt up all his sins. Surely when I ask his help – and you ask him, too – he will beget superb offspring in your brother's fields. For he said to me, at that time, "Remember me whenever there are things to be done." I will remember him now, if you wish, O great-armed Bhishma. For with your permission, the great ascetic will surely beget sons in the fields of Vicitravirya.'

When the great sage was mentioned, Bhishma cupped his hands in reverence and said, 'Anyone who sees into these three – dharma, profit, and pleasure; who sees that profit depends on profit, dharma depends on dharma, and pleasure depends on pleasure, but that separately they run contrary to one another; and who discriminates correctly between them after thinking about it carefully – he is an intelligent man. What you have just said is in keeping with dharma and for the welfare of our family; it is the best thing to do, and it pleases me best.'

When Bhishma had given this promise, the dark woman thought about the sage called Krishna of the Island. That wise man was expounding the Vedas when he realised that his mother had thought of him, and in a moment he mysteriously appeared. She honoured her son with the proper formalities, and then she embraced him in her arms and sprinkled him with her tears; the fisherman's daughter wept when she saw her son after such a long time. The great sage Vyasa, her first-born, sprinkled his anguished mother with water and greeted her; and then he said to his mother, 'I have come to do whatever you wish. Command me, you who know dharma truly, and I will do whatever pleases you.' Then the family priest honoured the great sage and welcomed him with verses recited in the proper way. And when Vyasa had sat down, and his mother had asked him about his health, Satyavati looked right at him and said, straight out, 'Sons are born as the common property of the mother and the father. As the father is their master, so is the mother; this is certain. Just as you are my first son, given to me by the creator, so too Vicitravirya is my last-born son. And just as Bhishma is Vicitravirya's half-brother, sharing a father, so you are his half-brother, sharing a mother, as you will agree; his father is Shantanu. Now, Bhishma keeps his word, and his word is his strength; and he has made a decision not to have children and not to rule the kingdom. Out of esteem for your brother, and for the continuation of the dynasty, and at the request of Bhishma, and at my insistence, and out of compassion for living creatures, and to protect everyone – you should listen kindly to what I say, and do it. The two wives of your younger brother are like the very best daughters of the gods, blessed with beauty and youth, and they want to have sons according to dharma. Beget children in them – you are quite capable of it, my little son – children that are appropriate for this family and for the continuation of its line.'

Vyasa said, 'You know dharma, Satyavati, both the higher and the lower. And because your thinking is within dharma, for you do know dharma, and is for the benefit of living creatures, and because you insist, therefore I will do what will bring about dharma, and what you wish. For this custom has been observed in ancient times. I will give my brother sons who are the equal of the gods Mitra and Varuna. But the two queens must observe a vow that I will prescribe, for a year, properly, so that they will become pure. For I will enter no woman unless she has entered this vow.'

'But you must make the queen pregnant *right away*,' said Satyavati. 'In kingdoms where there are no kings, there is no rain, there are no gods. How can a kingdom that has no king be maintained? So plant the embryo; Bhishma will make it grow.' 'If I must produce a son quickly, before the proper time,' said Vyasa, 'then let her take this as her highest vow: She must endure my ugliness. If she can bear my smell, my appearance, my clothes, and my body, then Kausalya will conceive a most extraordinary embryo on this very day. He will have a hundred sons, who will protect the Kuru dynasty and dispel its sorrows; this is certain.'

Then the sage vanished, awaiting the union. The queen went to her daughter-in-law and met her in private and spoke to her words that were full of dharma and considerations of profit, but were also for her own welfare: 'Kausalya, listen to what I say, which concerns dharma. The line of the Bharatas has been cut off, evidently because my good fortune has run out. Bhishma has seen how upset I am and how pressed his father's dynasty is; he has told me his idea about this and about the way to cause dharma to thrive. But this idea depends on you, my daughter; I will tell you what it is. Raise up again the ruined dynasty of the Bharatas; receive an embryo from your noble brother-in-law, good lady. Bring forth a son who will be like the king of the gods, O lady with good hips. He will bear the heavy yoke of the kingdom of our dynasty.' With some difficulty, (Satyavati) won (Kausalya) over by using dharma, for the princess was dedicated to dharma. And then (Satyavati) fed the Brahmins, the divine seers, and the guests.

Now, when her daughter-in-law had bathed at the time of her fertile season, Satyavati made her lie down on the bed and said to her gently, 'Kausalya, you have a brother-in-law, and he will come to you today. Stay awake and wait for him; he will come in the middle of the night.' When (Kausalya) heard the words of her mother-in-law, she lay there on the lovely bed, thinking that it would be Bhishma or one of the other bulls of the Kurus. Then, in the dead of the night, when most people were asleep, and the lamps were still shining, the seer entered her bed, for he always kept his word, and he had promised first to go to Ambika (Kausalya).

When the queen saw the tawny matted hair of Krishna (Vyasa), and his blazing eyes, and his red beard, she closed her eyes. For when Kausalya looked at him – and he was hard to look at – she thought, 'How ugly!', for she was not used to anything like that, and in her terror she shut her eyes as tight as buds. Indeed, the sage with his matted hair was ugly, a skinny man of a most peculiar colour, and his odour was the very opposite of sweet-smelling; he was in all ways hard to take.

He united with her that night, because he wanted to please his mother, but Kausalya, the daughter of the king of Kashi, was so frightened that she could not look at him. Afterwards, his mother met him as he came out, and she said to her son: 'My son, will a king's son with good qualities be born in her?' When Vyasya heard these words from his mother, he answered her, impelled by fate, though he was extremely intelligent and had knowledge beyond his senses. He said, 'He will have the vital energy of a million elephants; he will be a wise royal seer, with great fortune, great heroism, and great intelligence; and he will have a hundred powerful sons. However, because of his mother's deficiency in the quality (of sight), he will be blind.' 'But a blind man is not qualified to be king of the Kurus, you treasure of asceticism,' his mother said, when she heard her son's words; 'if this son is blind, then we don't have him, even though we have him. Because of this, you must beget a younger son to be king, to protect the dynasty and destroy the sorrows of its good people. The other wife of your brother has beauty, youth, *and* a good character; beget in her a child who will have even more virtues; do it as I tell you. You must give the Kuru dynasty a second king to protect the line of relatives and to nourish the line of fathers.' 'All right,' the great ascetic promised, and he went away. And after a while, Kausalya gave birth to a son who was blind.

Once again, the queen persuaded her (other) daughter-in-law (Ambalika) and, as before, the blameless Satyavati had the sage brought to her. Engaging Ambalika's co-operation, Satyavati once more caused her son to unite with her, to continue the family line. Ambalika, who was a good woman, sat down on the splendid bed; deeply depressed, she waited as she was constrained to do, thinking, 'Who is it who will come?' Then the great sage came to Ambalika in the same way. When she saw him, she too was so upset that she turned pale.

Vyasa, the son of Satyavati, saw that she was frightened and upset and pale, and so he said, 'Since you with your lovely face turned pale when you saw how ugly I am, therefore this son of yours will be pale, and his name will be Pale (Pandu).' And as the great seer said this, he went out.

Then Satyavati saw her son come out and spoke to him. Again he explained to his mother, and told her that the child was pale; and his mother asked him again for one more son. 'All right,' the great seer answered his mother. And when the right time came, the queen (Ambalika) brought forth a boy, pale but full of good signs, seeming to shine forth with good fortune; and from him were born five sons, the Pandavas, who were great archers.

Then she made Kausalya unite with him again during her fertile season. But when that woman, who was like the daughter of a god, merely thought of the appearance and the smell of the great sage, she was frightened, and she did not do what the queen told her to do. This daughter of the king of Kashi adorned in her own ornaments a slave girl as beautiful as a celestial nymph, and sent her to Krishna (Vyasa). The slave girl rose to meet the sage when he arrived, and bowed to him. When he invited her, she had intercourse with him, and did good things to serve him. The sage was completely satisfied by all the enjoyments of lust that he had in her; he spent the whole night with her, taking his pleasure in her. When he got up, he said to her, 'You will no longer be a slave girl. Lovely woman, your womb has received a glorious embryo who will be the very soul of dharma, the most intelligent man in the world.' This son born of Krishna of the Island was named Vidura, the brother of Dhritarashtra and Pandu, and his intelligence was immeasurable. As a result of the curse of the noble Mandavya, Dharma himself took the form of Vidura, who knew the principles of profit and was free of lust and anger.

When (Vyasa) had thus discharged his debt of dharma, he went back to his mother and told her about the (third) embryo; and then he vanished.

And that is how Vyasa of the Island begot in the field of Vicitravirya sons who were like children of the gods, to extend the dynasty of the Kurus. (*Mahabharata* 1.99–100)

3.1.2 The karma of Dharma: Mandavya on the stake

The whole of the first book of the Mahabharata *is a conversation between Vaishampayana, the narrator of the story, and a king named Janamejaya. Near the end of the previous selection, Vaishampayana casually referred to 'the curse of the noble Mandavya'. In response to this, Janamejaya asked, 'What deed had Dharma done that made him incur a curse? And by whose curse was he born in the womb of a Shudra?' Vaishampayana replied with this story:*

There was once a certain Brahmin known as Mandavya; he was steadfast, an expert on all dharma, firm in truth and asceticism. The great ascetic and great yogi would stand at the entrance to his hermitage at the foot of a tree with his arms above his head, and keep a vow of silence. He had stood there in this asceticism for a long time when there came to his hermitage robbers carrying plunder, closely followed by many policemen. They stashed their plunder in his house and hid there in fear as the police force approached. While they were hiding there, the police force soon arrived in pursuit, and they saw the seer. Then they asked the ascetic, who was still under his vow of silence, 'Great Brahmin, which way did the robbers go? We want to go the same way, to catch up with them.' But the ascetic did not say anything at all, good or bad, in reply to the question of the police. The king's men searched the hermitage and saw the thieves hiding there, and the loot, too. Then the police began to have doubts about the sage; they tied him up and reported him and the robbers to the king. The king passed judgement on him along with the thieves: 'Kill him.' The executioners did not know who he was, and so they impaled the great ascetic on a stake. And when the police had had the sage impaled on the stake, they went back to the king with the recovered wealth.

The Brahmin seer, who was the very soul of dharma, remained on the stake for a long time. Though he had no food, he did not die. He held fast to his vital breaths and summoned together the seers. The sages suffered terribly when they saw the noble ascetic suffering ascetically on the tip of the stake. In the night, they became birds and came back to him from all around, demonstrating their powers; and then they questioned that excellent Brahmin: 'We want to hear what evil deed you committed, Brahmin.' Then the tiger among sages said to the ascetics, 'Whom can I blame? For no one but me is guilty.'

The king heard the sage and came out with his counsellors; then he tried to appease the great seer who was still on the stake. He said, 'Greatest of seers, please forgive me for the mistake that I made in my delusion and ignorance; you shouldn't be angry at me.' When the king said that, the sage forgave him; and when he was forgiven, the king had him taken down from the stake. But when he had taken him down from the tip of the stake and started to pull the stake out of him, he was unable to pull it out, and so he cut off the stake at its base. And so the sage went about with the stake still inside him. As he moved around with the stake in his neck, ribs, and entrails, he started to think, '(The stake) could be used as (a pole) to carry flower baskets.' By means of this asceticism he conquered worlds that were hard for other people to conquer; and people used to call him, 'Tip-of-the-stake Mandavya'.

Then the Brahmin, who knew the highest meaning, went to the house of Dharma; when the powerful sage saw Dharma seated there, he scolded him, saying 'What *was* the bad deed that I did, without knowing what I had done, a deed which has earned me such a fruit of retribution? Tell me the truth at once; see the power of my asceticism.' Dharma said, 'You stuck blades of grass up the tails of little butterflies, and this is the fruit that you have obtained from that karma, ascetic.' Tip-of-the-Stake Mandavya said, '*When* did I do this? Tell me the truth.' To this question the king of dharma replied, 'You did it when you were a child.'

Then Tip-of-the-Stake Mandavya said, 'For a rather small offence you have given me an enormous punishment. Because of that, Dharma, you will be born as a man, in the womb of a Shudra. And I will establish a moral boundary for the fruition of dharma in the world: no sin will be counted against anyone until the age of fourteen, but it will be regarded as a fault for those who do it after that age.' And so, because he was cursed by the noble sage for the offence that he had committed, Dharma was born in the form of Vidura, in the womb of a Shudra. (*Mahabharata* 1.101)

3.1.3 Yudhishthira approaches heaven with his dog

Dharma, incarnate as a god, also becomes incarnate in the human hero Vidura, as we have seen above. But Dharma plays an even more important role as the father of Yudhishthira, whom he begets upon Kunti, the wife of Pandu, when Pandu (like his surrogate father, Vicitravirya) is unable to produce children himself. In the course of the Mahabharata, *Dharma reveals himself to Yudhishthira, and to others, in a variety of forms. When he appears at the very end of the Epic, he reminds Yudhishthira of one of those previous incidents: once, Dharma disguised himself as a forest spirit to test the virtue of the brothers when they were in search of water; all but Yudhishthira failed and were killed, but Yudhishthira survived and revived them all. When asked whom he would revive first, he chose Nakula (who, with Sahadeva, was born of Madri) rather than Bhima or Arjuna (who were, with Yudhishthira, born of Kunti), so that Nakula's mother and his own would each have a living son.*

The final encounter between Dharma and the Pandavas takes place when, after most of their relatives, male and female, have been killed, the five Pandava brothers – Yudhishthira (son of Dharma), Arjuna (son of Indra), Bhima (son of Vayu, the wind), and the twins Sahadeva and Nakula (sons of the Ashvins) – with their joint wife, Draupadi, go north toward the sacred mountain Meru. They are followed by a dog, regarded by Hindus as an unclean animal whose touch is polluting.

They gathered together their inner forces and entered into a yogic state and set out for the north. They saw the great Himalayan mountain and went beyond it until they saw the ocean of sand, and they gazed down upon mount Meru, the ultimate mountain. As they were all moving along quickly, absorbed in their yoga, Draupadi lost her yogic concentration and fell to the ground. When the mighty Bhima saw that she had fallen, he spoke to Yudhishthira, the king of dharma, about her, saying, 'The princess Draupadi never did anything against dharma; then what has caused her to fall to the ground?' Yudhishthira replied, 'Draupadi was greatly partial to Arjuna (among us, her five husbands); and now she has experienced the fruit of that partiality.' When Yudhishthira the son of Dharma had said this, he went on, never glancing at her, for he concentrated his mind; he was the very soul of dharma, a bull among men.

Then the wise Sahadeva fell to the ground, and when Bhima saw that he had fallen he said to the king (Yudhishthira), 'This man was always eager to serve us all, with no thought for himself; why has he fallen to the ground?' Yudhishthira said, 'He did not think that anyone was as wise as he was. This flaw in his character has caused the prince to fall.' And when he had said this, Yudhish-thira left Sahadeva behind and went on with his brothers, and with the dog.

When the warrior Nakula saw that Draupadi and Sahadeva had fallen, he was tormented, for he loved his family, and he himself fell to the ground. And when the handsome hero Nakula had fallen, Bhima spoke to the king again, saying, 'This man, my brother, Nakula, never violated dharma, and always did what he said he would do; and he was the handsomest man in the world. But now he has fallen to the ground!' When Bhima had said this about Nakula, Yudhishthira, the soul of dharma, the most intelligent of all men, replied: 'His philosophy was, "There is no one as handsome as me; I am the best, the only one." This thought stuck in his mind, and so Nakula has fallen. Come along, Bhima, Wolf-belly. Whatever is fated for anyone, that is what he must, inevitably, experience.'

But when Arjuna, the Pandava who rode on a white horse, the killer of enemy heroes, saw that they had fallen, he himself fell to the ground after them, overcome by grief. And when that tiger among men, the seed of Indra, hard to withstand, had fallen and was dying, Bhima said to the king, 'I cannot recall anything that this noble man ever did wrong, particularly on purpose. To whom, then, did he do some harm that has caused him to fall to the ground?' Yudhishthira replied, 'Arjuna said, "I will burn up my enemies in a single day." But, though he was proud of his heroism, he did not do this; and so he has fallen. He despised all (the other) archers; but a man who wishes for greatness must do what he says he will do.'

Having said this, the king went forth; and Bhima fell. As he fell, Bhima said to Yudhishthira, the king of dharma, 'Your highness! Look! I, whom you love, have fallen! What has caused me to fall? Tell me, if you know.' And Yudhish-thira replied, 'You ate too much, and boasted about your vital energy, and despised your enemy. That is why you have fallen to the ground.' And when he had said this, the great-armed Yudhishthira went on, never looking down. Only the dog followed him – the dog that I have already told you about quite a lot.

Then Indra came to Yudhishthira in his chariot, making heaven and earth reverberate everywhere, and he said to him, 'Get in.' But Yudhishthira, the king of dharma, had seen all his brothers fallen, and burning with grief he said to Indra, the thousand-eyed, 'My brothers have all fallen here; let them come with me. I do not want to go to heaven without my brothers. And the delicate princess (Draupadi), who deserves to be happy – let her come with us. Give your permission, O lord of the gods.'

'You will see all your brothers and your sons, who have reached heaven before you, together with Draupadi' said Indra. 'Don't be sad. They have cast off their human bodies and gone; but you will go to heaven with this body; this is certain.' Then Yudhishthira said, 'O lord of all that has been and is to be, this dog has been devoted to me constantly. Let him come with me; for my heart is incapable of cruelty.' 'Today, great king, you have become immortal, like me,' said Indra, 'and you have won complete glory and great fame, and all the joys of heaven. Abandon this dog; there is no cruelty in this.' 'Noble god, god of a thousand eyes,' said Yudhishthira, 'it is hard for one who is noble to commit an ignoble act like this. I do not want to achieve glory if I must do it by abandoning someone who has been devoted to me.'

'But there is no place for dog-owners in heaven,' said Indra, 'for the evil spirits called Overpowered-by-anger carry off their sacrificial merit (that would earn them a place in heaven). And so, king of dharma, you should think before you act; abandon this dog; there is no cruelty in this.' Yudhishthira said, 'People say that to abandon one who is devoted to you is a bottomless evil equal to murdering a Brahmin. Therefore, great Indra, I will never, in any way, abandon him now in order to achieve my own happiness.' Indra said, 'The evil spirits called Overpowered-by-anger carry off what has been offered, sacrificed, and given as an oblation into the fire, if it is left uncovered and a dog has looked at it. Therefore you must abandon this dog, and by abandoning the dog you will win the world of the gods. By abandoning your brothers, and even your darling Draupadi, you reached this world by your own heroic action; how is it then that you will not abandon this dog? Perhaps, having abandoned everything, you have now lost your mind.'

Yudhishthira said, 'There is no such thing as either union or separation for mortals when they are dead; this is common knowledge. I could not keep them alive, and so I abandoned them – but (I would not abandon) those who are alive. Handing over someone who has come to you for refuge; killing a woman; confiscating the property of a Brahmin; and betraying a friend; these four acts, Indra, are equalled by the act of abandoning someone who is devoted to you; this is what I think.'

When he heard these words spoken by the king of dharma, the god (who had been there in the form of the dog) took his own form, Dharma. He was satisfied with king Yudhishthira, and spoke to him with smooth words of praise: 'Great king, you are well born, with the good conduct and intelligence of your father, and with compassion for all creatures. Once upon a time, my son, in the Dvaita forest, I tested you, that time when your brothers were all killed as they went too far in their search for water, and you abandoned Bhima and Arjuna, your two brothers, and chose to save the life of Nakula, because you wanted to deal equally with the two mothers (yours and Nakula's). And now you abandoned the celestial chariot, for you insisted, "This dog is devoted to me." Because of this, great king, there is no one your equal in heaven. And because of this, you have won the undying worlds, won the supreme way of heaven, and won them with your own body.'

Then Dharma and Indra and the Maruts and the two Ashvins and all the other gods and celestial sages made Yudhishthira mount the chariot, and along with them, in their own chariots, went the perfected beings that go wherever they wish to go, all of the dustless gods with their great virtue and with their virtuous speech, thoughts, and actions. The perpetuator of the Kuru family

(Yudhishthira) flew swiftly upwards in that chariot, encompassing heaven and earth with his blazing glory. Then Narada, who knew all about everyone and lived among the gods, and who was a great ascetic and a great talker, said, out loud, 'This Kuru king has eclipsed the fame of all the royal sages who are here. For I have never heard of anyone but this Pandava who has won all the worlds with his own body, encompassing them with his glory and splendour and noble behaviour.'

But when king Yudhishthira heard what Narada said, he who was the very soul of dharma bade farewell to the gods and the kings of his own family, saying, 'Whether my brothers are right now in a good place or a bad place, that is where I want to be; I don't want any other worlds.' When Indra, the king of the gods, heard the words of king Yudhishthira, a speech utterly devoid of cruelty, he replied, 'Great king, live in this place, that you have won by your own good actions. Why do you still drag human affection about, even now? You have achieved supreme success, such as no other man has ever achieved; your brothers have not attained a place like this. Yet even now human emotion touches you. Look, this is heaven; look at the gods and perfected beings who inhabit this triple paradise.'

But the wise Yudhishthira answered the king of the gods with a speech full of meaning: 'O conqueror of demons, I cannot bear to live here without them. I want to go where my brothers have gone, and where Draupadi has gone, big, dark, wise, virtuous, incomparable Draupadi, the woman I love.' (*Mahabharata* 17.2–3)

3.1.4 Salvation and damnation in the *Bhagavad Gita*
On the eve of the great battle between the Pandavas and their cousins, Arjuna is overcome with misgivings and hesitates to kill his cousins. The god Krishna, who is incarnate as Arjuna's charioteer and bodyguard, reassures him by teaching him the meaning of human duty and the divine soul. Reassured, Arjuna enters into the battle that is the Armageddon of his race. This conversation between Arjuna and Krishna, known as the Bhagavad Gita, *has taken on a separate life outside of the Epic in which it is set and has become one of the central documents of Hinduism. The passage I have selected continues the ancient theme of the inevitable corruption of the demons by the gods; see above, 2.2.2 and 2.2.3.1.*

The Lord said, 'Fearless and pure in nature, steadfast in the practice of wisdom, generous and self-controlled, performing sacrifice, devoted to the study of scripture, ascetic, sincere, injuring no one, truthful, without anger, renouncing (everything), peaceful, never slanderous, compassionate to (all) beings, never greedy, gentle, modest, never fickle, ardent, patient, enduring, pure, never malicious, never arrogant – these are the qualities of a man who is born to have the fate of a god. But a hypocrite, proud and arrogant, angry, harsh, and ignorant – these are the qualities of a man who is born to have the fate of a demon.

'The fate of a god is release; the fate of a demon is bondage – that is what is generally believed. But do not worry, Arjuna; you were born to have the fate of a god. There are two classes of beings in this world – the godlike and the demonic. I have told you about the godlike at some length; now listen to the demonic.

'The demonic do not understand activity nor the cessation of activity; there is no purity in them, no morality, no truth. They say, "The universe has no reality, no firm basis, no lord; it has not come into existence through mutual causation; desire is its only cause – what else?" Since they insist upon this doctrine, their souls are lost and their wits are feeble; and so they commit horrible actions in their wish to harm and destroy the universe. Immersing themselves in insatiable desire, possessed by hypocrisy, pride, and madness, in their delusion they grasp at false conceptions and undertake impure enterprises. They are afflicted by countless worries that end only at doomsday, for their only aim is to enjoy what they desire, since they are convinced that this is all there is. Bound by the fetters of hope, by the hundreds, obsessed by desire and anger, they long to amass great wealth, by whatever foul means, to satisfy their desires.

"I got this today! I'll satisfy this whim. This is my money, and this, and this will be mine soon. I killed that man – he was my enemy; and I will kill the others, too. I'm master, here; I'm the one who enjoys this; I'm successful and powerful and happy. I'm rich and superior; who else is there the likes of me? I'll sacrifice, and I'll give to charities, and I will have *fun*." This is what people say when they are deluded by ignorance.

'They are led astray by their many notions; they are caught up in the net of delusion; they are addicted to the satisfaction of their desires – and so they fall into a filthy hell. Full of themselves, rigid, maddened by their pride in their wealth, in their hypocrisy they offer sacrifices that are sacrifices in name only, not performed in the proper manner at all. They rely on their egotism, brute force, pride, desire, and anger; and they hate me and are unable to stand me – though I dwell in their own bodies, as in the bodies of all others. I always throw these hateful, cruel, vile, bad men into the wombs of demons in the course of their rebirths; and when they have fallen into a demonic womb, they are deluded in birth after birth, and they never ever reach me; and so they go the lowest way.

'The door to hell, that destroys the soul, is three-fold: desire, anger, and greed; that is why you should abandon these three. For when a man is released from these three doors of darkness, he acts for the good of his soul; and then he goes the highest way. Whoever discards the laws of the Shastras, and acts to accomplish his desires, never achieves fulfilment, nor happiness, nor the highest way. Therefore let the Shastras be your authority, determining what you should do and what you should not do. When you know what the Shastras say about something, you should do what they tell you to do.' (*Bhagavad Gita* 16.1–24)

3.2 *Ramayana*

The Ramayana *is shorter than the* Mahabharata, *more elaborate in its poetry, and more consistent in its theme: the story of the abduction of Sita, the wife of Rama, by the ogre Ravana, and the successful expedition mounted by Rama (with the assistance of Hanuman and other monkeys) to kill Ravana and win Sita back.*

3.2.1 The birth of Sita and the bending of the bow

Rama and Lakshmana, two of the four sons of king Dasharatha, and descendants of king Raghu, have come from their capital city of Ayodhya to Mithila, the capital city of King Janaka, ruler of the kingdom of Videha; they are accompanied by their family priest, the sage Vishvamitra. They have come there to try their luck at winning the hand of the princess Sita by winning the contest set for all suitors, that consists in bending a certain bow. This is a bow that came into existence at the time when the god Rudra destroyed the sacrifice of King Daksha, a story that is told at length in the Mahabharata. *It is a bow that cannot be bent by demons (Asuras), ogres (Rakshasas), spirits (Yakshas), What?-men (Kinnaras, creatures that are half-horse, half-man), Gandharvas (demigods connected with horses and fertility) or Nagas (great serpents, sometimes cobras, sometimes half-serpents, snake from the waist down and anthropomorphic from the waist up, inhabitants of the water worlds below the surface of the earth). Rama alone is able to bend the bow and win the princess.*

In the clear light of dawn, King Janaka performed his rituals and then summoned the noble Vishvamitra and Rama and Lakshmana. The king, who was the very soul of dharma, honoured the sage and the two Raghu princes, honoured them with the ritual set down in the Shastras, and then he said, 'Welcome to you, sir. What can I do for you, sinless one? Command me, for I am yours to command.' When the sage, who was the very soul of dharma, and also clever with words, heard the speech of the noble hero, Janaka, he answered him with this speech: 'These two Kshatriyas are the two sons of king Dasharatha, and are famous throughout the world. They wish to see that special bow that you have. Do please show it to them, and when they have satisfied their desire by seeing the bow, the two princes will go back home as they please.'

When he heard this, Janaka replied to the great sage, 'Let me tell you the purpose for which that bow is here. The king called Devarata, sixth in descent from Nimi, received this bow in trust from the noble god Rudra, who placed it in his hands. For, once upon a time, when Daksha's sacrifice was destroyed, the mighty Rudra bent this bow and said to the gods, in mock fury, "Since you gods did not set aside any share in the sacrifice for me, and I want a share, I am going to knock your precious heads off with this bow." Then the gods trembled with fear, and they bowed low to Rudra and begged him to forgive them, and he was satisfied by them. In his satisfaction, he restored to their former condition all their limbs that the noble god of gods had lopped off or mutilated or shattered with his bow. That celestial bow remains even today in our family, where it is highly valued.

'Now, one day when I was in the sacrificial grounds, I saw the ultimate celestial nymph, Menaka, flying through the sky, and this thought came to me: "If I should have a child in her, what a child that would be!" As I was thinking in this way, my semen fell on the ground. And afterwards, as I was ploughing that field, there arose out of the earth, as first fruits, my daughter, who has celestial beauty and qualities, and can only be won by one whose bride price is his manliness. Since she arose from the surface of the earth, and was born from no womb, she is called Sita, the furrow.

'In the past, kings kept coming here and coming here, wooing her, and I told those kings, "She will be given to the man whose bride-price is his manliness." Then all the kings who sought my daughter came to my city to prove their manliness. I showed them the bow, to test their manliness, but they could not even lift up that bow. And when I saw how little manliness they had, I refused to let any of them have my daughter. Then all those kings became angry, and they surrounded the city of Mithila on all sides and laid siege to it. For those kings, each individually thinking that he had been insulted, were filled with great anger, and so they oppressed Mithila. For a full year they besieged Mithila, with firm determination, and when, as a result of that siege, all my resources were exhausted, I asked help from the god of gods, (Rudra) the husband of Uma. The lord was satisfied by my propitiation and gave me an army, complete with all four divisions (infantry, cavalry, chariots, and the armoured division [elephants]). Then the power of the kings was broken and they went away, for they had little manliness in the courage of their army, and they were too proud of the little manliness that they had. This, then, is the incomparable celestial bow, that I will show to Rama and Lakshmana. And if Rama can string this bow, I will give him Sita, who was born of no womb, to be the daughter-in-law of Dasharatha.'

When the great sage Vishvamitra heard king Janaka's words, he said to him, 'Show the bow to Rama.' Then king Janaka commanded his ministers: 'Adorn the celestial bow with perfume and garlands and bring it here.' At Janaka's command, the ministers entered the city, placed the bow in front of them, and went back out, as the king had commanded. Five thousand tall, noble men put the chest (containing the bow) on (a carriage with) eight wheels and dragged it, with considerable difficulty. And when they had brought the iron chest that contained the bow, the king's counsellors said to the godlike Janaka, 'Here, king, is the incomparable bow that all the kings revere; if you wish, great king of Mithila, it can be seen.' At their words, the king cupped his hands in reverence and spoke to the noble Vishvamitra, and to Rama and Lakshmana: 'Here is the incomparable bow that the Janakas revere, O Brahmin, and that all those kings with their great manliness were unable to draw. None of the hosts of gods, none of the demons or ogres, or the foremost Gandharvas or spirits, none of the What?-men or great Nagas can bend this bow or string it or fit an arrow to it or pluck the string or even lift it. What chance is there then for men? This bow is the very best; bull of sages, show it to these two sons of the king.'

When the sage Vishvamitra heard what the king said, he said to Rama, 'Rama, my little calf, look at the bow.' And Rama did as the sage said; he opened the chest in which the bow lay and looked at the bow and said, 'I touch this great bow with my hand; now I will make a great effort to lift it, and even to string it.' 'Very well,' said the king and the sage, and as the sage had told him to do, he grasped the bow in the middle, playfully. And then, as many thousands of kings watched him, Rama strung the bow as if he were playing. With his manliness, Rama strung the bowstring and then drew the bow; and that incomparable man of great fame broke that bow right in the middle. It made a loud noise, loud as a thunderclap, and a great earthquake, as if a mountain had been shattered. The noise so stunned all the men that they fell down – all except the great sage, the king, and the two Raghu princes.

When the people revived again, the king – whose worries were over – cupped his hands in reverence and spoke to the bull among sages, for he knew how to make speeches: 'Sir, now I have seen the manliness of Rama the son of Dasharatha; it is surpassingly marvellous, inconceivable; I had no idea what it was like. My daughter Sita will bring great fame to the family of the Janakas when she takes Rama, the son of Dasharatha, as her husband. And so I have kept my promise, that her only bride-price would be manliness; I will give Rama my daughter Sita, who is as precious as life itself. With your permission, please, Brahmin, my counsellors will go quickly to Ayodhya, hastening in chariots. With courteous words they will bring the king to my city and tell him all about the betrothal of the girl whose only bride-price was manliness. And they will tell the king that his two sons are under the protection of the sage; this will satisfy the king, and then they can bring him here right away.' 'Yes,' said Vishvamitra, and the king spoke to his counsellors and gave them orders and sent them to Ayodhya; for he was the very soul of dharma. (*Ramayana* 1.65–6).

3.2.2 The song of Kusha and Lava

After bringing Sita back from the ogre Ravana, who had abducted her, and killing Ravana, Rama banished Sita from his kingdom, because her reputation had been sullied during her stay with Ravana. Sita took refuge in the hermitage of the sage and poet Valmiki, and, unknown to Rama, gave birth to twin boys, Kusha and Lava, whom Valmiki took as his pupils.

Meanwhile, Rama had been ruling his kingdom, surrounded by his three brothers, Lakshmana, Bharata, and Shatrughna; by the monkeys, whose king, Sugriva, and general, Hanuman, had helped Rama to bring Sita back; and by the good ogres who had defected to him, headed by Ravana's brother, Vibhishana. As the present episode opens, Rama is in the midst of performing the horse sacrifice that will establish his kingdom firmly forever. Valmiki sends to this sacrifice his pupils, Kusha and Lava, whom he has trained as professional poets and singers: their names are taken from the name of the wandering bard the kushilava. *In particular, he has taught them the great poem that he has composed – a poem about the adventures of Rama and Sita, called the* Ramayana.

This involves a paradox of some complexity: Rama is told the story of the Ramayana *while he is still inside it and it is still incomplete. Thus an intended ambiguity colours the end of the episode: are we listening to the end of the* Ramayana, *as it happens to Rama after he hears the story of the beginning of the* Ramayana? *Or are we listening to the* story *of the end of the* Ramayana, *as Rama continues to listen to it?*

As that most wonderful sacrifice was taking place, Valmiki, the bull among sages, suddenly arrived there with his two pupils. He saw the sacrifice, marvellous to behold, seeming celestial, and he made some pleasant huts in a corner of the sacrificial grounds of the seers. Then he said joyously to his two pupils, 'Go, both of you together, and with great joy sing the entire poem of the *Ramayana*. Sing it in the sacred sacrificial grounds of the seers and in the dwellings of the Brahmins, along the chariot roads and the main streets, and in the houses of the princes. But especially you must sing it at the door of Rama's palace where the ritual is taking place, before the sacrificial priests. Here are all sorts of sweet fruits, that grow on the tips of the mountains; keep on eating them as you sing; when you eat these fruits, my little calves, you will not get tired; but stay away from those savoury roots that come from the city. If king Rama has you sing for the hearing of the seers who are seated around him, sing there. Sing, with great joy, twenty chapters every day, with many musical measures, just as I taught you before. Do not be even a little bit greedy for wealth; what use is wealth for people who live in a hermitage and live on fruits and roots? If Rama should ask you, "Whose little boys are you?", say to the king, "We are the two pupils of Valmiki." Sound the key tone on these sweet-sounding stringed instruments, as I showed you before, and then forget your nervousness and sing sweetly. Sing it from the beginning, and do not show disrespect for the prince; for the king is the father of all creatures, according to dharma. So, tomorrow at dawn, concentrate and with joyous hearts sing the sweet song to the beat of the stringed instruments.'

When Valmiki, the most noble and famous sage, had instructed them in that way many times, he became silent. The two boys placed in their hearts the wonderful, auspicious speech that the seer had uttered, like the two Ashvins when they had been instructed by Shukra, the family priest of the demons. And they spent the night in happy anticipation.

When the night turned into dawn, the two boys bathed, made their oblations into the fire, and began to sing here and there as the seer had told them to do before. Rama heard that combination of singing and reciting, of a kind that had never been heard before, telling about his own former deeds; it was adorned with song and combined with many musical measures, to the beat of the stringed instruments. When Rama heard this from the two boys, he was overcome by curiosity; and during an interval in the ritual, the king, a tiger among men, summoned the great sages, the princes, the pandits, those who knew the Vedas, the bards who knew the Puranas, the grammarians, and the old Brahmins. He summoned all these, and then he had the two singers brought in. The crowds of seers and the powerful princes waxed ecstatic as they seemed to drink in with their eyes the king and these two singers. All of them said the same thing to one another: 'The two of them look just like Rama, like two reflections of the same thing. If they did not have matted hair and wear bark garments, there would be no way of distinguishing between the two singers and Rama.'

As the audience were talking in this way, the sage's two little boys began to sing a song that brought great joy. The song began, sweet as a song of the Gandharvas, beyond anything human, and the whole audience could not get enough of it. They began at the beginning, from the chapter in which Narada appears (chapter one), and continued for twenty chapters from there. Then, in the afternoon, when Rama had heard the twenty chapters, he said to his brother Bharata, for whom he felt great fraternal affection, 'Give these two noble boys eighteen thousand pieces of gold, immediately; spare no effort.' But the two bards, the noble Kusha and Lava, did not take the gold that was given them; they stood there in amazement and said, 'What good is this? We are forest-dwellers who are quite satisfied with forest fruits and roots. What would we do with gold in the forest?'

When the two of them said this, the whole audience, and Rama, became filled with curiosity and amazement; and Rama was curious to hear the provenance of that poem. The mighty king asked the sage's two little boys, 'What is the authority for this poem? What is it based on? Who is the author of this great and noble poem? What bull among sages is he?' When the king asked this, the sage's two little boys replied, 'The lord Valmiki, who has come here for the sacrifice, is the author, who has revealed to you this narration – in five hundred chapters – of all your deeds from the very beginning, leaving none out. It is based on your whole life, O king, both its auspicious and its inauspicious parts. If, great king, great charioteer, you are inclined to listen to it, then in the intervals of the ritual you and your attendants may hear it, if you have a moment free.' 'Yes,' said Rama, and when the two of them had been given permission by Rama they took their leave of him and returned, rejoicing, to the place where the bull among sages was staying. And Rama, together with the sages and noble princes, kept listening to that sweet song and then returning to the sacrificial hall.

Rama listened for many days to that marvellous song, together with the sages and the kings and the monkeys. And as the song was sung, he recognised that Kusha and Lava were the sons of Sita.

Rama summoned Sita, who appeared in court and swore that, if she was in fact innocent, the earth, her mother, would open up and receive her. The earth did so, and Sita vanished forever.

When the princess from Videha had entered the subterranean world, all the humans and all the seers cried out, 'Bravo! Bravo!', in Rama's presence.

Supporting himself upon his sceptre, his eyes streaming with tears, head down, heart-sick, Rama sat there, thoroughly miserable. He cried for a long time, shedding copious tears, and then, filled with sorrow and anger, he said, 'A sorrow such as has never before existed seeks to touch my heart; as I sat looking on, Sita, like good fortune incarnate, vanished. Once upon a time, she vanished into Lanka, on the far shore of the great ocean; but I brought her back even from there; so surely I will be all the more able to bring her back from under the surface of the earth. O goddess earth, let Sita come back to me, or else I will show my wrath, so that you will appreciate me. Indeed, you are my own mother-in-law, since, once upon a time, the princess of Mithila was pulled up from your presence by Janaka when he was ploughing with a ploughshare in his hand. Therefore, let Sita come back to me; open up a chasm for me; I will live with her, whether it be in the subterreanean world or on the very back of the vault of heaven. Bring Sita back to me; I am going mad for the sake of the princess of Mithila. If you don't give Sita to me this very day, just as she was, on the surface of the earth, then I will waste you entirely, with all your mountains and forests; I will destroy the earth; there will be nothing but water here.'

As Rama was talking in this way, filled with sorrow and anger, Brahma came with all the gods and spoke to Rama, saying, 'Rama, Rama, you should not grieve. Remember your previous existence and your secret plan, O scourge of enemies. At this dangerous moment, remember that you were born from Vishnu. Listen while I tell you, here in the middle of this assembly, about this particular poem, incomparably famous among all poems. Rama, it will tell everything, in detail, certainly, beginning with your birth, and including all the happiness and unhappiness, and even what is going to be in the future – all of this (story) was made by Valmiki. This is the primeval poem, Rama, and it is all about you; for no one but Rama deserves the fame brought by poems. I, and the gods, have already heard the first part, and it is heavenly, marvellous; it tells the truth and conceals nothing. Now, tiger among men, when you have collected your thoughts with dharma, listen to the rest of the *Ramayana*, the poem that tells the future. This remainder of the poem is famous under the name of the Final Section (*Uttara Kanda*). Listen now, with the seers, to the end; for this ending is not to be heard by anyone else but the great seers and you, who are the supreme seer.'

When Brahma, the god who is lord of the triple world, had said this speech, he went to the triple heaven, together with the gods and the Vasus (solar gods). But all the noble seers there who live in the world of Brahma got permission to stay there, for they had their hearts set on hearing the Final Section, the future of Rama.

Now, when the supremely glorious Rama had heard the auspicious speech spoken by the god of gods, he said to Valmiki, 'Sir, the sages who live in the world of Brahma have their hearts set on hearing the Final Section, that is about my future. Let it begin tomorrow.' And having made this decision,

Rama got hold of Kusha and Lava, quickly dismissed the crowd of people, and returned to the sacrificial hall.

And when the night had turned to dawn, Rama assembled the great sages and said to his two sons, 'Sing, and do not worry.' Then, when all the noble great sages were seated, Kusha and Lava sang the Final Section of the poem, the future.

When the princess from Videha had entered the subterranean world . . . the sacrifice ended, and Rama suffered intensely in his heart, for when he did not see the princess from Videha he regarded the entire universe as empty. Wracked by the greatest sorrow, he found no peace for his heart. He dismissed all the princes and the bears and monkeys and ogres and the crowd of people, Brahmins and others, who had been filled with wealth. And when the lotus-eyed Rama had dismissed them all, he placed Sita in his heart and entered Ayodhya. He did not choose any wife other than Sita, for a golden image of Janaka's daughter appeared in all of his sacrifices and in the place of his wife. He performed ten thousand horse sacrifices, and ten times that many Soma sacrifices, in which he gave away a great deal of gold. And he sacrificed with many other sorts of sacrifices – fire-oblations, and overnight sacrifices, expensive offerings of cows, all with the appropriate fees to the priests. As the glorious and noble Rama ruled in this way, striving for dharma, a long time passed. The bears and monkeys and ogres remained under Rama's control, and kings were conciliated by him every day. The god of storms rained at the proper time, so that there was abundant food; the skies were clear. The city and the country were filled with happy, healthy people. No one died at the wrong time; no living creatures became sick; there was no violation of dharma at all, when Rama ruled his kingdom.

Then, after a long time, Rama's glorious mother succumbed to the dharma of Time, surrounded by her sons and grandsons; and she was followed by Sumitra and Kaikeyi (the mothers of Bharata, Lakshmana and Shatrughna). And as they had performed their various dharmas, they were firmly established in the triple heaven; all of them dwelt in heaven with king Dasharatha; together, they achieved the dharma of helping their husband. Time after time, Rama offered great gifts to the Brahmins and ascetics on behalf of all of his mothers, without distinguishing between them; and he performed funeral offerings to his fathers, involving many jewels, and the most extensive sacrifices. Thus Rama, who was the soul of dharma, nourished his fathers and the gods. (*Ramayana* 7.84, 85, and 89)

4 PURANAS

The Puranas, or 'ancient (texts)', are traditionally said to treat five topics; the creation and dissolution of the universe, the ages of the various Manus, or ancestors of the human race, who preside over great periods of time known as the intervals of the Manus (manvantarani), *and the solar and lunar dynasties. Some of them do treat these subjects (some do not), but this ancient armature was richly fleshed out with a sprawling Sanskrit literature containing some of everything: stories, rituals, moral lectures, recipes, medical advice, philosophy, and specialised subjects such as architecture, iconography, veterinary information about horses and elephants – everything. The Puranas are impossible to date with any accuracy, but some are obviously older than others, all of them are later than the Epics, the cores of several were composed during the Gupta period (the fourth to sixth centuries A.D.), and most of them reached their present state before the Mughal period (twelfth century).*

4.1 MYTHS

4.1.1 How Brahma created the universe

Brahma, who has four heads, emits from himself both the material elements of the universe and the abstract categories with which we understand those elements. Matter is divided into the three qualities (or gunas): tamas (*darkness, inertia*), rajas (*energy, passion, activity*), *and* sattva (*goodness, peace*). *Time is divided into the four Ages or Yugas, that combine to make a* kalpa, *or aeon, at the end of which comes doomsday, followed by a period of quiescence or latency, when all is a watery chaos; and then the universe is created anew from the waters. Within the realm of material creation, Brahma emits mythical beasts such as the* sharabha, *sometimes said to combine the parts of a bird, serpent, lion, and so fourth; but he also creates a number of highly technical elements of the Vedic ritual.*

As Brahma meditated, creatures were born from his mind, together with the causes and effects that arose from his body. The souls that know the field (that is the body) arose from his field, his body, as he meditated. Then he wanted to emit the fourfold group of gods, demons, ancestors (or fathers), and humans, by the millions, and so he put himself to work at that. As he put himself to work, the element of darkness (*tamas*) arose in him; and as Prajapati went on meditating in his effort to create, from his behind the demons were born, his first sons. People who know regard the breath (*asu*) as the vital breath (*prana*); and so those who were born from that (breath from his rectum) were known as the demons (*asuras*). Then he discarded the body with which the demons had been created. That body that he had discarded immediately became the night; and since it contained a great deal of darkness, so too the night that is divided into three watches (contains a great deal of darkness); and therefore in the night people are themselves always covered with darkness.

After he had emitted the demons, he took on another body, one that was unmanifest, containing a great deal of goodness (*sattva*). He put that body to work, and as he was putting that body to work, the lord became pleased. Then out of the mouth of his shining face there arose the gods; and since they were born from him when he was shining (*divyatas*), therefore they are known as the gods (*devas*). And when one speaks of the 'playing' (*divya*) of the creator, it refers to this game of his; that is why the divinities were born from that 'playing' body. When he had emitted the gods, he discarded that shining body; and the body that he discarded then became the day. Therefore people worship the gods with rituals performed during the day.

After he had emitted the gods, he took on another body, this one made entirely of goodness, and he put it to work. The lord was thinking like a father as he meditated on his sons, and so the ancestors (*pitaras*, literally, 'fathers') were born from him in the separate place between day and night; and that is why those ancestors, who are gods, are called the 'fathers'. Then he discarded the body with which those ancestors had been created, and that body that he discarded immediately became the twilight. And therefore, just as day belongs to the divinities and night to the demons, the period between them belongs to the ancestors, and that body is the most important. Hence the gods, demons, seers, and men when they put themselves to work worship that body that is in between dawn and daybreak. And hence the twice-born worship the junction between day and night.

Then Brahma took on yet another body, one that was made entirely of energy (*rajas*), a body that he emitted from his mind. And the sons born from his mind were born as his progeny (*prajas*), because he progenerated them (*prajanat*). They are known as humans (*manushyas*) because they were born from his thinking (*mananat*), and they are known as his progeny because he progenerated them. When he had created these progeny, he discarded that body of his, and that body that the noble one discarded immediately became the moonlight. And so all his progeny become delighted when moonlight arises. Thus these bodies that the noble one discarded immediately became night, day, twilight, and moonlight. Moonlight, twilight, and day are the three made entirely of goodness; night is the one made entirely of darkness, and therefore night is a period that overpowers and restrains people. Thus the gods were emitted from his mouth when he had a shining body, and since they were born in the day, the gods are powerful in the day. And since the demons were emitted out of the vital breaths from his behind when he had a body made of night, being born of night they are invincible at night. These four – moonlight, night, day, and twilight – became the causes of all the future gods and demons, ancestors and men, in all the intervals of Manus that are past and those that have not yet come. Since all four of them are luminous (*bhanti*), and the syllable 'bha' appears in all the words for lights, therefore he emitted the gods and demons and humans and ancestors, and all the other sorts of creatures, in the waters (*ambhas*).

Then the lord discarded that body made of moonlight and took on another one, a form pervaded by energy and darkness, and he put that body to work. Then he emitted in the darkness other creatures who were filled with hunger, and these creatures filled with hunger tried to eat the waters. Since they said, 'Let us keep (*rakshamas*) these waters', these creatures made of hunger, who wander in the night, came to be known as ogres (*rakshasas*). And those who said, 'Let us diminish (*kshinumas*) the waters,' and took delight in one another, by that action became spirits (*yakshas*) and goblins (*guyhakas*), who do cruel deeds. The verbal root *raksh* also means 'protect', and the root *kshi* has the etymology of 'destroy'. And so they are known as ogres (*rakshasas*) because of protecting, and as spirits (*yakshas*) because of destroying.

When the wise lord saw them, he became so displeased that the hairs of his head fell out. As soon as they fell out, they rose and kept climbing up again and again. These immature (hairs) that left his head became slithery reptiles; because they were immature (*bala*) they are called dragons (*vyalas*), and because they left (*hina*) they are called snakes (*ahi*). Because they move on their bellies (*panna*) they are called belly-goers (*pannagas*), and because they slithered out (*vyapasarpat*) they are known as serpents (*sarpas*). Their hiding place is in the earth, and they crowd together away from the light of the sun and the moon. Then from his anger there arose the terrible embryo of fire that is made entirely of poison, and it entered into those serpents as soon as they were born.

After he had emitted the serpents, out of his anger there were formed terrible yellow flesh-eating ghosts made entirely of anger. Since they were has-beens (*bhutas*), they are called ghosts (*bhutas*), and since they are flesh-eaters (*pishitashanat*) they are called ghouls (*pishachas*). While he was singing a song (*gam*), his sons the Gandharvas were born from him. Now, the poets say that the verb *dhaya* can be used in the sense of 'drink'; and so, as they were born drinking in his speech, they are known as the Gandharvas.

After he had emitted these eight types of creatures who come from divine wombs, the lord then emitted the chants (*chandas*) when he was pleased (*chantatas*), and the birds (*vayas*) from his prime of life (*vayas*). After he had emitted the winged creatures, he emitted the groups of beasts. Brahma emitted the goats from his mouth and the sheep from his chest, the cows from his stomach; and from his two sides and his two feet he fashioned the horses and elephants, the donkeys, oxen, deer, camels, boars, dogs, and other species; herbs, fruits, and roots were born from the hairs on his body.

When he had thus created the five sorts of plants, he put them to use in sacrifices in the first Age of the aeon (*kalpa*), before the advent of the Age of the Trey. The cow, the goat, man, the sheep, horses, mules, and donkeys – these are known as the seven domesticated, village animals; and there are seven types of other animals, wild forest animals: tigers and other beasts of prey, leopards, elephants, monkeys, wild birds as the fifth, aquatic beasts as the sixth type of animals, and serpents as the seventh. Buffaloes, oxen, camels, animals with cloven hooves, *sharabhas*, elephants, and monkeys as the seventh, are also wild animals.

Then, in the realm of sacrifices, from his first, eastern mouth he fashioned the Gayatri metre, the verses of the *Rig Veda*, the three-fold praise, the chariot verses, and the praise to the fire. The formulas, the triple praise, the chants, the fifteen-fold praise, and the great chant, he emitted from his southern mouth; the songs, the Jagati metre, the seventeen-fold praise, the transformed sacrifice and the overnight sacrifice, he created from his western mouth; and the twenty-one-fold praise, the *Atharva Veda*, the super-overnight sacrifice, the Anushtubh metre, and the Vairajya metre, he emitted from his fourth, northern mouth. The lord god created lightning, thunderbolts, clouds, and red rainbows, and all of this is known as the rainstorm. He fashioned the three Vedas – *Rig, Yajur,* and *Sama* – in order to achieve the sacrifice. Creatures high and low were born from the limbs of Brahma, the Prajapati, as he was emitting the creation of progeny.

Thus when he had emitted the first fourfold creation of gods, seers, ancestors, and humans, after that he emitted the creatures that move and those that are still; he created the spirits and the ghouls and the Gandharvas and the celestial nymphs and men and What?-men, and ogres, birds, domestic beasts, wild beasts, and serpents, things that are changeless and those that change, things that go and things that are still. And whatever actions were originally created for them, those come back to them when they are created again and again; harmful or harmless, gentle or cruel, with or without dharma, truthful or false, these qualities come back to them, and so that pleases him. The creator himself set out the variety in the great elements and in the shapes that are the objects of the senses, and the distinction between the various creatures. (*Brahmanda Purana* 1.2.8.1–61)

4.1.2 The four Ages

Indra explains to a sage the degenerative nature of time. At first, there is no need for the basic social system, the varnashramadharma, *that consists of the dharma of the four* varnas *or classes of society (Brahmin, Kshatriya, Vaishya, and Shudra) and the four* ashramas *or stages of life (Brahmacarin or chaste student of the Vedas,* grihastha *or householder,* vanaprastha *or forest-dweller, and* sannyasin *or renouncer). But as time decays, the need for such a system arises; and as time further decays, it is no longer possible even to maintain such a system. Human life subsides back into the wilderness, and the next cycle of civilisation is born again.*

First, you should know, comes the Golden Age, and then the Age of the Trey; and the Age of the Deuce and the Fourth Age come next: these are the four Ages, in brief. The Golden Age is the age of goodness (*sattva*); the Age of the Trey is the age of energy (*rajas*); the Age of the Deuce is a mixture of energy and darkness (*tamas*); and the Dark Age is the age of darkness; each age has its characteristic ways of behaving. Meditation is the main thing in the Golden Age; sacrifice in the Age of the Trey; worship in the Age of Deuce; purity and charity in the Dark Age. The Golden Age lasts for four thousand years, and is followed by a twilight of four hundred years. And the lifespan of living creatures lasts for four thousand human years in the Golden Age.

After the twilight of the Golden Age has passed, one of the four feet of the dharma of the Ages is gone in all of its aspects. The excellent Age of the Trey is one fourth less than the Golden Age; the Age of the Deuce lasts for half the time of the Golden Age, and the Dark Age lasts for one half the time of the Age of the Deuce. The last three twilights last for three hundred, two hundred, and one hundred years; this happens in aeon after aeon, Age after Age. In the first Age, the Golden Age, the eternal dharma walks on four feet; in the Age of Trey, on three feet; in the Age of Deuce, on two feet. In the fourth Age it lacks three feet and is devoid of the element of goodness.

In (every) Golden Age, people are born in pairs; their livelihood consists in revelling in the taste of what exists right before one's eyes. All creatures are satisfied, always, and take delight in all enjoyments. There is no distinction between the lowest and the highest among them; they are all good, all equal in their life-span, happiness, and form, in the Golden Age. They have no preferences, nor do they experience the opposing pairs of emotions; they do not hate or get tired. They have no homes or dwelling-places, but live in the mountains and oceans; they have no sorrow, but consist mostly of goodness and generally live alone. They go wherever they wish, constantly rejoicing in their minds; in the Golden Age, people do not engage in any actions, good or bad.

At that time there was no system of separate classes and stages of life, and no mixture (of classes or castes). But in the course of time, in the Age of the Trey, they no longer revelled in the taste (of existence). When that fulfilment was lost, another sort of fulfilment was born. When water reaches its subtle state, it is transformed into clouds; from thundering clouds, rain is emitted. As soon as the surface of the earth was touched by that rain, trees appeared on it, and they became houses for the people, who used those trees for their livelihood and all their enjoyments. People lived off those trees at the beginning of the Age of the Trey.

But then, after a long time, people began to change; the emotions of passion and greed arose, for no apparent cause, as a result of a change in the people that arose out of time. Then all the trees that they regarded as their houses vanished, and when they had vanished, the people who were born in pairs became confused. They began to think about their fulfilment, considering the matter truthfully, and then the trees that they regarded as their houses appeared again. These trees brought forth clothing and fruits and jewellery; and on the very same trees there would grow, in bud after bud, honey made by no bees, powerful honey of superb aroma, colour, and taste. People lived on that honey, lived happily all their life long, finding their delight and their nourishment in that perfection, always free from fever.

But then, as another time came, they became greedy. They lopped off the limbs of the trees and took by force the honey that no bees had made. As a result of that crime that they committed in their greed, the magic trees, together with their honey, vanished, first here, then there, and as time exerted its power, very little of that fulfilment was left. As the Age of the Trey came on, the opposing pairs of emotions arose, and people became quite miserable as a result of the sharp cold and rain and heat. Tortured by these opposing pairs, they began to cover themselves; and then they made houses on the mountain to ward off the opposing pairs. Formerly, they had gone wherever they wished, living without fixed dwellings; now they began to live in fixed dwellings according to their need and their pleasure. . . .

Then, by the force of that Age, all the people were so crazy with rage that they seized one another and took their sons, wives, wealth, and so forth, by force. When he realised all this, the lotus-born (Brahma) created the Kshatriyas to protect people from getting wounded (*kshatat-tratum*), in order to establish a firm support for the moral boundaries. Then by means of his own brilliance, the god who is the soul of all established the system of the classes and stages of life, and he himself established the livelihood for each profession to live on. Gradually, the institution of sacrifice evolved in the Age of the Trey, but even then some good people did not perform animal sacrifices. For eventually Vishnu, who sees everything, performed a sacrifice by force, and then as a result of that the Brahmins prescribed the non-violent sacrifice.

But then, in the Age of the Deuce, men began to have differences of opinion, to differ in mind, action, and speech, and to have difficulty making a living. Then, gradually, as a result of the exhaustion of their bodies, all creatures became subject to greed, working for wages, working as merchants, fighting, indecision about basic principles, lack of interest in the schools of the Vedas, confounding of dharmas, destruction of the system of the classes and stages of life, and, finally, lust and hatred. For in the Age of the Deuce, passion, greed, and drunkenness arise.

And in (every) Age of the Deuce, a sage named Vyasa divides the Veda into four. For it is known that there was a single Veda, in four parts, in the Ages of the Trey; but as a result of the shrinking of the life-span, it was divided up in the Ages of the Deuce. And these divisions were further divided by the sons of the (Rig Vedic) seers, according to their deviant opinions; they transposed the order of the (Rig Vedic) mantras and the Brahmanas, and they changed the accents and the syllables. Wise men compiled the collections of the *Rig Veda, Yajur Veda,* and *Sama Veda*; though they were composed in common, they have been (subsequently) separated by people of various opinions, divided into Brahmanas, Kalpasutras, and explications of the mantras. Now, some of these works still follow the line of (the Vedas), and others depart from them.

The Epics and Puranas are distinguished according to the weight of their age; thus the (eighteen) Puranas are divided as follows (beginning with the oldest): the Brahma, Padma, Vishnu, Shiva, Bhagavata, Bhavishya, Narada, Markandeya, Agni, Brahmavaivarta, Linga, Varaha, Vamana, Kurma, Matsya, Garuda, Skanda, and Brahmanda. The *Linga Purana*, the eleventh, was established in the Age of the Deuce. There are thousands of sages, including Manu, Atri, Vishnu, Harita, Yajnavalkya, Ushanas, Angiras, Yama,

Apastamba, Samvarta, Katyayana, Brihaspati, Parashara, Vyasa, Shankha, Likhita, Daksha, Gautama, Shatatapas, and Vasishtha.

Drought, death, disease, and other plagues cause sufferings born of speech, mind, and action, and as a result one becomes numb. From this numbness people begin to think about release from suffering. From this thinking there arises detachment, and from detachment they begin to see their faults. As a result of seeing their faults, knowledge arises in the Age of the Deuce. Now, it will be recalled that the behaviour characteristic of the Age of the Deuce was a mixture of energy and darkness. But there was dharma in the first age, the Golden Age, and that dharma still functions in the Age of the Trey; in the Age of the Deuce, however, it becomes disturbed, and in the Dark Age it vanishes.

In the fourth Age, men's senses are disturbed by darkness and they fall prey to illusion and jealousy; they even kill ascetics. In the Dark Age, there is always carelessness, passion, hunger, and fear; the terrible fear of drought pits one country against another. Scripture has no authority, and men take to the violation of dharma; they act without dharma, without morality; they are very angry and not very smart. . . . When scripture is destroyed, and the dharma that is known from the Shastras, then people will kill one another, for they will have no moral boundaries, no check to their violence, no affection, and no shame. When dharma is destroyed, and people attack one another, they will become stunted and live only twenty-five years; their senses will become confused with arguing, and they will abandon their sons and wives. When they are struck by drought, they will abandon agriculture; they will leave their own countries and go to lands beyond their borders, seeking water in rivers, oceans, wells, and mountains.

Suffering greatly, they will live on honey, raw meat, roots, and fruits; they will wear garments of bark, leaves, and antelope skins; they will perform no rituals and have no possessions. They will fall away from the system of classes and stages of life and fall prey to the terrible mingling of classes. Then there will be very few people left, caught up in this calamity. Afflicted by old age, disease, and hunger, their minds will be numbed by suffering. But from this numbness there will arise thought, and thought makes the mind balanced. Understanding comes from a balanced mind, and from understanding comes a dedication to dharma. The people who are left at the end of the Dark Age will have a kind of formless mental peace.

Then, in a day and a night, the age will be transformed for them, deluding their wits as if they were dreaming or insane. And then, by the power of the goal of the future, the Golden Age will begin. And when the Golden Age has begun again, the people left over from the Dark Age become the people born in the Golden Age. . . . (*Linga Purana* 1.39.5–34, 48–70; 1.40.1–3, 66cd–76)

4.1.3 How Rudra destroys the universe

The Puranas tell of several different sorts of doomsday, on different levels; the one described here is the occasional dissolution, which occurs when Brahma sleeps, in distinction from the elemental dissolution, which occurs at the end of Brahma's life. It is the particular task of Rudra to destroy the universe; but as this text was composed by a worshipper of Vishnu, and therefore regards Vishnu as responsible for everything that happens in the universe, it simply frames the work of Rudra within the command of Vishnu.

The text describes several different levels of worlds within the universe. Within the encompassing ocean of eternity and infinity, Vishnu sleeps on the great serpent of eternity, Ananta, also called Shesha, 'What is Left' – i.e. what remains when all else is destroyed. Above the triple world inhabited by men is the fourth world, the Maharloka, that remains intact during doomsday, during which certain perfected beings sojourn in it. Though it is not destroyed, it is uncomfortably heated, and some of its denizens move out. The Janaloka is the fifth world, where the sons of Brahma and other perfected beings live; in some cosmologies, the world of Brahma is beyond the Janaloka; in others, it is equated with it. Above this world, in the sky, live the Seven Sages, mind-born sons of Prajapati, the seven stars of the Plough, in Ursa Major.

Twelve thousand divine years constitute a period of the four Ages, and a thousand of the four Ages is called a day of Brahma, or an aeon (*kalpa*), in which there are fourteen Manus. At the end of the aeon there occurs the occasional dissolution brought about by Brahma. It is very terrible; I will tell you about it. Listen. Later on, I will tell you about the elemental dissolution.

At the end of a thousand cycles of the four Ages, when the surface of the earth is mostly exhausted, a very fierce drought occurs and lasts for a hundred years. As a result, the creatures who live on earth lose most of their vital essence, and then they are so afflicted that they perish; none are left. Then the unchanging lord Vishnu takes the form of Rudra and sets to work to destroy all those creatures that dwell in him. The lord Vishnu enters into the seven rays of the sun and drinks up all the waters, leaving none. When he has drunk up all the waters that are inside living creatures that breathe, he dries up the entire surface of the earth. Whatever water there is in rivers and oceans and mountain streams, or in the subterranean watery hells – he absorbs it all.

All the water that he has taken away goes directly, by his authority, to the seven rays of the sun, which, enlarged by those waters, become seven suns. These seven suns blaze above and below, burning the entire triple world, including the subterranean watery hells. When it is burnt by these blazing fires, the triple world with its mountains, rivers, and oceans becomes entirely devoid of moisture; the moisture of its trees is burnt up, and the earth becomes like the back of a tortoise. When Vishnu has become Rudra of the doomsday fire, the one who withdraws everything, he becomes the hot breath of the serpent of Infinity and burns down the subterranean watery hells. And when it has burnt all the hells, the great fire goes to the earth and burns up the whole surface of the earth. Then a most terrible whirlwind haloed in flames envelops the middle realm of space and the world of heaven, and now the entire triple world, enveloped by this flame whirlwind that destroys all creatures, moving and still, looks like a frying pan. When the creatures that live in these upper two worlds are enveloped by heat, those who have discharged their duties go up to the great world above heaven (Maharloka). But since they are still heated by that great heat, those creatures go from there to the world beyond, the World of People (Janaloka), turning away from their present condition of life in their wish to go beyond.

When Vishnu in the form of Rudra has thus burnt the entire universe, he creates clouds that are born out of the breath from his mouth. These are the terrible, thick clouds called whirlwinds, that look like herds of elephants as they roar and send bolts of lightning through the sky. Some are as dark as blue lotuses; some are as pale as water lilies; some are thick, the colour of smoke; some are yellow; some are dun, like donkeys; some as red as lac; some the colour of lapis lazuli; some the colour of a sapphire. Some are as white as a conch shell or jasmine; some are as black as collyrium. Some are as red as cochineal; some are red as red arsenic; some are like the wings of the blue jay. Thus the thick masses of clouds arise. In shape, some of these fat clouds are like big cities; some are like mountains; some are like huts or houses.

Roaring loudly, they fill the sky with their huge bodies. Sending down their rain in great torrents, they extinguish the terrible fire that has penetrated everywhere inside the triple world. When the fire has gone out, they continue to rain ceaselessly for a thousand years, flooding the entire universe. Inundating the whole earth with drops the size of dice, they flood the middle realm of space in the same way, and heaven above, too. And when the whole world, moving and still, has been destroyed in blind darkness, the great clouds go on raining for a hundred years more.

When the water reaches the dwelling-place of the Seven Sages, the entire triple world becomes nothing but a single ocean. Then a wind comes out of the breath from the mouth of Vishnu, that blows for more than a hundred years and destroys those waters. Then the Lord, the Unthinkable, the existence of all beings, the one of whom all beings are made, who has no beginning, who is the beginning of everything, drinks up that wind, leaving nothing. Then the lord lies down in that single ocean, using the serpent Shesha as his bed; and the lord Hari (Vishnu), who creates the beginning, takes the form of Brahma. Praised by all those perfected creatures who had gone to the World of People, the sage Sanaka and the others, and contemplated by all those creatures desirous of Release who had gone to the world of Brahma, the supreme lord partakes of the celestial yogic sleep that is made of his own divine illusion; and he contemplates his own self in the form known as (Krishna), the son of Vasudeva.

This is the dissolution that is called occasional (*naimittika*), because it takes place on the occasion (*nimittam*, occasion or cause) when Vishnu takes the form of Brahma and sleeps. (*Vishnu Purana* 6.3.11–40; 6.4.1–7)

4.2 PHILOSOPHY

4.2.1 The fruits of hearing a Purana: Devaraja the sinner

Most Hindu sacred texts announce, at the end, the benefits that will accrue to the person who knows them; we have already encountered this formula at the end of passages in the Brahmanas and Upanishads. The Puranas are more baroque in their claims for the 'fruits of hearing' (phalashruti), and the following is by no means the most extreme example. The hero (if one may call him that) is a Brahmin, referred to as a 'god upon the earth', a term normally used for a Brahmin, though here it seems to be used with some sarcasm. It may also be significant that Devaraja's name, 'King of the gods', is the name of Indra, the greatest sinner among the gods.

Once upon a time, in the city of the Kiratas, there was a Brahmin who was not at all strong when it came to sacred knowledge. He was a poor man, a seller of liquors, and he turned away from the gods and from dharma. He had ceased to perform the ritual of bathing at twilight and he devoted himself instead to making a living like a Vaishya; he was called Devaraja ('King of the Gods'), and he used to deceive people who trusted him. He took as his prey various sorts of people – Brahmins, Kshatriyas, Vaishyas, Shudras, and even people lower than that – and he would kill them and take their money. Through this violation of dharma he eventually accumulated great wealth, but he was such an evil man that he didn't use even a small part of his money for dharma.

One day, that god upon the earth went to a pond to bathe, and there he saw a whore named 'Gorgeous' who excited him wildly. The beautiful woman was delighted when she realised that a rich Brahmin was in her power; and she satisfied his mind with her professional banter. He decided to make her his wife, and she to make him her husband; thus overpowered by lust, they made love for a long time. Sitting, lying, drinking, eating, and playing, the two of them constantly seduced one another, like newly-weds. Though his mother and father and (first) wife kept trying to stop him, he paid no attention to their words, so intent was he on his evil ways.

One day he became so impatient that he completely lost control, and in the night he killed his mother, father, and wife as they slept; and then that wretch took their money. He was so out of his mind with lust that he gave that whore all his own money as well as the money that he had taken from his father and the others. Then that sinner, the lowest of Brahmins, took to eating what should not be eaten, and he became addicted to drinking wine; he always ate out of the same plate as his whore.

Now, as fate would have it, one day he came to the town of Pratisthanam, and there he saw a Shiva temple filled with good people. While he stayed there, constantly hearing the *Shiva Purana* recited from the mouths of the Brahmins, that Brahmin was laid low by a fever. At the end of a month, Devaraja was dead of that fever; the minions of Yama bound him with nooses and led him by force to the city of Yama. At the same time, the hosts of Shiva, shining with their tridents in their hands, smeared with white ashes all over their bodies, wearing the rosaries of Shiva, set out from the world of Shiva and came in fury to the city of Yama. They beat up the messengers of Yama and reviled them over and over; they set Devaraja free, put him up on their marvellous celestial chariot, and got ready to go to Kailasa (the mountain of Shiva).

Then a great tumult arose in the middle of the city of Yama, and (Yama) the King of Dharma heard it and came out of his palace. There he saw the four messengers like four more Rudras before his eyes, and as he knew dharma, the King of Dharma honoured them with the proper ritual. Then, through his eye of knowledge, Yama realised all that had happened, but he was too frightened to ask a single question of the noble messengers of Shiva. When they had been honoured and asked for their blessings, they went to Kailasa and gave (Devaraja) to Shiva, the ocean of compassion, and to Amba (the wife of Shiva).

Precious is the reciting of the *Shiva Purana*, the highest purification, by the mere hearing of which even a very evil person attains Release. It is the great place of the eternal Shiva, the highest dwelling, the high spot; those who know the Vedas, say that it stands above all worlds. That evil man who, in his greed for money, injured many Brahmins, Kshatriyas, Vaishyas, Shudras, and even other creatures that breathe, the man who killed his mother and father and wife, who slept with a whore and drank wine, the Brahmin Devaraja went there and in a moment became released. (*Shiva Purana* 1.2.15–40)

4.2.2 The *Mahabharata* expiated

The Epic itself is obsessed with the problem of dharma inherent in the battle between cousins; this dilemma is taken up again in the Puranas, where it is given a typically Puranic solution: pilgrimage to the sacred spot of Prayaga, the junction of two rivers above Benares.

When King Yudhishthira, together with his brothers, had killed all the Kauravas, he was overwhelmed by great sorrow and became bewildered. Soon afterwards, the great ascetic Markandeya arrived at the city of Hastinapura and stood at the king's gate. The gate-keeper saw him and immediately told the king, 'The sage Markandeya is standing at the gate, wishing to see you.' Quickly, Yudhishthira the son of Dharma went to the gate and said to the other, 'Welcome to you, wise sage; welcome to you, great sage. Today my life has borne fruit; today my family has been carried across; today my ancestors have been satisfied, if you are satisfied, great sage.' Then Yudhishthira seated the sage on his throne and honoured him with water to wash his feet and so forth, thinking, 'He is a Mahatma, a great-soul.' And Markandeya was satisfied with Yudhishthira and said to him, 'Why are you bewildered, you who are so wise? I came here because I know about it all.' Then King Yudhishthira bowed to the great sage and said, 'Tell me – briefly – how I may be released from my sins. Many men who had committed no offence were killed in the battle between us and the Kauravas. Please tell me how one may be released from the mortal sin that results from injuring living creatures, even if it was done in a former life.'

Markandeya said, 'Listen, your majesty, noble descendant of Bharata, to the answer to what you have asked me: going to Prayaga is the best way for men to destroy evil. The god Rudra, the Great God, emperor of all the immortals, lives there, as does the self-born lord Brahma, together with the other gods.' Yudhishthira said, 'Sir, I wish to hear the fruit of going to Prayaga. Where do people who die there go, and what is the fruit of bathing there? And tell me the fruit of those who live in Prayaga; for you know this, and so you should tell me. I bow to you... . ' (*Kurma Purana* 1.34.5–18)

4.2.3 Karma transferred in hell: Vipashcit

King Vipashcit arrives in Hell and asks the servant of Yama why he has been condemned to hell, since he has performed so many good deeds. In the course of his answer, the servant implies that the king has already paid his small debt to Yama by remaining just for those few moments in hell, and now may enjoy the fruits of his good deeds in heaven. At the king's request, Yama's servant tells him why all the people there are suffering. This passage is translated below, in section 5.5.2. Then the story continues along lines somewhat parallel to the Mahabharata *story of Yudhishthira and his dog (above, section 3.1.3).*

When the servant of Yama had been questioned by the king, he replied politely, fierce though he was, 'Great king, what you said is true, without any doubt. However, you did commit one small sin; let me remind you about it. Your wife, a princess from Vidarbha, named Fatso (Pivari), came into her fertile season on one occasion in the past, but you left her barren, for you were infatuated with your other wife, the very beautiful Kaikeyi. And because you transgressed the rule that requires a man to have intercourse with his wife during her fertile season, you have come to this terrible hell. Just as the fire expects the purified butter to fall into it at the time of the oblation, even so Prajapati expects the seed to fall at the fertile season. If a man who cares for dharma overlooks that duty because he is distracted by lust, he commits a sin because he neglects the debt (of a son) that he owes to his ancestors, and so he falls to hell. But this is the full extent of your evil; no other sin is found in you. Therefore come and enjoy the fruits of your many meritorious deeds. . . . Let us go somewhere else. You have seen everything now; and you have seen hell. So let us go somewhere else.'

At that, the king prepared to go, letting the servant precede him. But then all the men who were being so hideously tortured there cried out, 'Have mercy on us, your majesty! Stay here just a little moment more! For the wind that comes from contact with your body refreshes our hearts and dispels the pain that we feel when our limbs are burnt and crushed and beaten all over. Tiger among kings, have pity on us.'

When he heard what they said, the king asked Yama's man, 'How can I have the power to refresh these people? Have I committed some great meritorious karma in the mortal world of which this gift of refreshment is the reward? Tell me.' (The servant replied,) 'Your body has been nourished by the food that remained after the ancestors, gods, guests, and ghosts (were fed); and since your heart went out to (these people in hell), therefore the wind that comes from contact with your limbs grants them refreshment, and these people who have committed evil deeds are not tormented by their torture. Since you sacrificed properly with the horse sacrifice and other sacrifices, therefore by the mere sight of you Yama's torture machines, knives, fires, and birds, that are the causes of great suffering from crushing, cutting, burning, and so forth, become gentle, for they are counteracted by your splendour.'

The king said, 'Men cannot obtain in heaven or in the world of Brahma such happiness as arises from giving peace (*nirvana*) to suffering creatures; this is what I think. If their torture does not hurt these people in my presence, then I will be one of those people whose faces confer prosperity on those who see them, and I will stay here, like an immovable pillar.' Yama's man said, 'Come, your majesty, let's go. Enjoy the pleasures that you have won by your own merit, and let these men of evil karma enjoy their torture.'

The king said, 'For that very reason, I *won't* go, as long as these people suffer. The people who live in hell are happy in my presence. What use is the life of that man who does not show favour to a man in trouble, even a confirmed enemy who comes to him for help? Sacrifice, charity, and asceticism do no good to a man in the world beyond if he has no heart to help people in trouble. A man who is hard-hearted toward children and people who suffer and old people and so forth, I do not regard as human; he is an ogre. The torture of hell that these people experience from being heated by fire or smelling revolting smells or from hunger or thirst that make them faint – that torment is destroyed as a result of my presence; and I regard that, good sir, as a happiness greater than heaven. If many people become happy while I suffer, what can there be that I have not attained? Tell me that, right away.'

Yama's servant said, 'Here is Dharma and here is Indra; they have come to take you away. You can't help going away from here; so go, your majesty.' Dharma said, 'I myself will lead you to heaven, for you have served me properly. Mount this celestial chariot; do not delay; come.' But the king said, 'Dharma, men are being tortured in hell by the thousands. "Save us!" they cry out to me; and so I will not go away from here'. Indra said, 'These people reached hell as a result of their own most evil karma; but you, on the other hand, are supposed to go to heaven as a result of your good karma.'

The king replied, 'Dharma, if you know – or you, Indra, who have performed a hundred horse sacrifices – just how far my authority extends, you should tell me that right away.' 'Like the drops of water in the ocean, or like the stars in the sky, or like the streams of water in the rain or the grains of sand in the Ganges, or like all the creatures in the various wombs – as these cannot be counted, great king, so too it is impossible to count your merits. And by evincing this compassion right now, here in hell, you brought the count to hundreds of thousands. Therefore, go, matchless king, and enjoy all those merits in the home of the immortals; but let these wear away here in hell the evil born of their own karma.' 'How,' replied the king, 'will men ever take pleasure in associating with me if these people are not uplifted in my presence? Therefore, let whatever good deeds I have done be used to release these people of evil karma from their torments in hell.'

Then Indra said, 'By this, great king, you have reached an even higher place; and see how these people of evil karma are released from hell.' Then a rain of flowers fell on to the king, and Indra had him mount the celestial chariot and led him to heaven. And all who were there were released from their tortures – though they all went from there immediately to another womb that was determined by the fruits of their own karma. (*Markandeya Purana* 14.1–7, 15.47–80)

4.2.4 Ethics: how to stay out of trouble

This passage is an amalgam of moral exhortations, medical advice, superstition, and general folk wisdom. It is evidently a combination of several different texts; there are abrupt transitions in tone, repeated lines, and contradictions.

No one is anyone's friend. No one is anyone's enemy. Friendships and enmity arise out of a specific cause. A shelter in sorrow, a shelter in danger, and a receptacle of affection and confidence – who created this jewel, this word, 'friend'? A person who continuously utters 'Hari' (Vishnu) in the same way (as if he uses the word 'friend') girds his loins to set out for Release. A man does not have the same sort of confidence in his mother or his wives or his blood brother or his own son that he has in a person who of his own nature becomes his friend. If you want to have someone's affection for ever, avoid these three mistakes: do not gamble with him or do business with him; and do not see his wife when he is not present.

Do not, for that matter, live in a lonely place with your own mother, sister, or daughter; for the powerful cluster of the senses drags away even a wise man. Lust takes pleasure in perversity; a man doesn't lust for the things that belong to him; but where it will result in ruin, murder, or physical punishment, lust moves in. It is possible to know the deep currents of a hurricane, or a horse, or the great ocean, but not to know the current of a mind that lacks affection. When there is no opportunity; or no private place; or no man who wants her – only then do women remain chaste wives. She may serve the bed of one man always, but in her mind she is pleasuring another; when a woman cannot get (other) men, she is true to her husband. The things that a mother does in secret when she is mad with passion – those things should not be imagined by her sons, lest they conceive ideas that are incompatible with their belief in her good character.

As for a whore, even her sleep is controlled by others, and she must do what the hearts of others dictate, conforming to them; she pretends to laugh all the time, because she is constrained to do so; and she is deprived even of the right to her own sorrow. Her body is bought for money, her throat ripped open by the hooves of sensualists. She makes her living on the longings of the masses; thus is the whore highly esteemed among the people.

Fire, water, women, fools, snakes, and the members of the royal family – these six are always made use of by other people, but they mean sudden death. Is it surprising if a Brahmin who is clever at scripture and texts becomes a Pandit? Is it surprising if a Brahmin who is clever at the science of politics becomes full of dharma? Is it surprising if a woman who has youth and beauty is *not* virtuous? Is it surprising if a man, even if he has no money, never *does* commit a crime?

Do not reveal your weaknesses to someone else, but learn what his weakness is; note the other man's parts and his nature, sitting like a turtle in your own house. If the sprouts of rash passion break out even in a woman who lives in the nether worlds and is hemmed in by high ramparts, who can truly possess a woman? An enemy who hates you but is outside of your family cannot harm you as much as you can be harmed by someone who shares your dharma, knows your weak spots, is sharp, and is a thorn to his own people.

A true pandit is a man who can please a child with sweets, a pupil with good precepts, a woman with money, the gods with asceticism, and all the people with lavish entertainment. But men who try to get a friend by means of a trick, to get dharma by means of dirty work, wealth by means of hurting other people, knowledge by means of happiness, or a woman by cruelty – these are not pandits. A man who cuts down a fruit tree because he wants fruit is a stupid man; it should be used whole; you spoil it if you try to get the root.

'An ascetic is efficient; you can get exhausted from a distance; a woman who drinks wine is virtuous' – I don't believe any of this. Do not trust someone who is not trustworthy, and do not even trust a friend; for one day your friend may get angry and reveal all your secrets. But having trust in all creatures, and being good to all creatures, while concealing his own good nature within himself – this is the sign of a good man. Whatever action is committed, the results adhere to the one who commits it; and so, after turning over all the possible consequences, you should act with firmness and intelligence.

Older women, new wine, dry meat, strong radishes, yogurt in the night, sleep in the day – a wise man avoids these six things. A household is poison to a poor man; a young woman is poison to an old man; knowledge is poison to someone badly taught; and food is poison to a man who has indigestion. Charity is welcome to a man who does not stint; praise is welcome to the lowly; generosity is welcome to a poor man; and a young woman is welcome to a young man. Drinking too much water, sitting on hard seats, loss of vital fluids, suppression of the urge to defecate, lying down during the day, staying awake at night – these six things cause diseases to afflict men. Exposure to the rays of the young sun, too much sexual intercourse, exposure to the smoke of the cremation grounds, warming the hands, looking upon the face of a menstruating woman – these sap your long life-span. Dry meat, older womem, the rays of the young sun, unripe yogurt, sex in the morning, and falling asleep immediately afterwards – these six things are sudden death. Freshly made butter, grapes, a young wife, a dish of milk and rice, warm water, and the shade of a tree – these six immediately revive you.

The water of a well, the shade of a banyan tree, and the breasts of women are warm in the winter and cool in the summer. Three things immediately produce strength: a young woman, a massage, and a good meal. Three things immediately sap strength: a journey, sex, and a fever. You should never eat dry meat or milk in the company of your wife or friends, nor with kings; this might lead to separation (from them) in a moment. Prosperity abandons even the man who holds the wheel of power in his hands if he has torn clothes, dirty teeth, eats too much, talks crudely, or lies down at sunrise or sunset. Pulling out grass all the time, scratching the ground, rubbing your feet together, or brushing your teeth, wearing dirty clothes, having filthy hair, sleeping at dawn and dusk, lying down without your clothes on, eating too much and laughing too much, beating time to music on your own lap or on your chair – such behaviour would even drive Lakshmi (or: prosperity) away from Vishnu. But a well-cleaned head, well-washed feet, sex with a fine woman, eating lightly, not sleeping naked, not having intercourse on the nights of the new and full moon – these six would retrieve your prosperity even if it had been lost for a long time.

Wearing any flower, but particularly a white one, on your head wards off misfortune. The shadow behind a lamp or a bed or behind the riverside place where a washerman works – these are places where misfortune lurks. The young sun, the smoke from a corpse, an old woman, unripe yogurt, or the dust from sweeping will be avoided by a man who wants to live a long life. The dust from an elephant, horse, chariot, grain, or cows is auspicious; the dust from a donkey, camel, goat, or sheep is inauspicious. The dust of cows and of grain, as well as the dust that comes from the body of your son – this is greatly recommended dust, that destroys great sins. The dust of goats and donkeys and the dust from sweeping is very bad and causes great sins. The wind from a winnowing fan, the water from (cleaning) the tips of your nails, or from bathing or washing clothes, the dust of sweeping, and the water from washing hair – these destroy the merit that has already been earned. You should not walk between two Brahmins, or between a Brahmin and a fire, or between a husband and wife, or between a horse and a bull.

What wise man would place his trust in women, kings, fire, snakes, his own learning, the service of his enemy, the enjoyment of pleasures, and such things? You shouldn't trust people who are not trustworthy; but you should not place too much trust even in people who are trustworthy. For danger comes from trust, and might cut you down right at the root. A man who trusts in a treaty made with an enemy is like a man who falls asleep on top of a tree and wakes up when he falls down.

Do not be too gentle, or too cruel; a kind person they kill with kindness, and they kill a harsh person with harshness. Do not be too straight or too soft; straight trees are cut down, but crooked trees remain standing. Trees full of fruit bend low; people full of virtues bend low; but dry trees and fools break, instead of bending. Miseries come and go unsought; a man seeks (happiness) and is ready to pounce on it, like a cat. Much happiness always walks before and after a noble man; the opposite is true of an ignoble man; so do as you wish. A plan heard by six ears breaks out; heard by four ears, it is kept. But even Brahma could not discover the plan heard by just two ears.

What use is a cow who does not calve or give milk? What use is a son who is neither wise nor virtuous? But a single son who is wise and virtuous, a lion among men, illuminates the family as the moon illuminates the sky. A single good tree, sweet-smelling and in flower, perfumes the entire wood; so does a single good son perfume the family, a single son who has good qualities. But what use are a hundred sons without good qualities? The moon alone dispels darkness, but the thousands of stars do not.

You should fondle a son for five years, and then beat him for the next ten years. But when he gets to be sixteen, you should treat your son like a friend. As soon as a son is born, he takes away your wife; when he grows up he takes away your money; and when he dies he takes away your vital breath; there is no enemy the equal of a son.

There are tigers with the faces of deer, and deer with the faces of tigers; to find out the true form of each, you must distrust every step they take. The one flaw in a person who is forgiving – there is no second flaw – is that the man he forgives thinks he is weak. One thing you must never forget: pleasures perish in a moment; the opinions of people who are slick and sophisticated are always cold-blooded. The eldest brother becomes like the father when the father is dead; he should be the father of all (the brothers) and protect them all. He should act with equal fairness to all his younger brothers, giving them the same enjoyments and livelihoods, as if they were his sons.

The co-operation of many men of little substance is awesome; a rope made of straws may tie down an elephant. A man who steals other peoples' possessions and then gives them away as charity goes to hell even though he is a donor, and the people whose money it is get the fruits of his generosity. If a man destroys what belongs to the gods or steals from Brahmins or transgresses against Brahmins, his family falls from caste. Good men have established restorations for killing a Brahmin, drinking wine, stealing, and breaking a vow; but there is no way to make up for ingratitude.

The gods and ancestors do not eat the offerings of a wretch who marries a low-caste woman, or a man who is controlled by his wife, or a man who lets his wife's lover live in his house. The ungrateful man, the ignoble, the man whose anger lasts a long time, and the insincere – know that these four are Untouchables (Candalas); the fifth kind of Untouchable is the one who is born into that caste. A bad idea or an enemy, however small, should not be overlooked by a wise man; even a small fire if unchecked can reduce the whole universe to ashes. Anyone who is free from passion when he is still in the first flush of youth is really free from passion; this is my opinion. But anyone can be free from passion when the elements of his body are worn out with age. Good luck, like the public roads, belongs to everyone in common; if you think, '(Good luck) is mine,' you will not stay happy. The body that is controlled by the physical elements in it depends on the mind; and when the mind is destroyed, the physical elements are destroyed. Therefore the mind should always be guarded in health, since the physical elements arise in the mind.

. . . . .

The shadow of a cloud, a grass fire, the attentions of low people, water on the road, the love of a whore, and the affection that you place in a cad – these six are evanescent, like bubbles. People are never made happy by well-meaning advice. Since honour is the very root of life, where can happiness come from when honour wanes? The king is the strength of the weak; crying is the strength of a baby; silence is the strength of a fool; lies are the strength of a thief. In whatever way a man is able to comprehend a science, that is precisely the way that he should study it, and then he will take pleasure in learning. In whatever way a man forms an opinion about beauty, he should stick to that precisely in everything, and then people will like him very much.

A man is destroyed by three things; greed, rashness, and trust; therefore you should not be greedy or rash or trusting. Fear a danger until it fails to arrive; but if a sharp danger does arise, withstand it as if you were not afraid. The residue of a debt, the residue of a fire, and the residue of a disease may grow strong over and over again; therefore you should not allow such residues to remain. Repay a good deed with a good deed, and an injury with an injury; I see nothing wrong in this procedure; you should do wrong to people who do wrong. If someone slanders you when you are absent and speaks well of you when you are present, avoid such an illusory friend as you would an enemy. Even a good man is destroyed by the company of a bad man; even clear water is made filthy by mud.

The man who gives money to a Brahmin is enjoying it properly; hence Brahmins should be honoured carefully and assiduously. What is left over from a Brahmin's food is to be eaten; a man who does nothing wrong is wise. What is done when you are absent is friendship; what is done without hypocrisy is dharma. There is no assembly where there are no elders; and those who do not speak dharma are not elders. There is no dharma where there is no truth; and it is not truth when it is discovered through deceit.

A Brahmin is the highest of men; the sun the highest of fiery things; the head the highest of all the limbs; and truth the highest of all vows. What sets the mind at peace is truly auspicious; what involves no serving of another man is fully a livelihood; what is enjoyed by your family is truly earned; and a boast made to your enemies in battle is truly a boast. A wife who has no passion is truly a wife; a man who has abandoned all thirsts is truly happy; a man you can trust is truly a friend; one who has conquered his senses is truly a man. When a friendship is broken off, affection and respect are lost. Only what you would praise in yourself should be regarded as commendable.

You should never hunt for the source of rivers, priests of the fire-altar, the land of India, or your family; for there may be a serious flaw at the root. Rivers end in the salt ocean; sex ends with breaking up with the woman; slander ends with the person hearing the rumour; and wealth ends in misery. The prosperity of a king may end in a Brahmin's curse; the glory of a Brahmin may end in evil; good conduct ends when one lives in a noisy place; and a family is ruined when a woman is in charge. All hoardings end in loss; all risings end in falls; unions end in separations; and life ends in death.

If you want to come back, don't go very far away; you should turn back from the edge of water or from (the branch of) a slippery tree. Don't live in a country where there is no ruler, or where there are many rulers, or where a woman rules, or a child rules.

A father protects her when she is a little girl; her husband protects her when she is a young woman; and her son protects her in old age; a woman should never be independent. A man may abandon a barren wife in the eighth year, and he may leave in the ninth year a woman whose children die; in the eleventh year he may abandon a wife who bears him only daughters; and he may immediately abandon a woman who says unpleasant things to him. Husbands wander away from moral boundaries for three reasons: because they are useless to people, because they are afraid of their entourage, and because of money.

A tired horse, an elephant in rut, a cow who has just brought forth her first calf, and frogs in a place where there is no water – a wise man will keep far away from all of these. A man tormented by the need for money has neither a friend nor a relative; a man tormented by lust has neither fear nor shame; a man tormented by worry has neither happiness nor sleep; a man tormented by hunger has neither grace nor brilliance. A poor man or the slave of another man or a man in love with another man's wife or one who has stolen another man's wealth – where would any of these find sleep? But the man who has no debts, who has no disease, who has free opportunities and is not attached to a wife – he sleeps well.

A lotus becomes elevated up to the level of the water; a servant becomes boastful according to the power of his master; water and sun are friends to the lotus as long as it stays in its own place; but they cause it to rot and dry up when it falls from its place. The friends that a man has when he stays in his position become his enemies (when he loses it); the sun is pleasant to the lotus in the water but dries it up when it is taken out of its place. They are respected when they stay in their place and when they stay in their position; but when they fall from their position they are not respected – this is true of hair, teeth, nails, and men.

A man's behaviour, and his form, and his speech, reveal his family; eagerness reveals affection; and the body indicates what one has been eating. Rain is useless to the ocean; food is useless to a man who is sated; generosity is useless to a rich man; and a good deed is useless to a bad man. If you dwell in someone's heart, you stay close to him even when you are far away; but when you have gone out of a person's heart, you are far away even when you are near.

A twisted face, a low voice, sweating limbs, and great fear – these are the signs of death, and they are also the signs of a beggar. A lifetime spent as a hunchback, or afflicted by worms, or driven out by a wind, or living on the peak of a mountain, would be better than begging. Even Vishnu, the lord of the universe, became a dwarf when he begged (from the demon Bali); so who else could be greater than him, and not become lightweight when he begs?

The mother is an enemy and the father an opponent to their children if they do not teach them to read; without reading, a man cannot shine in the midst of the assembly, but is like a heron in the midst of swans. Knowledge is the beauty of an ugly person; knowledge is greater than any hidden wealth. Knowledge makes a man good and beloved of other people; knowledge is the guru of gurus. Knowledge destroys the afflictions of one's relatives; knowledge is the highest divinity; knowledge is honoured among kings; a human without knowledge is a beast. The possessions that one has inside a house, to which one is so attached, may all be stolen; but knowledge cannot be taken away by other people.

Vishnu told this synopsis of ethics, with all the vows, to Shaunaka; Shaunaka heard it and told it to Vyasa; and from Vyasa it came to us. (*Garuda Purana* 114.1–75; 115.39–83)

4.3 RITUALS

4.3.1 An animal sacrifice

Animal sacrifices play a part in many different sorts of rituals. This animal sacrifice takes place in the course of the initiation of a Vaishnava pupil by his guru. The text uses technical terms to designate various ritual and philosophical concepts. It speaks of 'closing the eyes' as a euphemism for killing the sacrificial animals, where the Vedic texts used a different euphemism, speaking of 'quieting' the animal. And it imitates the Vedas in measuring the sacrificial thread in direct proportion to the height of the sacrificer, as the Vedic gods build their fire-altar in proportion to Prajapati (above, section 2.1.2.1.2). Then the text meditates upon the sacrificial victims in conjunction with various combinations of the five elements, the tattvas *of which Nature (Prakriti) is composed. The slaughtered animals are placed in a pit, and a 'red thread', also called the thread of Nature, is used to consecrate them.*

Enter the temple of worship and worship (the image of) Vishnu while circumambulating him to the right, saying, 'You alone are the refuge for Release from the bonds that bind the beasts sunk in the ocean of rebirth; O god, you always look upon your devotees as a cow looks upon her calf. God of gods, have mercy; by your favour, I will release all these beasts that are bound by the nooses and bonds of Nature.' When you have announced this to the lord of gods, have the beasts enter there; purify them with the chants and perfect them with fire. Place them in contact with the image (of Vishnu) and close their eyes. Then scatter on them handfuls of flowers and leaves, while uniting them with the name (of Vishnu). Perform the worship in the usual order, but without any mantras; and whatever image a flower falls on, call it by the name of that image.

Take a red thread spun by a maiden, and measure it from the tuft of hair on your head to the tip of your big toe; multiply that figure by six and then again by three. Meditate upon Nature, in whom all of this dissolves and out of whom all of this is given birth, and who becomes present in Her various manifestations. Then make Nature-nooses with that thread, counting according to the number of elements, and place it on an earthenware tray by the side of the pit. Meditate upon all the elements, beginning with creation and continuing through Nature till you end with the element of earth, and (mentally) place them in the body of your pupil. Divide them into three, or into five, or into ten, or into twelve; count them with all the possible groupings of the elements. Then draw over the body of the beast the thread of Illusion, that is the essence of the particles, the whole form of the five limbs of Nature. (*Agni Purana* 27.17–28)

4.3.2 The origin of the lingam

Vishnu tells the sages the story of the first appearance of the lingam, or phallus of Shiva, in the form of a pillar of fire.

Once upon a time, when the whole triple world was unmanifest, in darkness, swallowed up by me, I lay there alone, with all the creatures in my belly. I had a thousand heads and a thousand eyes, and a thousand feet; I held in my hands the conch shell, discus, and mace, as I lay in the immaculate water. Then, all of a sudden, I saw from afar the four-headed (Brahma), the great yogi, the Person with golden luminosity, infinitely luminous, as bright as a hundred suns, blazing with his own brilliance. The god was wearing a black antelope skin and carrying a water-pot; and in the space of the blinking of an eye, that supreme Person arrived. Then Brahma, to whom all people bow, said to me, 'Who are you? And where do you come from? And why are you staying here? Tell me, sir. I am the maker of the worlds, self-created, facing in all directions.' When Brahma had spoken like that to me, I said to him: '*I* am the maker of the worlds, and also the one who destroys them, again and again.' As the two of us were talking together in this way, each wishing to surpass the other, we saw a flame arising in the northern quarter. As we looked at that flame we were amazed, and its brilliance and power made us cup our hands in reverence and bow to that light from Shiva. The flame grew, a surpassing marvel, and Brahma and I hastened to run up to it. It broke through heaven and earth with its halo of flame, and in the middle of the flame we saw a lingam of great lustre, measuring just a handsbreadth, unmanifest and full of supreme light. In the middle, it was neither gold nor stone or silver; it was indescribable, unimaginable, visible and invisible again and again. It had a thousand garlands of flames, amazing, miraculous; it had great brilliance, and kept getting much bigger. It was covered with a halo of flame, terrifying all creatures with its monstrous form, excessive, bursting through heaven and earth.

Then Brahma said to me, 'Quickly, go down and find out the (bottom) end of this noble lingam. I will go up until I see its (top) end.' We agreed to do this, and went up and down. I kep going down for a thousand years, but I did not reach the end of the lingam; and then I became afraid. In the very same way, Brahma did not find its end above, and came back to join me right there in the expanse of water. Then we were amazed and frightened of the noble one; deluded by his power of illusion, we lost our wits and became confused. But then we meditated on the lord who faces in all directions, the origin and resting place of the worlds, the unchanging lord. Cupping our hands in reverence, we paid homage to Shiva, the trident-bearer, who makes the great, terrifying sound, who has a frightening form, and fangs, who is manifest, and great:

'We bow to you, O lord of the gods and people; we bow to you god, noble lord of all creatures. We bow to you, the eternally successful yogi, the support of all the universe, the highest ruler, the highest ultimate reality, the undying, the highest place. You are the eldest, the lovely god, the ruddy one, the jumper, the lord Shiva; you are the sacrifice; you are the utterance of 'Vashat!' and the utterance of 'Om!'; the heater of enemies; the utterance of 'Svaha!'; you are obeisance and the perfection of all holy rituals; you are the utterance of the sweet drink, 'Svadha!'; you are the sacrifice, the vows, and the observances; the Vedas, the worlds, the gods, the true god everywhere. You are the quality of sound in space; you are the origin and dissolution of creatures. You are the perfume in the earth, the fluidity of the waters, the brightness of fire, great lord. You are the touch of the wind, lord of gods, and the form of the moon. You are the knowledge in intelligence, lord of gods, and the seed in nature. You destroy all the worlds; you are Time, the Ender, made of death. You alone maintain the three worlds, and you alone create them, o lord. With your eastern face you act as Indra, and with your southern face you withdraw the worlds again. With your western face you act as Varuna; this is certain. With your northern face you are Soma, o best of gods. In one way or in many ways, you create the worlds and destroy them, O god. You are the Adityas, the Vasus, the Rudras, the Maruts, and the Ashvins. You are the Perfected Beings, the magicians, the Nagas, the sorcerers, the ascetics; the noble Valakhilya sages, and those who have achieved success in their asceticism, and who have kept their vows. O lord of gods, from you all of these goddesses, firm in their vows, and others, have been born: Uma, Sita, Sinivali, Kuhu, Gayatri, and Lakshmi; and the goddesses Fame, Fortitude, Wisdom, Modesty, Loveliness, Form, Sweetness, Contentment, Growth, and Activity; and Sarasvati, the goddess of speech; and, O lord of gods, from you have sprung Twilight and Night. We bow to you who have the power of a million million suns, who are as white as a thousand moons; we bow to you who hold the thunderbolt and the bow called Pinaka; we bow to you who hold the bow and arrows in your hand.

We bow to you whose body is adorned with ashes; we bow to you who destroyed the body of Kama (the god of erotic love); we bow to you, god of the golden embryo, the golden robe, the golden womb, the golden navel, the golden semen, variegated with a thousand eyes; we bow to you, god of the golden colour and the golden hair, you the golden hero and the giver of gold; we bow to you, god, master of gold with the sound of gold. We bow to you with the Pinaka bow in your hand, Shankara, the blue-necked.'

When he had been praised like that, he became manifest, the one of great intellect, the god of gods, womb of the universe, shining as bright as a million suns; and filled with pity, the great god, the great light, spoke to us, as if he would swallow up the sky with his thousands of millions of mouths. His neck was shaped like a conch shell; his belly was lovely; he was adorned with various kinds of jewels; his body was variegated with all sorts of gems, and he wore various kinds of garlands and unguents. The lord had the Pinaka bow in his hand and he held the trident; he was fit to be worshipped by the gods. He wore a great serpent for his sacred thread, but he did not frighten the gods.

He sent forth a great laugh, with the noise of the sound of the *dundubhi* drum, like the roar of thunder, a laugh that filled the entire universe. The two of us were terrified by that great sound, but then the great god said, 'I am satisfied with you two, best of the gods. See my great yoga, and lose all your fear. Both of you, eternal, were born from my limbs in the past; Brahma here, the grandfather of all people, is my right arm, and Vishnu is my left arm, always unconquered in battles. I am satisfied with the two of you, and so I will give you a boon, whatever you ask.'

Then the two of us were ecstatic, and we bowed to the feet of the lord, and we said to the great god, who was standing there inclined to favour us, 'If you are really satisfied, and if you are going to give us a boon, then let the two of us always have devotion for you, O god, lord of the gods.' The god of gods said, 'So be it, fortunate ones. Create masses of progeny.' And when he had said this, the lord god vanished. (*Brahmanda Purana* 1.2.26.10–61)

4.3.3 The origin of the shrine of the lingam

To humble the sages of the Pine Forest, Shiva appeared to them naked and ithyphallic, and seduced their wives; in their fury, they cursed his lingam to fall to the ground. The world was immediately plunged into darkness, nor was any new life born, since Shiva's lingam is the source of all heat and light and life in the world. Realising their mistakes, the sages sought help from Brahma. He helped them to restore the lingam, but this led to new problems: the gods complained that an undesirable desegregation of castes (men and gods) was taking place in heaven, together with overcrowding. (A similar problem arises when mortals become immortals – above, section 2.1.2.1.2 – or when Yama complains that men are going to heaven instead of to hell – section 4.2.1.). To remedy this, Brahma tries to conceal the power of the primordial lingam (the one that had fallen from the body of Shiva) by covering it up with a false, ordinary stone lingam; but this, too, fails. The lingam, fortunately for us, cannot be destroyed.

As this passage opens, the sages have just discovered the consequences of their action in causing Shiva's lingam to fall.

The sages asked Brahma how they could do what was best for the universe. Brahma said, 'Let us go to seek refuge with Shiva, the three-eyed god who holds the trident in his hand. By the grace of the god of gods, you will be as you were before.' When Brahma had said this to them, they went with him to the highest mountain, Kailasa, and there they saw Shiva seated next to Uma. Brahma, the grandfather of the universe, began to praise Shiva, the god above all gods, the one who gives boons, the lord of the triple world:

'We bow to you, the Endless, boon-giver, wielder of the Pinaka bow, great god, god, the Pillar, the highest soul; we bow to you, lord of the universe, always the saviour, donor of all knowledge. You are the one god, the supreme Person. Honour to you, womb of the lotus, lord of the lotus, honour, honour, honour to you, the very form of what is horrible and what is peaceful, fierce in your anger. We bow to you, lord of all, leader of the gods, with the trident in your hand; honour to you, honour to you, creator of everything.'

When the great god was thus praised by Brahma and by the sages, he said, 'Do not be afraid. Go. My lingam will be there for you again. Do what I say, quickly, if you wish to please me. Establish my lingam again. Do not hesitate. Those who worship my lingam in a spirit of complete devotion will find nothing hard to achieve, ever. Anyone who commits all sorts of bad deeds, even knowingly, is purified by worshipping my lingam; don't worry about this. You caused my lingam to fall; now move it to the great lake that is called Near Presence, and establish it there. Then, Brahmins, you will obtain whatever you desire. This lingam, that people call the Pillar, will be worshipped by those who dwell in heaven. And since it is situated at the place of the Lord of the Pillar, it will be known as the Lingam of the Lord of the Pillar. Any people who think constantly about the Pillar will be freed from all their sins. Their bodies will become purified by the sight of it, and they will obtain Release.'

When the sages and Brahma heard what the god said, they made an effort to take the lingam from the Pine Forest. But the gods and sages were not able to move it. Thoroughly exhausted, overheated with exhaustion, they asked Brahma for help, and he said to them, 'What use is all your exhaustion? You are not able to carry the lingam that the god of gods, the god of the trident, caused to fall by his own wish. Therefore, all of you gods must go together to seek his help, and if he is satisfied with you, the great god himself will carry it.'

At these words, the gods and sages went with Brahma to Mount Kailasa, hoping to see Rudra. But when they did not see the god, they became worried, and the sages said to Brahma, 'Where is the great lord, the god?' Brahma meditated for a long time and realised that the great lord, the god, was standing in the form of an elephant, receiving the praise of the mind-born sages. Then all the (Pine Forest) sages and the gods went with Brahma to the holy great lake where the god himself was standing. Still they did not see him, though they sought him everywhere, and again all the gods and Brahma became worried.

But then they saw the Goddess standing there cheerfully holding a gourd, and as she was pleased, she said, 'You have exhausted yourselves in your search for the great lord. Drink this ambrosial liquid, gods, and then you will know Shankara.' When the gods heard what the Goddess said, they were filled with happiness, and they drank that pure ambrosial liquid. Immediately afterwards, they sat down comfortably and asked the supreme Goddess, 'Where is the god who has come here and taken the form of an elephant?' The Goddess pointed out where he was standing in the middle of the lake. When all the gods and sages saw him they were filled with joy; led by Brahma, they said, 'O great god, you abandoned the lingam that is revered by the triple world. But no one else is capable of bringing it (here), great lord.'

When Brahma and the others had said this to him, the lord god Hara (Shiva) went with the sages to the Pine Forest hermitage. And when the great god, the greatest lord, arrived there, still in the form of an elephant, he grasped (the lingam) playfully with his trunk. The great god took it and set it down on the western bank of the lake, while the great sages praised him. Then all the gods and the sages rich in ascetic power, seeing that they had reaped their reward, began to praise the great lord:

'We bow to you, supreme soul, of endless wombs, witness of all people, highest ruler, omniscient god, knower of the Self, knower of higher and lower, knowable through sacred knowledge, lord of all, great ultimate reality, great knower of the Self, great Person, dwelling-place of all beings, dwelling in the heart, primeval god, great god, eternal Shiva, ruler, hard to know, hard to propitiate, great lord of creatures, highest lord, great lord of yogis, three-eyed, great yogi, highest ultimate reality, highest light, supreme knower of ultimate reality, the syllable Om, the utterance "Vashat!", the utterance "Svaha!", highest cause, omnipresent, all-seeing, all-powerful, god of all, unborn, possessing a thousand rays, possessing many rays, shining beautifully, with the lustre of Shiva, with endless lustre, whirlwind, absorber, fire of the submarine mare, soul of fire and ambrosia, purifier, great purifier, great cloud, possessing great illusion, great desire, destroyer of the god of desire, swan, highest swan, great sovereign, great lord, great lover, great swan, destroyer of fire, worshipped by the gods and perfected ones, bearer of gold, golden seed, golden navel, with golden tips of hair, with hair like rushes, giver of boons to all people, showing grace to all, lying on the lotus, lying on sacred *kusha* grass, lying in the heart, ocean of knowledge, ruler, lord, great sacrifice, great sacrificer, made of all sacrifices, heart of all sacrifices, praised in all sacrifices, unsupported, lying in the ocean, born of Atri, full of pity to your devotees, of unbroken yoga, supporter of yoga, whose body is illuminated by the great gem in the head of the serpent Vasuki, green-eyed, three-eyed, with matted hair, blue-necked, bearing the crescent moon, you who took away half the body of Uma, wearing the elephant skin, great destroyer of the cycle of rebirth that is hard to cross over – favour us, O you who are to your devotees like a cow to her calf.'

When he was thus praised with true devotion by the hosts of gods, led by Brahma the Grandfather, the great-souled Shiva abandoned the form of the elephant and became present in the lingam. Then the great god spoke to Brahma and the other gods, right before the eyes of the sages, and told them about the supreme glory of the shrine: 'This great and most holy lake is known as the Near Presence. Because I have come to it, it grants Release. Whatever men come here, Brahmins or Kshatriyas or Vaishyas, by the mere sight of the lingam they will look upon the highest place. Day after day, when the sun reaches its zenith, the ocean, lakes, and (other) shrines will unite in the shrine of the Pillar. And whatever man praises me devotedly with this hymn of praise will always find me easy for him to reach; this is certain.' When the lord Rudra had said this, he vanished; and the gods and all the sages went back to their own places.

From then on, men mingled (with gods) in heaven, since the power of the Pillar lingam is such that by the mere sight of it one wins heaven. Then all the gods went to Brahma for help, and Brahma said to them, 'What is your purpose in coming here?' The gods said, 'We are in great danger from men, grandfather; protect us.' Brahma, the leader of the thirty gods, said, 'Fill the lake with dust right away. Indra, help them out.' So Indra, the chastiser of the demon Paka, caused a rain of dust to fall for seven days and filled that lake, as the gods asked him to do.

But when the great lord, the god of gods, saw that rain of dust, he took hold of the lingam and the banyan tree that grew at the shrine, grasping them with his hand (or trunk). And that is why the holiest part of the shrine is the part where the water is; a man who bathes in it is the equal of one who has bathed in all the shrines. And whoever performs the funeral ritual near the lingam and the banyan tree satisfies his ancestors, so that they will give him what is difficult to get on earth.

When all the sages saw that the lake was full, with great faith they touched all the limbs of their bodies with the dust, and by means of the dust all the sages shook off all their sins; honoured by the bands of gods, they went forth to the place of Brahma. And the perfected beings of great souls who worship the lingam achieve the supreme perfection that is hard to attain in any number of rebirths. When Brahma realised this, he placed a stone lingam on top of that primordial lingam; but after a long time, the glory of the primordial lingam stained the stone lingam, so that by the mere touch of it, too, a perfected being reaches the highest place.

Again the gods reported to Brahma, 'These men are achieving supreme perfection by the mere sight of the lingam.' When he heard this, the lord Brahma placed seven lingams there, one on top of the other, for he wished to help the gods. But even so, perfected beings who desire Release and are intent upon tranquillity worship the dust zealously and go forth to the highest place. Even the dust that is scattered by the wind over Kurukshetra enables a man who has committed a most evil act to go forth to the highest place.

The power of the shrine of the Pillar destroys the evil deed that a woman or a man has committed knowingly or unknowingly. By the sight of the lingam and the touch of the banyan tree, Release is achieved; and by bathing in the water near it one obtains the fruit that one longs for. Whoever offers the libation to the ancestors in that water enjoys endless fruits in every drop of the water. And whoever stands, full of faith, behind the lingam and offers the libation to the ancestors with black sesamum oil – he satisfies (his ancestors) for three Ages. His ancestors, satisfied, drink the supreme water for as long as the interval of a Manu is said to last, for as long as the lingam stands.

In the Golden Age is was called the Near Presence; in the Age of the Deuce, it was called the Lingam of the Wind; and between the Age of the Trey and the Dark Age it became known as the Well of the Lake of Rudra. That most fortunate man who bathes in the shrine of the Lake of Rudra on the fourteenth day of the dark fortnight of the month of Caitra achieves the highest place. And anyone who stands by the banyan tree in the night and meditates on the highest lord, gets whatever he is thinking of in his heart, by the grace of the banyan tree of the Pillar. (*Vamana Purana, Saromahatmya* 23.1–36, 24.1–31)

5 SHASTRAS

The Shastras are the textbooks of Hinduism. The most important are those devoted to each of the three human goals: dharma (the Dharma Shastras), profit (the Artha Shastras), and pleasure (the Kama Shastras, of which the Kamasutra *is the most famous). But there are also Shastras for medicine (of which those by Caraka and Sushruta are the most important) the Shastras for the care of horses (Ashva Shastras) and elephants (Gaja Shastras), and so forth. They share a common mode of discourse: each point is debated in the light of the opinions of various authorities.*

5.1 THE BODY

Medicine is known in India as the science of long life (ayur-veda). *Since the goal of many religious texts was to prolong the human life-span* (ayur), *medicine is a sacred science, a part of religion. The medical texts teach the Hindu to care for his mind and body in ways that supplement the advice offered, on this same subject, by the Dharma Shastras, the teachings of yoga, Tantras, and other school of Hinduism.*

5.1.1 Second opinions on the aetiology of disease

Once upon a time, when all the great sages had assembled before lord Punarvasu, who was dharma incarnate, this dispute arose in order to determine the primordial origin both of this creature called the person – who is a mass of soul, senses, mind, and sense objects – and of his diseases. Then Vamaka, the king of Kashi, who understood the subject, approached the assembly of sages, greeted them, and uttered this speech: 'Good sirs, is the origin of the person also thought to be the origin of diseases, or not?' When the king had said this, Punarvasu said to the sages, 'Every one of you has dispelled all doubts through your unlimited knowledge and understanding. You should dispel the doubt of the king of Kashi.'

Parikshi, the son of Mudgala, thought about this and said, 'The individual person is born from the Soul, and so the diseases are also born from the Soul; this is their cause. (The Soul) collects and enjoys karma and the fruits of karma. Happiness (health) and unhappiness (disease) cannot function without this seat of all consciousness.'

But Sharaloman said, 'No. The soul never by itself yokes the soul with diseases or other unhappinesses, for it hates unhappiness. But when the mind that is conscious of goodness (*sattva*) is overwhelmed by energy and darkness (*rajas* and *tamas*), then it causes the origin both of the body itself and of pathological changes in the body.'

Varyovida, however, said, 'No. The mind alone cannot be the cause. Neither the diseases of the body nor one's state of mind can exist without the body. But all creatures are born from *rasa* (the fluid essence of digested food), and so the various diseases are also born from *rasa*. And since the waters abound in *rasa*, they are said to be the causes of origins.'

But Hiranyaksha said, 'No. The soul is not regarded as born from *rasa*, nor is the mind, that is beyond perception by the senses. But there are diseases caused by sound and so forth. Indeed, the individual person is born of the six elements of matter (earth, water, fire, wind, space and mind or soul), and so diseases are also born from the six elements. That the person is a mass of the six elements is well known from the Sankhya school of philosophers, among others.'

But as he said this, Kaushika said, 'No. How could someone be born out of the six elements, without a mother and a father? A person is born from a person; a cow from a cow, and a horse from a horse. Diseases such as urinary disorders are known to be hereditary. So the two parents are the cause.'

'No,' said Bhadrakapya. 'For a blind person is not born from a blind person. And how could you explain the primordial origin of the first mother and father? But a creature is known to be born of his karma, and so diseases are also born from karma. Neither a person nor diseases are born without karma.'

But Bharadvaja said, 'No. An agent must always precede an action (karma). And no person can be the result of an action that has not been done; this is clear enough. No, nature is the cause, one's own nature, the cause of both diseases and the person, just as it is the nature of earth to be rough, water to be fluid, wind to move, and fire to be hot.'

But Kankayana said, 'No. If this were so, there would be no fruits of individual efforts. Success or failure would simply result from the very nature of creatures. Prajapati, the child of Brahma, had an unlimited imagination, and it was he who created the happiness and unhappiness of this universe, sentient and insentient.'

'No,' said Bhikshu Atreya. 'Prajapati constantly wished for the welfare of his offspring, and so he would never yoke them with miseries as if he were not a good man. No, the individual person is born of time, and diseases are born of time. The whole universe is in the power of time; time is the cause of everything.'

Now, as the sages were arguing in this way, Punarvasu said, 'Don't talk like this. It is hard to get to the truth when people take sides. People who utter arguments and counter-arguments as if they were established facts never get to the end of their own side, as if they were going round and round on an oil press. Get rid of this collision of opinions and think about the heart of the matter. Not until you shake off the darkness of factionalism from what you want to know will true knowledge emerge. The same factors that give birth to man when they are working in harmony give rise to the various diseases when they are in disharmony.'

When he heard Punarvasu say this, Vamaka the king of Kashi asked him again, 'Sir, what *is* the cause of the growth of a person who is born of harmonious causes and of the diseases that are born from disharmonious causes?' Punarvasu said to him, 'The use of good food is one cause of the growth of a person, and the use of bad food is a cause of diseases.' As Punarvasu said this, Agnivesha said to him, 'Good sir, how can we recognise, without fear of contradiction, the signs that distinguish the sorts of food that are good and bad? For we find that contrary effects result from the foods regarded as good and the foods regarded as bad, as a result of variations in the amount, time, method of use, geographical area, constitution of the body, condition of the humours, and age of the individual.'

Punarvasu said to him, 'Agnivesha, the foods that maintain the elements of the body in balance according to nature, and that even out their disequilibrum – consider these to be good foods. The opposite kind are bad foods. This is an irrefutable way to distinguish between good and bad foods.' When he said this, Agnivesha replied, 'Sir, physicians have an abundance of different opinions. Not all of them will understand this sort of teaching . . .' (Caraka 1.1.15.3–34)

5.1.2 The humours of the mind and body

The group of causes of the diseases that take hold of both (mind and body) are three fold: wrong use, non-use, and excessive use of time, thought, and the objects of the senses. The body and the consciousness are regarded as the grounds in which diseases and health appear; balanced use (of time, thought, and sense objects) is the cause of health and happiness. The highest self undergoes no changes through the sense objects or the basic elements; it is the cause of consciousness, the eternal observer who sees all actions. Wind, bile and phlegm are said to be the group of humours, the sources of disease, in the body; and energy (*rajas*) and darkness (*tamas*) are said to be the source of disease in the mind. Pathological changes that are regarded as curable are counteracted by medicines possessing qualities opposite (to the humours of the changes), applied with proper regard for place, dose, and time. But no cure is prescribed for diseases that are incurable. (Caraka 1.1.1.54–62a)

5.1.3 How not to get sick

This list, which contains some of the same precepts that are listed in the Garuda Purana *section on ethics – see above, 4.2.4 – differs from that list primarily in its emphasis on food and the body. Much of its advice makes sense to us, though some of it seems irrelevant, if not superstitious, or – in the case of the exhortation to smoke – downright wrong.*

If you desire your own well-being, you should always, everywhere, entirely, keep your wits about you and behave well. If you observe all of these things simultaneously you achieve both of your aims: freedom from disease and conquest of your senses. I will now describe that proper behaviour in its entirety.

(1. Moral exhortations)

You should: honour gods, cows, Brahmins, gurus, old people, those who have perfected themselves spiritually, and teachers; perform the proper rituals for fire, make use of the prescribed herbs, perform the twilight ritual at dawn and sunset; clean your rectum and your feet all the time; cut your hair, beard, body hair, and nails three times every fortnight; wear clothes that are not torn; be cheerful and smell good; dress well, comb your hair, and always put oil on your head, ears, nostrils, and feet; smoke; speak before you are spoken to; smile; help people in trouble; perform oblations and sacrifices; be generous; pay respects to crossroads; offer food to various minor divinities; honour guests; offer funeral oblations of rice to the ancestors; speak useful, measured, sweet, and significant words at the right time; control yourself; observe dharma; be jealous about the causes of actions but not about their fruits; be free of anxiety and free of fear, modest, thoughtful, energetic, clever, patient, and virtuous; believe in the gods; be respectful to teachers who have attained spiritual perfection or who are old, or who excel in decorum, intellect, knowledge, nobility, or vigour; carry an umbrella and a cane; wear a turban and shoes; look just six feet ahead of where you are walking; have auspicious behaviour and character; avoid ground where there are tattered clothes, bones, thorns, filthy hair, chaff, rubbish, ashes, skulls or broken potsherds, baths, or offerings to minor deities; stop exercising before you get overtired; be a friend to all creatures, reconcile the angry, calm the frightened, help the poor, keep your promises, be conciliatory, put up with the words of other people, conquer your envy, seek the quality of peace, and get rid of the causes of passion and hatred.

(2. Moral precautions)

You should not: tell a lie, take what belongs to other people, lust for another man's wife or his property; take pleasure in enmity or do bad deeds or be bad even towards someone bad; talk about other peoples' faults or tell other peoples' secrets; associate with people who do not follow dharma, who are hated by the kind, or who are insane, fallen from caste, abortionists, low, or corrupt; ride on dangerous vehicles or sit on a chair that is hard and knee-high, or sleep on a bed that lacks a coverlet or that is cheaply built or too narrow or uneven; walk on the rough peaks of mountains, or climb a tree, or swim where the water has a strong current; step on the shadow of a member of your family, or a member of any good family; go near a conflagration; laugh loudly; break wind audibly; yawn, sneeze, or laugh without covering your mouth; pick your nose, grind your teeth; snap your nails; crack your joints; scrape the ground; pull up grass; pulverise dry mud; move with disorderly limbs; look at the planets or at anything that is undesirable, foul, or forbidden; say 'Hum' in front of a corpse; cross the shadow of a sacred tree, a flag, a guru, or a person who is to be honoured or who is reviled; go at night into a temple, sacred grove, courtyard, crossroads, garden, burning ground, or slaughterhouse; go alone into an empty house or a forest; enjoy the company of wicked women, wicked friends, or wicked servants; oppose the highest men or wait upon the lowest; take pleasure in crooked acts or indulge in ignoble acts; frighten people; indulge in violent or excessive sleeping, wakefulness, bathing, drinking, or eating; sit for a long time with your knees up; go up close to snakes or animals that have big teeth or horns; expose yourself to easterly winds, sun, hoar-frost, or hurricanes; provoke a quarrel; approach a fire when you are not mentally calm or have not washed your hands after eating; get warm by putting (fire) below you; bathe when you have not yet recovered from exhaustion or when you have not yet washed out your mouth (after eating) or when you are naked; touch your head with the garment you wore in your bath; touch the tips of your hair; wear (after a bath) the same clothes you wore before you bathed; go out without touching a jewel, butter, respectable people, auspicious objects, or flowers; pass by respectable people or auspicious objects on the left side, or others on the right side.

(3. Food)

You should not eat without: wearing jewels on your hand; bathing; wearing intact clothing; muttering prayers; offering oblations to the gods or giving oblations to the ancestors, or giving to gurus and guests and dependants; putting on auspicious perfume and garlands; washing your hands, feet, and mouth; washing your face; first making an offering into the fire; sprinkling the place with water; saying mantras over the place.

You should not eat: facing north; with a disturbed mind; surrounded by people who are undevout, uncouth, impure, or hungry; on plates that are foul;

at the wrong place or time, or in a crowd; with loathing; loathsome food; or food that has been served by people who are against you.

You should not eat: stale food, except for meat, green vegetables, dried vegetables, fruits, and sweets; without leaving something over, except for yogurt, honey, salt, roasted coarsely ground meal, and clarified butter; yogurt at night; roasted coarsely ground meal by itself or at night or in large quantities or twice (in a day) or interrupted by drinks of water or by tearing it with your teeth.

(4. Excretions)

You should not: sneeze, eat, or sleep when you are not sitting up straight; do any other job when you are agitated (by the need to defecate); emit spit, excrement, or urine in the face of wind, fire, water, the moon, the sun, a Brahmin, or a guru; urinate on the road or in a public place or at the time of taking food; emit phlegm or mucus during prayer, oblation, religious studies, offerings to minor gods, or auspicious rituals.

(5. Sex)

You should not: insult women, nor rely upon them too much; tell them secrets or give them too much authority; have sexual intercourse with a woman who is menstruating, diseased, impure, or cursed, or who has undesirable looks or behaviour or manners, or who is not clever, or who is inexperienced or devoid of desire, or who desires some other man or is married to some other man, or who belongs to another caste.

You should not have intercourse: in anything but a vagina; in a sacred grove, public courtyard, crossroads, garden, burning ground, slaughterhouse, water, medical clinic, or in the houses of gurus, or in temples, or at dawn or sunset, or on special days of the month, or when you are impure, nor without taking (aphrodisiac) drugs, or when you lack sexual excitement, or when you don't have an erection, or when you haven't eaten, or when you have overeaten, or on an uneven surface, or when you are under pressure to urinate; or when you are suffering from exhaustion, too much gymnastic exercise, fasting, or fatigue; or in a place where there is no privacy.

You should not, when you are impure (after sex): speak against good people or teachers, or perform spells, rituals, puja to sacred groves or to people worthy of honour, or study.

(6. Study)

You should not study: if there is lightning at the wrong season, or when the quarters of the sky are lit up, or in an earthquake, or during a big festival, or when meteors are falling, or during an eclipse, or at new moon, or at dawn or dusk; nor with a guru who is not first-class. (Caraka 1.1.8.17b–24a)

5.2 BIRTH

5.2.1 Embryology

Embryology is a particularly religious aspect of Hindu medicine, due to the importance of the doctrine of rebirth; as rebirth is a wheel, any discussion of birth also involves a discussion of death, but I have rather arbitrarily separated them, and begun with birth, in the Western manner. We have already encountered an early speculation on embryology in the Chandogya Upanishad *discussion of karma – above, section 2.3.2.3; but the Puranas discussed the subject in far greater detail. There are several different explanations of conception and birth, but the one underlying the present text assumes that the menstrual blood* (rajas, *also the term for the quality of energy) is the woman's seed; hence the seed of which the child is born is regarded as twofold, male and female.*

(The sage Jaimini asks the birds,)

O tigers of twice-born ones, dispel my doubts when I ask you about the appearing and vanishing of creatures. How is a living creature born? How does it grow? How does it exist when it stays in the middle of the stomach, squeezed in all its limbs? When it comes out of the stomach, how does it grow? And how does it become separated from its feelings at the moment when it departs? A person who has died consumes both his good deeds and his bad deeds; how, then, do they cause his fruits to arise? How is the foetus not digested like a lump of food there in the stomach? For even very heavy foods are digested there in the woman's stomach; so how is the little creature not digested? And how will it experience all of the karma of its good deeds? Tell me all this, without any ambiguity; for it is a very great secret, about which men are quite confused.

(The birds answer by repeating a conversation that took place between a young boy and his father; the boy, nicknamed Jada ('Impotent') because he was regarded as an idiot, in fact remembers his former lives and deaths, and tells his father about them:)

The impregnation of human women is the emitting of the seed in the menstrual blood. As soon as (the soul) is released from hell, or from heaven, it arrives (in the womb). Overpowered by that (soul), the two-fold seed becomes solid, father. It becomes a spec of life, and then a bubble, and then flesh. And just as a shoot of a plant is born from a seed, so from the flesh the five limbs (two arms, two legs, and the head) are born, with all their parts. The subsidiary limbs, too – fingers, eyes, nose, mouth and ears – grow out of the (five) limbs; and out of the subsidiary limbs, in the same way, grow the nails and so forth. The hair on the body grows in the skin, and the hair of the head grows after that.

The birth-sheath grows larger as it takes on flesh. Just as a coconut grows big along with its shell, so the sheath of the embryo, that opens out on the bottom, grows bigger. The embryo grows up in the bottom of the womb, placing its two hands beside its knees, with its two thumbs on top of its knees, the fingers in front; behind the two knees are the two eyes, and in between the knees is the nose; the buttocks rest on the two heels, and the arms and shanks are outside. In this way, the living (human) creature gradually grows up inside the woman's womb; other living creatures position themselves in the stomach according to their shapes.

The fire inside the stomach makes the embryo hard, and it lives on what is eaten and drunk (by the mother). The sojourn of the living creature inside the stomach is meritorious and is made of retained merit. A channel called the 'Strengthener and Nourisher' is attached to the inside of the embryo's navel and to the channel from the woman's entrails, and the embryo stays alive by that means. For what the woman eats and drinks goes into the embryo's womb, and the living creature's body is strengthened and nourished by that so that it grows.

Then it begins to remember its many previous existences in the wheel of rebirth, and that depresses it, and it tosses from side to side, thinking, 'I won't ever do *that* again, as soon as I get out of this womb. I will do everything I can, so that I won't become an embryo again.' It thinks in this way as it remembers the hundreds of miseries of birth that it experienced before, in the power of fate.

Then, as time goes by, the embryo turns around, head down, and in the ninth or tenth month it is born. As it comes out, it is hurt by the wind of procreation; it comes out crying, because it is pained by the misery in its heart. When it has come out of the womb, it falls into an unbearable swoon, but it regains consciousness when it is touched by the air. Then Vishnu's deluding power of illusion assails him, and when his soul has been deluded by it, he loses his knowledge. As soon as the living creature has lost his knowledge, he becomes a baby.

After that he becomes a young boy, then an adolescent, and then an old man. And then he dies and then he is born again as a human. Thus he wanders on the wheel of rebirth like the bucket on the wheel of a well . . . (*Markandeya Purana* 10.1–7, 11.1–21)

5.2.2 A strange birth

The birth of a son to couples who are childless is one of the perennial problems discussed in Hinduism. When the husband is alive, but unable to produce a child, a sage or god may impregnate his wife in his stead; thus, as we saw (in 3.1.1), the Mahabharata *heroes were begotten by proxy. Often a sage produces a child by consecrating a special pot of milk and rice (symbolic of the female and male elements) which the wife eats, and thereby becomes pregnant. When the husband has died, his widow may burn herself on his pyre, but often she is prevented from doing so by a divine announcement that she is to have a child, perhaps because she was impregnated by the now dead father, before his death, or perhaps because she was subsequently impregnated by a sage or god, or by the dead man's brother. The present text combined these various themes to produce a text that is bizarre even in*

Hindu terms but that does represent the reductio ad absurdum *of a very serious problem. It also demonstrates the extreme implications of a basic Hindu medical belief, namely that the hard parts of a child – bones, teeth, sinews, and so forth – are contributed by the father's seed, the soft parts – blood, flesh, and so forth – by the mother.*

King Dilipa had no son, and after a long time, he died. His two wives were constantly sad. They went to the hermitage of the sage Vasishtha and said to him, 'The dynastic line descended from King Sagara has been broken, and the kingdom has been attacked by enemies. Tell us what to do.' When he heard this, the great sage thought deeply about the matter, and when he had made his decision he said to the two queens, 'This human dynasty will not be terminated. A noble son will be born to the two of you, fine ladies with beautiful eyes. I will make a supreme effort on your behalf.' When he had said this, Vasishtha cooked up a consecrated pot of rice and milk (*caru*) that was infused with all the good qualities, using the proper ritual for one who wishes to have a son. Then he said to the two noble women, 'One of you must eat this consecreated pot of rice and milk, and the other must have intercourse with her in the manner of a man.'

When the women heard this, they did what the great sage had told them to do. The eldest queen became pregnant, and after the usual time brought forth a son. But since the boy had been born without any semen of a man, he was born without any bones, and was just like a ball (*pinda*) of flesh. The two queens named him Bhagiratha because he had been born from a mere portion (*bhaga*) (of the usual parents), and they raised him to be a person of supreme dharma. Even as a child he learned all of the Vedas, but because he had no bones he was deformed; all the parts of his body were crooked.

One day, he set out for the home of his guru (Vasishtha) in order to study the Vedas with him. On the way, the little boy saw the sage Ashtavakra ('Crooked in Eight Ways'); he bowed to him in a twisted way, and spoke to him with twisted speech, as he was by his very nature forced to do. The sage became furious and said to him, 'If you thought to laugh at me, and bowed to me in such a way to demonstrate how twisted my body is, then you will be burnt to ashes by my curse; there is no alternative. But if this twisted form of yours is yours by your very nature, then you will immediately become powerful and very handsome.' As soon as Bhagiratha was addressed in this way by the sage, he became a mighty hero, as handsome as Kama the god of love himself. And Bhagiratha became ecstatic with joy and bowed to the sage over and over and praised him and circumambulated him many times; finally the sage gave him permission to depart, and the boy went on to his guru's home, in his celestial beauty.

When Vasishtha saw the boy so powerful and so handsome, he anointed him king, with the help of the previous counsellors of the king; and when the boy, whose power and courage were great, had been anointed, he won back his paternal kingdom from the enemies who had taken it. (*Padma Purana, Svarga*

Khanda 16.6–24)

5.2.3 The perils of growing up

Suffering takes thousands of different forms, as it arises from conception, birth, old age, disease, death, and hell. The living creature that has a very delicate body becomes encased in abundant filth inside the embryo, where he is enveloped by the membrane and his back, neck, and bones are all twisted out of shape. As he grows, he suffers greatly from the excessively acrid, bitter, spicy, salty, and burning hot food (that his mother has eaten). He can't stretch out his own limbs or contract them or anything else, and he is squashed on all sides, lying there in the faeces and urine and slime. Though he is unable to breathe, he is conscious, and he remembers his hundreds of former births. Thus he sits there in the womb bound by his own karma, and very miserable.

As he is born, his face is smeared with faeces, blood, urine, and semen, and his bones and sinews are hurt by the wind of procreation. He is turned head downwards by the powerful winds of childbirth, and he comes out from his mother's stomach bewildered by pain. He faints, and when he is touched by the outside air he loses his understanding, and is born. His body is hurt as if pierced by thorns, as if split open by saws; he falls from his pustulent wound like a worm upon the ground. Incapable of even scratching himself, or of turning over, totally without any control, he obtains his food, such as the milk he drinks at the breast, by the will of another person. Lying asleep on a bed, unclean, he is bitten by insects' stings and other things, and can do nothing to ward them off.

There are many sufferings in birth, and many that come right after birth; and there are many that he encounters in childhood, inflicted by elemental factors and so forth. Covered over by the darkness of ignorance, a man's heart becomes stupefied; he does not know, 'Where have I come from? Who am I? Where am I going? What am I made of? What bond is it that binds me? What is the cause, and what is not the cause? What is to be done, and what is not to be done? What is to be said, and what is not to be said? What is dharma, and what is against dharma? What does it consist in, and how? What is right to do, and what is not right to do? What is virtue and vice?'

Thus, confused like an animal, a man stumbles into the great misery that arises from ignorance, for he is primarily intent upon his penis and stomach. Ignorance is the source of inertia (*tamas*), and so the undertakings of ignorant men are deficient in good karma. But the seers say that hell is the reward for a deficiency in good karma, and so ignorant men suffer the most, both here and in the other world.

When old age shatters the body, gradually the limbs become loose; the old person's teeth decay and fall out; he becomes covered with wrinkles and sinews and veins; he can't see far, and the pupils of his eyes are fixed in space; tufts of hair appear in his nostrils, and his body trembles. All his bones become prominent; his back and joints are bent; and since his digestive fire has gone out, he eats little and moves little. It is only with pain and difficulty that he walks, rises, lies down, sits, and moves, and his hearing and sight become sluggish; his mouth is smeared with oozing saliva. As he looks toward death, all of his senses are no longer controlled; and he cannot remember even important things that he had experienced even at that very moment. Speaking takes a great effort, and he repeats himself; he is wakeful and very tired because of his heavy breathing and coughing. An old man is lifted up by someone else, and dressed by someone else; to his servants, his own sons, and his wife he is an object of contempt. He has lost all his cleanliness, though he still has his desire for amusement and food; his dependents laugh at him and all his relatives are disgusted with him. Remembering the things that he did in his youth as if he had experienced them in another birth, he sighs deeply and becomes very sad. (*Vishnu Purana* 6.5.9–35)

5.3 MARRIAGE

All Hindu texts agree that marriage is very important, and that it must be done by the rules, carefully; but different texts, such as the Lawbook of Manu – *the standard work on dharma, the* Kamasutra – *the standard work on sex, and the Tantras, have different ideas about precisely what the rules are.*

5.3.1 Women to marry and not to marry

Even within the standard text, the Lawbook of Manu, *various opinions are attributed to other lawmakers such as Atri and Gautama. Nor does a single law apply to all men; on the contrary. The book is intended primarily for men who are twice-born (so called because they are born again as members of Hindu society – Brahminis, Kshatriyas, and Vaishyas – on the occasion of their ritual initiation at maturity), in contrast with those beyond the Hindu pale, Shudras and the even lower Untouchable castes, though it also gives rules for Shudras (for the sake of symmetry, if nothing else). But each of the three twice-born classes has its own rules for marrying, eating, and every other human function.*

When, with the permission of his teacher, he has bathed and performed the ritual for homecoming (at the end of his studies) according to the ritual rules, a twice-born man should take a wife who is of the same class and has the right marks. A woman who does not come from the same blood line on her mother's side, nor belong to the same ritual line on her father's side, is considered proper as a wife and a sexual partner for a twice-born man. When it comes to relations with a woman, a man should avoid the ten following families, even if they are great or prosperous with cattle, rich in sheep, or possessing other wealth: a family that has abandoned the rituals, one that does not have boys, or a family that does not chant the Veda; and those families in which they have hairy bodies, piles, consumption, weak digestion, bad memories, and families with white leprosy, or black leprosy. A man should not marry a maiden who is a redhead or has an extra limb or is sickly or who is bald or too hairy or talks too much or is sallow or who is named after a constellation, a tree, or a river, who has a low caste name, who is named after a mountain, a bird, a snake, or has a slave name, or who has a fearsome name. He should have nothing to do with a woman who is too fat or too thin, too tall or too dwarfish, who is past her prime or lacks a limb, or who is fond of quarreling.

He should take a woman whose limbs are complete and who has a pleasant name, who walks like a swan or an elephant, whose body hair and hair on the head is fine and whose teeth are not big, with delicate limbs. A wise man, out of concern for the dharma of daughters will not marry a woman who has no brother or whose father is unknown.

Taking a woman of the same class is recommended to twice-born men for the first marriage; but for men in whom sexual desire has arisen, these should be the choices, listed in order: according to the tradition, only a Shudra woman can be the wife of a Shudra; she and one of his own class can be the wife of a Vaishya; these two and one of his own class for a Kshatriya; and these three and one of his own class for the high-born (Brahmin). A Shudra woman is not mentioned as the wife of a Brahmin or a Kshatriya even when they are under duress, even in a story. Twice-born men who are so infatuated as to take as wives women of low caste quickly reduce their families, including the children, to the status of Shudras. A man falls from his caste when he weds a Shudra woman, according to Atri and to (Gautama) the son of Utathya, or when he has a son by her, according to Shaunaka, or when he has any children by her, according to Bhrigu. A Brahmin who beds a Shudra woman goes to hell; if he begets a child on her, he forsakes the status of Brahmin. The ancestors and the gods do not eat the offerings to the gods, to the ancestors, and to guests made by such a man, and so he does not go to heaven. No expiation is ordained for a (twice-born) man who drinks the froth from the lips of a Shudra woman or who is tainted by her breath or who begets a son on her.

Now listen to the summary of these eight marriage rituals for the four classes, that are both for good and for ill, in this life and after death. Now, the eight are the marriages named after Brahma, the gods, the sages, Prajapati, the demons, the Gandharvas, the ogres, and the ghouls. I will tell you all about which one is within the dharma of each class, and the faults and qualities of each, and their merits and demerits when it comes to offspring. It should be understood that the first six as they are listed above are within the dharma of a Brahmin, the last four are for a Kshatriya, and these same four, with the exception of the ogre marriage, are for a Vaishya or a Shudra. Some sages think that the first four are enjoined for a Brahmin, only one, the ogre marriage, for a Kshatriya, and the demonic for a Vaishya and a Shudra. But here, in this law book, three of the (last) five (the marriages in the manner of Prajapati, the Gandharvas, and the ogres) are within dharma, but two – the marriages in the manner of the ghouls and the demons – are not within dharma and are never to be performed. Two of the marriages mentioned above, those according to the

Gandharvas and the ogres, are regarded as within the dharma of Kshatriyas, whether they are used separately or combined.

A marriage is known as following the dharma of a Brahma marriage when a man dresses his daughter and adorns her and summons a man who knows the Vedas and is moral, and himself gives her to him as a gift. They say a marriage is in the dharma of the gods when a man adorns his daughter and gives her as a gift to a sacrificial priest, in the course of a properly performed sacrifice. It is called a sages' dharma when he gives away his daughter according to the rules, after receiving from the bridegroom, in keeping with dharma, a cow and a bull, or two cows and bulls. The tradition calls it the rule of Prajapati when a man gives away his daughter after adorning her and saying to the couple, 'May the two of you together fulfil dharma.'

It is called a demonic dharma when the maiden is given to a man because he desires her himself, when he has given as much wealth as he can to her relatives and to the maiden herself. The ritual is known as a Gandharva marriage when the bride and her groom unite with one another because they want to, as a result of the desire for sexual intercourse. The wedding is called the rule of the ogres when a man forcibly carries off a maiden out of her house, screaming and weeping, after he has killed, wounded, or beaten (her and/or her relatives). The lowest and most evil of marriages, known as that of the ghouls, takes place when a man secretly seduces a girl who is asleep, drunk, or out of her mind.

. . . .

A man should approach his wife sexually during her fertile period, and always find his sexual pleasure in his own wife; and when he desires sexual pleasure he may go to her to whom he is vowed, except on the days at the junctures (*parvans*). The natural fertile season of a woman lasts for sixteen nights, according to the tradition, though these include four special days that are disapproved of by good people. For among these nights, the first four, the eleventh, and the thirteenth are disallowed; the other ten nights are allowed. On the even nights, sons are conceived, and on the uneven nights, daughters; therefore, a man who wants sons should unite with his wife during her fertile season on the even nights. A male child is born when the seed of the man is greater (than that of the woman), and a female child when the seed of the woman is greater (than that of the man); if both are equal, a hermaphrodite is born, or a boy and a girl; and if the seed is weak or scanty, there will be a miscarriage. A man who avoids women on the disallowed nights and on eight other nights is regarded as a chaste student, no matter which of the four stages of life he is in. (Manu 3.4–34, 3.45–50).

5.3.2 Women not to sleep with

Note how much shorter this is than the Kamasutra's *list of (married) women to sleep with, below, sections 5.3.3 and 5.3.4; Manu, by contrast (5.3.1), gives for more prohibitions than permissions.*

The following women are not to be approached for sex: a leper, a lunatic, a woman who has fallen from her caste, or who tells secrets, or who asks (for sex) publicly, a woman whose youth is almost entirely gone, one who is too light or too dark, bad-smelling, a close relative, a good friend, a female ascetic, or the wife of a relative, of a friend, of a learned Brahmin, or of a king. (*Kamasutra* 1.5.29)

5.3.3 Married women to sleep with

This passage is a good example of 'alternative Hinduism': for a religion that puts so much emphasis on marital chastity, such detailed attention to the actualities of adultery is an important counterpoise, showing just how theoretical the 'mainstream' texts on this issue are.

When men of the four classes enjoy sex according to dharma, with virgins of their own caste, it is a means of getting lawful progeny and a good reputation, and does not conflict with the customs of the world. But one is not allowed to enjoy sex with women of classes higher than one's own, or with women of one's own class who have already been had by other men. However, it is neither required nor forbidden to enjoy sex with women of classes below one's own, with women who have been banished from their own caste, with professional whores, or with women who have already been 'married' twice. There is only one reason to have sex with such women, and that is for the sake of pleasure. The women with whom one may have sex (Nayikas) are, therefore, of three sorts: maidens; women who have been 'married' twice; and professional whores.

Gonikaputra, however, has argued that there is a fourth sort of woman to whom one may make love, even if she has already been married to another man; this is a woman whom one takes because of some special reason. For example, when a man thinks, 'This woman does whatever she wants to do, and has ruined her virtue already with many lovers other than me; even though she is of a class higher than mine, I can go to her as I would go to a whore, without injuring my dharma.' Or he may think, 'This woman was widowed as a virgin and remarried; she has been mounted by others before me; there is no reason to hesitate here.' Or, 'This woman has her husband under her thumb, and he is a great and powerful man who is very close with my enemy. If she becomes very close to me, out of her love for me she will get her husband to turn away from my enemy.' Or, 'Her husband, who is powerful, is against me and wishes to harm me; she will change his attitude to me.' Or, 'If I make her my friend, I will be able to do favours for my friends, or hurt my enemies, or accomplish some other difficult undertaking.'

Or, 'If I become intimate with this woman, and kill her husband, I will get for myself his great wealth and power, which ought to be mine.' Or, 'There is no danger involved in my having this woman, and there is a chance of wealth. Since I have no property and no way of making a living, this is the way that I will get a lot of money, from her, with very little trouble.' Or, 'This woman is madly in love with me and knows all my weaknesses. If I don't want her, she will ruin me by publicly exposing my faults. Or she will accuse me of some fault which I don't in fact have, but which will be easy to believe of me and hard to clear myself of, and this will be the ruin of me. Or else maybe she will cause a break between me and her husband, who is an important man but under her control, and she will get him to join my enemies; or she herself will attach herself to my enemies.' Or, 'This woman's husband has defiled the women of my harem; I will therefore defile *his* wives in return.' Or, 'The king has ordered me to kill his enemy, who is hiding (in this woman's house). I will kill him (by seducing her).'

Or, 'Another woman, whom I love, is in the power of this woman. I will get to the one I want by my connection with this one.' Or, 'This woman will help me to get a maiden who is under her control, a maiden hard to get, rich and beautiful.' Or, 'My enemy is a close friend of this woman's husband. I will get him to have an affair with her.'

For these and similar reasons one may resort even to the wife of another man. But it should not be done merely because of passion, rashly. So much for the reasons for taking another man's wife. (*Kamasutra* 1.5.1–21)

5.3.4 Married women who will sleep with you

The following are women who can be gotten without any trouble, who can be had by means of mere perseverance: a woman who stands at the door; who looks out from her porch on to the main street; who hangs about the house of the young man who is her neighbour; who is always staring (at you); a woman sent as a messenger, who looks sideways at you; one whose husband has taken a co-wife for no good reason; who hates her husband, or is hated by him; who has no one to look after her; who has no children; who is always in the house of her relatives; whose children have died; who is fond of society; who is addicted to pleasure; the wife of an actor; a young woman whose husband has died; a poor woman fond of enjoying herself; the wife of the oldest of several brothers; a woman who is very proud; a woman whose husband is inadequate; a woman who is proud of her skills; a woman who is distressed by her husband's foolishness or by his lack of distinction or by his greediness; a woman who was chosen as a bride when she still a young girl, but somehow was not obtained by that man, and now has been married to someone else; a woman who longs for a man whose intelligence, nature, and wisdom are compatible with hers and not contrary to her own personality; a woman who is by nature given to taking sides; a woman who has been dishonoured (by her husband) when she had done nothing wrong; one who is put down by women whose beauty and so forth are the same as hers; whose husband travels a lot; the wife of a man who is jealous, foul-smelling, too clean, impotent, lazy, unmanly, a hunchback, a dwarf, deformed, a jeweller, vulgar, bad-smelling, sick, or old. (*Kamasutra* 5.1.52–4)

5.3.5 Married women who will not sleep with you

The Kamasutra classifies men and women into animal types, according to the intensity of their passion and the size of their sexual organs; men are (in descending order) stallions, bulls, and hares; women are elephants, mares, and deer. This physiological factor is mentioned in the discussion of adultery, but is by far outweighed by the subtle attention to psychological and even sociological factors – among which the concern for dharma (so central to most Hindu discussions of law and ethics) is merely a casual, last-minute consideration.

A woman desires whatever attractive man she sees, and so does a man desire every attractive woman. But for various considerations, the matter goes no farther. This is what Gonikaputra says . . .

Here are the reasons why a (married) woman rejects a man: affection for her husband, regard for her children, the fact that she is past her prime, or overwhelmed by unhappiness, or unable to find an opportunity to get away from her husband; or because she gets angry and thinks, 'He is propositioning me in an insulting way'; or because she lacks imagination and thinks, 'This is unthinkable'; or because she thinks, 'He will soon go away' or 'He has no tie to me; he is attached to someone else'; or because she is frightened and thinks, 'His face cannot keep a secret,' or, 'His affection and regard are all for his friends'; or because she fears that his attachment to her is light; or because she is diffident, regarding him as glamorous; or if she is a 'deer-woman' of slight build and little passion she may fear, 'He is too passionate and forceful'; or she may be embarrassed when she thinks, 'He is a man about town and accomplished in all the arts'; or she may feel, 'He has always treated me just as a friend'; or she may be displeased with him for his lack of knowledge of the right time and place, or despise him for his low status; or she may be disgusted when she thinks, 'Though I have given him hints with my face and gestures, he does not understand'; or if she is an 'elephant-woman' of large build and strong passion she may think, 'He is a "hare-man" of weak passion'; or she may feel pity for him and think, 'I would not want anything unpleasant to happen to him because of me'; or she may become depressed when she sees her own shortcomings, or afraid when she thinks, 'If I am discovered, I will be thrown out by my own people'; or she will not respect him because he has grey hair; or she may worry that he has been employed by her husband to test her; or she may have regard for dharma. (*Kamasutra* 5.1.8, 5.17–43)

5.3.6 The karma of marriage: the king's wife, the Brahmin's wife, and the ogre

This is a story about the dharma of marriage, the transfer of karma, the 'eating' or 'enjoying' of sex, food, and karma (the same Sanskrit verb applies to all three); and the interwining of the lives of the king and his people, especially Brahmins.

King Uttanapada had a son named Uttama ('Supreme'), the child of his queen Suruci, famous, powerful, and courageous. He was the very soul of dharma, noble, a king wealthy in aggressiveness, surpassing all creatures, like the sun in his valour. He was the same to an enemy and to a friend, to an opponent and to his own son, since he knew dharma; to an evil man he was like Yama, king of the dead, but to a good man he was like Soma. And, knowing dharma, that son of Uttanapada married a woman named Bahula, of the race of Babhru, just as the supreme Indra married Saci. His heart was always excessively affectionate toward her, just as the moon's heart always takes its place in the constellation Rohini. His mind did not become attached to any other object; the heart of that king depended upon her even in his dreams. Simply from looking at her lovely body his eyes made his body hot; and when he touched her body, he melted into her.

But the voice of the king, even though it was so loving, disturbed her hearing; and she regarded even his great respect for her as a humiliation. She disdained the garland that he gave her, and all the beautiful jewels. She would get up as if half-drunk when he was drinking the finest liquor; and when the king was eating and would hold her hand just for a moment, she would eat only a very little food and show that she was not very happy. Thus, though he was so loving toward her, she was not very loving toward him; but this simply made the excessive passion of the king grow even greater.

Then, one day, when the king was engaged in drinking, and all the other kings were looking on, and they were surrounded by courtesans and were being serenaded by sweet sounds, he very respectfully placed in the queen's hand a drinking goblet full of wine. But she did not wish to take that goblet, and she turned away, before the eyes of all the kings. That made the king furious; he summoned a door-keeper, hissing like a snake – for she whom he loved had repelled her unloved husband – and he said, 'Door-keeper, take this hard-hearted woman to a deserted forest and leave her there right away; do not hesitate about this command of mine.' Then the door-keeper, regarding the king's command as something about which there must be no hesitation, put the beautiful queen in a carriage and abandoned her in a forest. And when the king had had her abandoned in the forest in this way, and she didn't see him, she considered that he had done her a great favour. But the king, the son of Uttanapada, was tormented by his passion for her; his heart and soul ached, and he found no other wife. He remembered her, with her lovely body, day and night, ceaselessly. He carried on governing his kingdom, protecting his subjects with dharma, caring for his subjects as if he were a father and they were the sons sprung from his loins.

Then a certain Brahmin came there and with an aching heart said to the king, 'Great king, I am very unhappy; listen while I tell you about it, for the cure for the sufferings of men comes from nowhere but the king. While I was asleep, during the night, someone stole my wife, without even breaking open the door of the house. You must bring her back.' The king said, 'Don't you know who stole her or where she was brought to? Who am I to fight with? Where am I to bring her back from?' The Brahmin said, 'While I was sleeping in my house, with the door shut just as tight as could be, someone stole my wife

– I've already told you that. You are our guardian, your majesty, whom we hire by giving you a sixth of our wealth. And therefore men sleep at night without worrying about your dharma.'

The king said, 'I've never seen your wife. What sort of looks does she have, what sort of body? How old is she, and how patient? Tell me, what sort of character does your Brahmin lady have?' The Brahmin said, 'She has piercing eyes and is very tall; she has short arms, and a bony face. Her belly hangs down, and she has flat buttocks and small breasts. She is very ugly, your majesty; I am not blaming her, that's just the way she is. Her speech is coarse, too, your majesty, and her nature is not at all gentle. That is how I would describe my wife; she is hideous to look at. And she has ever so slightly passed her prime. That is what my wife looks like; I am telling you the truth.'

The king said, 'You've had enough of her, Brahmin; I will give you another wife. A pretty wife will bring you happiness; that sort is a source of misery. Lack of beauty may sometimes be a cause of a very good character; but a woman who lacks both beauty and character should be abandoned. Yours was carried off by someone else.' The Brahmin said, 'It is written in scripture, your majesty: "Protect your wife." When the wife is protected, the offspring are protected. For one's self is born in one's offspring; and when the offspring are protected, the self is protected. So she must be protected, your majesty. If she is not protected, the various classes will become commingled, and that will cause one's previous ancestors to fall from heaven, your majesty. Every day that I live without a wife, I lose dharma, because I have ceased to perform the obligatory rituals, and that, too, will cause me to fall. My future line of descendants is in her, your majesty; she is the one who will give you the sixth part (of our income); she is the cause of dharma. That is why I have described to you the wife that was stolen from me, my lord; bring her back, since you are the supreme authority for protection.'

When the king heard this speech, he thought about it. Then he mounted his chariot, that was equipped with all the things that one might want. He wandered this way and that way over the earth in that chariot until he saw in a great forest a superb hermitage for ascetics; he dismounted and entered in, and there he saw a sage seated on a silk cushion, blazing with glory, as it were. When the sage saw that the king had arrived, he stood up hastily and welcomed him respectfully; then he said to his pupil, 'Bring the water to greet the guest.' But the pupil said to him, quietly, 'Why should he be given the water of greeting, great sage? Think about it and command me, and I will do what you command.' Then the Brahmin realised what had happened to the king, and he honoured him merely by giving him conversation and a place to sit. The sage said, 'For what reason have you come here, and what do you wish to do? I know that you are king Uttama, the son of Uttanapada.'

The king said, 'Great sage, someone – I don't know who – stole a Brahmin's wife right out of the house, and I have come here in search of her. I have come to your house and bow before you; and I hope that out of your pity for me you will tell me what I ask of you.' 'Ask me, your majesty', said the sage, 'and do not worry about what can be asked. If it is something that I can tell you, I will tell you truly.' The king said, 'When you first saw me arrive at your house, great sage, you were about to give me the water with which a guest is welcomed; why, then, was it withheld?' The sage said, 'The minute I saw you, in my haste I gave a command to this pupil, but then he admonished me. By my grace, he knows what is to come in this universe, just as I know what has happened and is happening everywhere. When he said, "Consider, and then command", then I knew. That is why I did not give you the water for a guest. In truth, your majesty, you deserve the water, since you, Uttama, are born in the family of the self-created Manu; nevertheless, we think that you are not fit to receive the water.'

The king said, 'What did I do, Brahmin, knowingly or unknowingly, so that I do not deserve the water from you, though I have arrived from a great distance?' The sage said, 'What, have you forgotten that you abandoned your wife in the forest? Your majesty, you abandoned your entire dharma along with her. A man whose ritual life has been ruined becomes untouchable for a fortnight; so you whose obligatory rituals have been ruined (are untouchable) for a year. Just as an affectionate wife must put up with a husband even if he lacks good character, so too, even if a wife has a bad character, she must be supported. The wife of that Brahmin, the one who was stolen, was unpleasant; but, nevertheless, because he wished for dharma, he has outshone you. You set other people straight when they deviate from their dharma, great king; but who else is there who will set you straight when you deviate from your own dharma?'

The king was truly embarrassed when that wise man talked to him like that. 'Yes', he said. And then he asked the sage about the Brahmin's wife who had been stolen: 'Sir, who stole the Brahmin's wife, and where did he take her? You know the past and the future in this universe, without any error.' The sage said, 'An ogre named Balaka, the son of Adri, took her. You will see her today in the Utpalavataka forest, your majesty. Go and reunite the Brahmin with his wife right away. Don't let him become a breeding ground for sin day after day, like you.'

The king bowed before the great sage and mounted his chariot and went to the Utpalavataka wood that he had mentioned. And there the king saw the Brahmin's wife, who looked just as her husband had described her. She was eating bilva fruits. He asked her, 'Good woman, how did you come to this forest? Tell me plainly: are you the wife of Susharman Vaishali?' The Brahmin lady said, 'I am the daughter of Atiratra, a Brahmin who lives in the forest, and I am the wife of Vaishali, whose name you just uttered. I was stolen by a bad ogre named Balaka; while I slept inside my house, I was separated from my brothers and my mother. Someone should burn to ashes that ogre who separated me in this way from my mother and brothers, and from others; I am living here in great misery. He brought me into this very deep forest, but then he abandoned me; I don't know why it is that he enjoyed me neither carnally nor carnivorously, neither for the pleasures of the flesh nor for the pleasure of flesh.'

The king said, 'Do you happen to know where the ogre went when he had let you go? Your husband sent me here, O giver of joy to Brahmins.' The Brahmin lady said, 'The night-wandering ogre is staying inside this very forest. Go in and see – unless you're afraid.' He entered on the path that she had indicated, and saw the ogre, who was surrounded by his troops. The moment that the ogre saw the king, he made haste from afar to touch his head to the earth, and then he approached the king's feet and said, 'By coming here to my house you have done me a great favour. Command me; what can I do for you? For I live within your political domain. Please accept this welcoming water and take this seat. We are your servants; you are our master. Command me absolutely.'

The king said, 'You have done everything, and rendered me all recompense. But for what purpose did you bring the Brahmin's wife here, night-wanderer? She is not good-looking; there are other wives, if you stole her for that. And if you brought her here to eat her, why haven't you eaten her? Tell me that.' The ogre said, 'We don't eat people; those are other ogres, your majesty. But we eat the fruit of a good deed. And I will tell you about the fruit of a good deed: that is how I came to be reborn in the cruel and terrifying womb of an ogre. When we are dishonoured, we eat the very nature of men and women. But we do not eat flesh; we do not eat living creatures. When we eat the patience of men, they become angry; when we have eaten their evil nature, they become virtuous. We have gorgeous female ogres who are the equal of the celestial nymphs when it comes to beauty. While they are here, how could we take sexual pleasure in human females?'

The king said, 'If you want her neither for your bed nor for your table, night-wanderer, then why did you enter the Brahmin's house and steal her?' The ogre said, 'That Brahmin is outstanding when it comes to knowing mantras; as I went to sacrifice after sacrifice, he would recite the mantra that destroys ogres and prevent me from doing my job. We're starving because of the ritual of mantras that he uses to keep us from making our living. Where can we go? That Brahmin is the officiating priest in all the sacrifices. Therefore we brought this deficiency upon him: without a wife, a man is not fit to perform the rituals of sacrifice.'

When he said the word 'deficiency', referring to the Brahmin, the king became deeply depressed, thinking, 'He is talking about the Brahmin's deficiency, but truly I am the one that he censures. And that excellent sage also said that I did not deserve the water for a guest. Since the ogre, too, spoke to me about the deficiency of that Brahmin, I must really be in a very tight spot as a result of not having a wife.' As the king was thinking these thoughts, the ogre spoke to him again, bowing low to the king and cupping his hands in reverence: 'Your majesty, do me the favour of giving me a command as I bow before you, your servant who lives in your realm.' The king said, 'Night-wanderer, since you did say, "We eat the very nature . . .," listen to what we would like you to do. Eat the evil nature of this Brahmin lady, right now. When you have eaten her evil nature, she may become nice. Then take her to the house of the man whose wife she is. When this is done, you will have done all that can be done for me as one who has come to your house.'

Thereupon, by the king's command, the ogre used his own power of illusion to enter inside the woman and eat her evil nature. And when he had stripped the Brahmin's wife of her extremely fierce evil nature, she said to the king, 'By the ripening of the fruits of my own karma, I was separated from my noble husband; this night-wanderer was merely the proximate cause of that. The fault was not his, nor that of my noble husband; the fault is mine, no one else's; one eats the fruit of what one has done oneself. In another life, I separated myself from some man; and that separation has now fallen upon me; what fault could there be in my noble husband?'

The ogre said, 'My lord, I will take her to her husband's house, as you command. But command me to do whatever else can be done for you, your majesty.' The king said, 'When this is done, you have done everything for me, heroic night-wanderer. But come to me whenever I think of you, when the times comes for something to be done.' 'Yes!' said the ogre, and then he took the Brahmin's wife – who was purified and without her evil nature – and brought her quickly to her husband's house.

Now, when the king had sent the woman to her husband's house, he sighed and thought, 'What good deed could there be in this? The noble sage said that I was wretched because I was unfit for the offering of water to a guest, and this night-wanderer spoke of deficiency, referring to the Brahmin. I abandoned my wife. How shall I act? I shall ask that incomparable sage, who has the eye of knowledge.' Reasoning in this way, the king mounted his chariot and went to the dwelling of the great sage – the soul of dharma, knower of past, present and future. He dismounted from his chariot, approached the sage, bowed to him, and told him what had happened to him: how he had met the ogre, and seen the Brahmin woman, and how her evil nature had vanished, and how he had sent her to her husband's house, and the reason for his own return.

The sage said, 'I already knew what you had done, your majesty, and your reason for coming back to me with an aching heart: you came to ask me, "What am I to do about this?" Now that you have come, your majesty, listen to what you must do. A wife is a powerful cause of dharma, profit, and pleasure for men; in particular, a man who abandons a wife is abandoned by dharma. A man who has no wife, your majesty, is not fit to perform the obligatory rituals, whether he is a Brahmin, a Kshatriya, a Vaishya, or a Shudra. When you abandoned your wife, you didn't do a very good thing; for just as women should not abandon a husband, so too men should not abandon a wife.'

The king said, 'Sir, what shall I *do*? This was the ripening of my karmas, that made me abandon her because she was not affectionate to me when I was affectionate toward her. Whatever one does one endures with an aching heart and an inner soul that fears separation. But she was abandoned in the forest, and now I do not know where she has gone. Maybe she was eaten in the forest by lions or tigers or night-wandering ogres.'

The sage said, 'She has not been eaten, your majesty, by lions or tigers or night-wandering ogres. She is now in the subterranean watery world, but there is still no stain on her character.' The king said, 'Who took her to the subterranean world? And how did she come to remain unstained? This is most marvellous, Brahmin; you must tell me how it happened.'

The sage said, 'In the subterranean world there is a Naga king, the famous Kapotaka. He saw her when you had abandoned her and she was wandering around in the great forest. And since the young woman has both beauty and good character, he fell in love with her, declared his intentions to her, and carried her to the subterranean world. Now, the wise Naga king has a beautiful daughter named Nanda, your majesty; and he also has a charming wife. When the daughter saw your queen, more beautiful than her mother, she thought, "This woman will become the rival co-wife of my mother," and so she brought her to her own house and hid her in the inner apartments of the women there. But when Nanda was asked (for the queen), she refused to give any answer; and so her father said to his daughter, "You will become mute." The daughter remained there, under this curse; and your wife, that was carried off by the Naga king, is still kept there by his daughter, and is still chaste.'

The king, rejoicing, asked that outstanding Brahmin the cause of his own bad luck with regard to the woman he loved: 'Sir,' said the king, 'everyone likes me very much, but my own wife is not very fond of me; what is the cause of this? I long for her excessively, even more than for my own vital breath, great sage; but she is badly disposed toward me. Tell me the reason for that, Brahmin.' The sage said, 'At the moment when you took her hand in the marriage ceremony, the sun, Mars, and Saturn looked down on you, and Venus and Jupiter looked down on your wife. At that moment, the moon was for you, and Mercury, the son of the moon, was for her. These two groups are inimical to one another, and very inimical to you, your majesty. Now, go and protect the earth according to your own dharma; with your wife as your assistant, perform all the rituals of dharma.' When king Uttama heard this, he bowed to the sage, mounted his chariot, and went back to his own city.

When he arrived at his own city, the king saw the Brahmin, now joyously united with his wife, who now had a good character. The Brahmin said, 'Best of kings, I have achieved my aims, since you who know dharma have protected dharma and brought my wife back to me.' The king said, 'You have indeed achieved your aims, incomparable Brahmin, by protecting your own dharma. But we are in a tight spot, since we do not have a wife in the house.' 'Great king,' said the Brahmin, 'if she has been devoured by beasts of prey in the forest, you should not disregard dharma by allowing anger to overpower you. Enough of her; why don't you take the hand of another woman in marriage, your majesty? There are beautiful maidens in the houses of kings.' The king said, 'The woman I love was not eaten by beasts of prey; she is alive, and her character is still unstained. How shall I act in this matter?'

The Brahmin said, 'If your wife is alive and has not gone astray in her virtue, why do you ruin your whole life by living without a wife?' The king said, 'Because even if I brought her back, she is always unpleasant to me; she causes me misery, not happiness. Enough of her! She is no friend of mine. Whatever you did, Brahmin, to gain power over your beautiful wife, make the same effort to give me power over my wife.' The Brahmin said, 'There is a ritual called "the desire of a lover" that will make her fond of you, and I will also perform the ritual of "finding a friend", which people use when they want friends. For it produces fondness between two people who are not fond of one another, and it generates the greatest affection between a wife and husband. I will do that sacrifice for you, your majesty. Wherever your lovely wife is, bring her here from there; she will become extremely fond of you, your majesty.' When he heard this, the king collected all the things needed for the ritual, and the Brahmin performed the sacrifice. Seven times the Brahmin performed that sacrifice, again and again, in order to give the king his wife. And when the great Brahmin sage thought that he had made her friendly to her own husband, he said to the king, 'Bring here, close to you, the woman you long for, your majesty. Enjoy all pleasures with her, and perform the sacrifices with reverence.'

The king was amazed at the Brahmin's words, and then he remembered that most virile night-wanderer, who kept his promises. As soon as he thought of him, he came to the king immediately, bowed to him, and said, 'What can I do for you?' Then the king told him, at great length; and the ogre went to the subterranean world, took the king's wife, and returned. As soon as she was brought back, she looked upon her husband with ecstatic joy and said, 'Forgive me,' over and over, overflowing with happiness. The king embraced her violently and said to the proud woman, 'My darling, I do forgive you. Why do you keep saying that?' His wife said, 'If your heart has truly forgiven me, then I want to ask you for a favour; do it to honour me.' The king said, 'Speak without hesitation and tell me what you desire from me. There is nothing you cannot get from me, my darling; I am entirely at your disposal.'

His wife said, 'My friend, the daughter of the Naga, was cursed by him for my sake: "You will be mute," he said, and she became mute. If, out of your fondness for me, you are able to find a cure for her and to remove the impediment to her speech, then there is nothing that you will not have done for me.' The king said to the Brahmin, 'What ritual is there for this, to dispel her muteness?' The Brahmin replied to the king, 'Your majesty, I will perform a sacrifice to Sarasvati, the goddess of speech, by your command; and your wife here will pay her debt by restoring her friend's speech.' Then that excellent Brahmin performed the sacrifice to Sarasvati on her behalf, muttering all the verses to Sarasvati with deep concentration.

In the underworld, the girl regained her speech, and a sage there, named

Garga, said to her, 'This very difficult favour was done for you by your friend's husband.' When she learned this, Nanda the Naga's daughter went quickly to the city and embraced the queen, her friend, and praised the king over and over again with sweet and auspicious words. Then the Naga woman sat down and said, 'Great hero, you have just done me a favour, and so my heart goes out to you. Listen to what I say. You will have a son of great heroism; he will wield an unchallenged wheel of power upon the earth. He will truly know all the Shastras on politics and will be intent upon the practice of dharma; he will be a Manu, the wise ruler of this interval of Manu.' And when she had given him this boon, the daughter of the Naga king embraced her friend again and went back to the underworld.

The noble king made love to his wife for a very long time, while he continued to rule his subjects, and then she bore him a son, like the lovely full-orbed moon that is born on full-moon day. When he was born, all the people rejoiced, together with the gods; the drums of heaven roared, and showers of flowers fell from heaven. Seeing that his form and character would be lovely, all the assembled sages called him Auttama ('The best'), saying, 'The boy was born in the family of Uttama ('Supreme'), and he was born at the best time, and he has the best limbs; so he will be "The Best". And so Uttama's son became famous under the name of Auttama; he was a Manu, with the power of a Manu.

Whoever listens constantly to the story of Uttama and to the life of Uttama will never be hated by the wives he loves or by his sons or relatives; nor will anyone who hears or recites this story ever experience separation from anyone. (*Markandeya Purana* 66.3–37, 43–69; 67.1–39; 68.1–29; 69.1–41)

5.4 PUBLIC LIFE: HOW TO TEST YOUR MINISTERS

The Arthashastra, *or textbook on politics, is attributed to Kautilya, the minister of the Mauryan emperor Candragupta in the second century B.C. It is a compendium of advice for a king; and its advice is cynical to the point of Machiavellianism. In addition to much technical information on the running of a kingdom, it also contains – like all* shastras *– a good deal of thought on the subject of human psychology; this, too, is cynical.*

Determine the purity or impurity of ministers by means of temptations. With the assistance of his prime minister and his domestic chaplain, the king should use temptations to purify his ministers in order to establish them in offices which are appropriate to them.

The king should command his domestic chaplain to teach the Vedas or perform a sacrifice for someone for whom it is forbidden to perform a sacrifice, and then, when the chaplain cannot bear to do this, the king should dismiss him. Then the chaplain, through his agents, should approach each of the ministers, one by one, and swear an oath and whisper, 'This king violates dharma. Very well. Let's set up in his place another king who respects dharma, one who comes from the same family, or has been kept in prison, or an independent king from a good family, a neighbouring king, perhaps, even a tribal chieftain, or an arriviste. This suits all of us; what about you?' If anyone refuses, he is pure. This is the temptation of dharma.

The king should dismiss his general for taking things that he shouldn't take. Then the general, through his agents, should approach each of the ministers, one by one, and whisper to them about killing the king in order to get wealth that they are greedy for; they should say, 'This suits all of us; what about you?' If anyone refuses, he is pure. This is the temptation of wealth.

A (woman disguised as a) wandering female ascetic should gain the confidence of the harem; then she should do favours for each of the prime ministers, and whisper to them, one by one, 'The chief queen is in love with you and has found a way for you and her to be together; there will be a lot of money, too.' If anyone refuses, he is pure. This is the temptation of lust.

One minister should get all the other ministers to sail with him on a ship, and the king, becoming anxious about this, should arrest them all. Another man should be there in prison, pretending to have been arrested already, and he should approach them, now that they have been stripped of their money and their honour, and whisper to them, one by one, 'This king has set out to do a bad thing. Very well. Let's kill him and set up another king in his place. This suits all of us; what about you?' If anyone refuses, he is pure. This is the temptation of fear.

Those who prove to be pure after the temptation of dharma should be employed by the king in jobs to purify the country of the human thorns in the side of dharma; those who prove to be pure after the temptation of wealth should be employed in jobs involving the collecting of funds, such as tax-collector or treasurer; those who prove to be pure after the temptation of lust should be used as guards in the women's quarters, both the inner apartments and the outside pleasure grounds; those who prove to be pure after the temptation of fear should be used as the king's bodyguards. And those who remain pure in the face of all temptations he should make his ministers. Those who prove impure in all ways he should employ in managing mines, forests, and elephant farms.

Our teachers have determined that the king should employ, each in his own appropriate job, according to his particular purity, ministers who have proven pure with respect to each of the three goals of human life (dharma, wealth, and desire), plus fear. But the king should definitely not make himself or his queen a target to test the purity of his ministers; this is Kautilya's opinion. Nor should he ever corrupt someone who is not corrupt, as one might befoul water with poison; for there may not be any cure for someone who has become corrupt; the intellect of good people, once it has been made foul by the four kinds of temptation, may go on to the end and stay there stubbornly, never turning back. Therefore the king should use some external object in this four-fold undertaking and use his agents to track down the purity and impurity of his ministers. (*Arthashastra* 1.10.1–20)

5.5 DEATH

5.5.1 How to die and go to hell

This story is a continuation of the conversation between the young man nicknamed Jada and his father. In section 5.2.1, above, Jada, who remembers his past lives, explained how embryos were conceived and born; here he tells what happens after death – or, if you prefer (as the Hindus do), before conception.

(The boy said to his father:)

Listen, father, and I will tell you truly, just as I experienced it repeatedly, the whole wheel of rebirth, that never ages or stands still. I will tell it all to you, father, if I have your permission, beginning with the moment of departure, as no one else will tell it.

Heat, impelled by a sharp wind, is agitated upward in the body; it bursts the vital places open, blazing without any fuel. Then the upward-moving vital breath starts upward, thus obstructing the downward movement of water and food that has been digested. If a man has been habitually generous about giving water and food and liquids, all that he has given now brings him refreshment in his moment of distress. A man who gave food with a mind purified by faith now becomes satisfied even without any food at all. And if a man has never told lies, or ruined anyone else's pleasure, and if he is a faithful believer in the gods, he experiences an easy death. People who have always taken pleasure in worshipping the gods and Brahmins, and who have never envied others, who have spoken fairly and been generous and modest, those men die happy. A man who has never abandoned dharma because of lust or rashness or hatred, who has done as he is told and is gentle, he finds an easy death.

But men who have not been donors of water or food find burning thirst and hunger when the time of their death comes upon them. People who have given money overcome cold; those who have given sandalwood paste overcome heat; and those who have never caused anyone any distress overcome the painful suffering that destroys the vital breath. Those who have caused delusion and ignorance find great fear, and the worst men are oppressed by terrible torments. A false witness, a liar, and a man who teaches wrong things, they all die in delirium, and so do those who revile the Vedas.

Then come the hard-hearted men of Yama, terrifying, foul-smelling, with hammers and maces in their hands. When they have come within the dying man's line of sight, he begins to tremble; ceaselessly he screams for his brother, mother, children. His voice stutters and has a single pitch; his gaze wanders in terror, and his mouth grows dry with his fast breathing. His breath becomes loud, and his sight fails; he is full of pain, and then he leaves his body. Preceded by his vital wind, he takes on another body of the same form, a body born of his own karma in order for him to be tortured, not a body born of the mother and father; and its life-span and constitution are the same as those of the one before.

Then the messenger of Yama quickly binds him with cruel bonds and drags him to the south, bewildering him with blows of his stick. To a place that is rough with sharp *kusha* grass, thorns, ants, stakes, and rocks, where there is a blazing fire and hundreds of pits, and a blazing hot sun burning with its rays, he is dragged by Yama's messengers, who terrify him with their jackal howls. Dragged about by these horrible messengers, and eaten by hundreds of jackals, the man of evil karma sets out on the terrible road to the house of Yama. Humans who have been donors of umbrellas and sandals, or of clothing, travel that road in comfort, and so do people who are donors of food; and men who have given away land ride in shining carriages. But a man who is oppressed by evil helplessly experiences pain as he is led for twelve days to the city of the king of dharma. When his corpse is being burnt, he experiences terrible burning; and when it is beaten he suffers too, and when it is cut he suffers intense agony. When a man('s body) stays wet for a very long time he suffers miserably, even if by the ripening of his own karma he has gone to another body. But whatever water, together with sesamum seeds, his relatives offer (in the rites for dead relatives), and whatever balls of rice they offer, he eats that as he is being led along. When his relatives rub his (dead) body with oil and massage his limbs, that nourishes and strengthens a man (in hell), and so does whatever his relatives eat. A dead man who does not (take the form of a ghost and) bother his relatives on earth too much when they are asleep and dreaming is nourished and strengthened by them as they give him gifts (in the form of the offerings to his departed soul). As he is being led, he sees his own house for twelve days, and he consumes the water and balls of rice and so forth that are given to him then on earth.

Then, after twelve days, as he is dragged forward, the man sees the horrible, terrifying dwelling-place of Yama. As soon as he has arrived there, he sees Yama himself, who looks like a mass of powdered black collyrium with very red eyes, standing in the midst of Death, Time, the Ender, and so forth. His mouth gapes open with monstrous teeth, and his face is terrible when he frowns; and he is surrounded by hundreds of diseases, deformed, terrifying, twisted. He holds his big stick and has great arms; he is dreadful with his nooses in his hands. And then the man goes to the good or bad place that Yama points out for him.

The man who bears false witness or tells lies goes to the hell called Terrible (Raurava), and so does a man who kills a Brahmin, when he himself has not been stung by murder, or who kills a cow or who kills his father. Also a man who takes away the wife who has been pledged to another man, or who violates the boundary of someone else's land, or who sleeps with his guru's wife or seduces a virgin. Listen while I describe to you the exact form of that Terrible hell. It extends over two thousand leagues, and is a knee-high pit, very difficult to cross over; coals are heaped up in it, level with the ground, blazing fiercely with the fuel of the heated coals. Into the middle of that pit the followers of Yama throw the man of evil karma; he runs about in it, being burnt by the intense fire. At every step, his foot is injured and torn apart, again and again, and he goes on lifting up his foot and putting it down again, day and night. When he has thus crossed over a thousand leagues, he is released; but then he goes to another hell of that sort, called Joyless (Niraya), in order to purify his evil . . .

Thus I have told you about the first hell, called Terrible. Now listen, father, to the description of the hell called the Great Terrible hell (Maharaurava). Men who have intercourse with women who are not permitted for intercourse, and who take pleasure in things that should not be eaten, who harm their friends and betray the confidence of their masters, who find their sexual pleasure in the wives of other men and shun their own wives, people who destroy roads or ruin ponds and gardens, these and other men of evil behaviour are burnt by the servants of Yama in this hell. It extends for seven times five thousand leagues. The ground there is made of copper, and under it is a blazing fire. Heated by that heat, the whole ground glows like a burst of lightning and radiates heat in a way that is intensely painful to the sight, touch, and other senses. His hands and feet bound by the followers of Yama, the man of evil deeds is thrown into the middle of that hell, and he rolls over and over in it. Then he is dragged fast along the road, where he is eaten by crows, herons, wolves, owls, scorpions, and mosquitoes, and also by vultures. As he is being burnt, he cries out over and over again, in terror and confusion and anguish, 'Father! Mother! Brother! My son!', but he finds no peace. Foul-minded men who have transgressed and committed evils are released from that hell after millions and millions of years.

Then there is another hell named Darkness, that is very cold by nature. It is as long as the Great Terrible hell and is enveloped in thick darkness. A man who has killed a cow or his brothers or an infant is brought to this cold hell. There men run about in horrible darkness, tormented by the cold, huddling up to one another and embracing one another for refuge. Their teeth fracture, chattering with the intense cold; and others run about tormented by hunger and thirst. A vicious wind carrying pieces of ice pierces their bones, and they are so tormented by hunger that they eat the marrow and blood that comes out of those bones. They wander about embracing one another, licking one another. Thus humans experience great anguish in that darkness, until the evil that they have done is used up.

Then there is another great hell, called Cutting-off. In it, father, potters' wheels revolve constantly. A man who says he has seen what he has not seen, or says he has heard what he has not heard; or a man of bad conduct who does not honour the sacred syllable 'Om' and his guru; or a man who does not listen to his guru's words or the words of the sacred texts – these evil men of bad conduct are brought to this hell by Yama's men. These men are mounted upon the wheel and cut apart by the thread of Time held in the fingers of the followers of Yama, from the soles of their feet to the tip of their heads. But they do not lose consciousness; and when they are cut into hundreds of pieces, the pieces reunite again. Men of evil karma are cut up like this for thousands of years, until there is nothing left of their evil and it is all gone.

Now listen while I describe the hell called Unsupported, where the inhabitants experience unbearable suffering. Anyone who causes obstacles to Brahmins who delight in their own dharma is bound by terrible bonds and tied to turning wheels; and on the other side are wheels and well-buckets that are used to produce pain. Men of evil karma are put on these wheels and revolve on them for a thousand years, without interruption, without ever standing still; and then another man is bound to the well-bucket wheel, and dipped into the water like a bucket. The men whirl around, vomiting blood over and over; their entrails come out in their mouths, and their eyes hang out in front. The suffering that they experience could not be borne by living creatures.

Now hear of another hell, called Sword-leaf-forest, where the ground over a thousand leagues is covered with blazing fires. People who make obstacles for chaste students or ascetics go to the Sword-leaf-forest hell, as do others who annoy good people. The living creatures that dwell in hell are constantly falling down there, where they are burnt by the fierce, cruel rays of the sun. In the middle of it there is a lovely forest with glossy leaves; but the leaves are the blades of swords. And brindled dogs howl there, by the millions, on all sides, with big mouths and big teeth, as terrifying as tigers. Now, creatures who are oppressed by thirst and heat see that forest, with its cool shade, in front of them, and they go forth into it, moaning, 'O Mother! O Father!', in their great torment, as their feet are burnt by the fiery surface of the earth. But as soon as they get there, a wind causes the sword-leaves to fall on them, and then, driven by the wind, the swords fall on top of them. At this, the creatures fall on the ground, that is a heap of blazing fire, an earth entirely pervaded by a flame that licks at them. Then those terrible brindled dogs immediately tear them apart, limb from limb, tearing up their organs and their skin as they scream. Thus, I have described the Sword-leaf-forest hell to you.

Now let me tell you about the Hot-pot hell, that is even more frightening than that one was. Everywhere it is filled with flames and red-hot pots, and those pots, heated by blazing fires, are filled with hot oil and iron filings. People who have amassed the karma of bad deeds are thrown into these pots, head downwards, by the servants of Yama – people who have defiled the Dharma Shastras or people who have defiled the holy places of pilgrimage; or a man whose wits are so deluded that he abandons a desirable woman, loving and beautiful, whom he has enjoyed – abandons her even when no fault is seen in her. Such people are brought there and cooked right away in the iron pots; they are boiled, and the hot marrow that flows from their bursting limbs clouds the water. Terrible swift vultures tear them apart, cutting off the eyes and bones from their bursting skulls, and then drop them back into the pots again. Again and again, in the bubbling and crackling oil, their bodies become whole again, united with their liquified heads, limbs, sinews, flesh, skin, and bones. Then the minions of Yama stir them up and stir them with the stirring spoons, making great eddies in the hot oil, churning up the evil-doers. Thus, father, I have told you, in considerable detail, about the Hot-pot hell.

Now, when he has crossed over all the hells, the evil man becomes born as an animal, among the worms, insects, moths, beasts of prey, mosquitoes, and so forth. Then he is born in elephants, trees, and so forth, and in cows and horses, and in other wombs that are evil and painful. When he finally becomes a human, he is a despicable hunchback or dwarf, or he is born in the womb of a woman of some tribe of Untouchables. When there is none of his evil left, and he is filled with merit, then he starts climbing up to higher castes, Shudra, Vaishya, Kshatriya, and so forth, sometimes eventually reaching the stage of Brahmin or king of men. That is how men of evil karma fall down into hells.

Now listen while I tell you how men of meritorious deeds go forth. These men go along the way of merit that Yama points out for them. There the Gandharvas sing to them and the bevies of celestial nymphs dance for them; glowing with various celestial garlands, and shining with the sweetness of pearl necklaces and anklets, they go forth immediately on very high divine carriages. And when they get down from those carriages, they are born in the families of kings and other noble people. There they maintain and protect their good conduct, and they enjoy the very best pleasures. After that they go upward; or they go down, and become men as they were before.

Thus I have told you all about what happens to a man when he dies. Sometimes a man goes to heaven; sometimes he goes to hell. Sometimes a dead man experiences both hell and heaven. Sometimes he is born here again and consumes his own karma; sometimes a man who has consumed his karma dies and goes forth with just a very little bit of karma remaining. Sometimes he is reborn here with a small amount of good and bad karma, having consumed most of his karma in heaven or in hell.

A great source of suffering in the hells is the fact that they can see the people who dwell in heaven; but (the people in hell) rejoice when (the people in heaven) fall down into hell. Likewise, there is a great misery even in heaven, beginning from the very moment when people ascend there, for this thought enters their minds: 'I am going to fall from here.' And when they see the hells they become quite miserable, worrying, day and night, 'This is where I am going to go.'

When one is dwelling in the form of an embryo, one experiences great misery because of the womb; and when one is born one has the misery of childhood and growing up. Adolescence is very hard to bear because of the pressures of lust, jealousy, and anger; old age consists mostly of misery; and death is the greatest misery of all. Dragged along by the servants of Yama and thrown into the pits of hell, again one experiences birth as an embryo, and then death, and then hell. Thus creatures are wracked on this wheel of rebirth, revolving like the buckets on the wheel of a well; they wander about, bound by the bonds of nature, and are killed over and over again. Father dear, there is no happiness at all here in this world crowded with hundreds of miseries; how, therefore, should I who am striving for release observe the religion of the three Vedas? (*Markandeya Purana* 10.47–87; 12.3–48; 10.88–97; 11.22–32)

5.5.2 The punishment to fit the crime

King Vipashcit, who is sojourning in hell, finds a way to transfer some of his good karma to the sinners there; see above, section 4.2.3 While he is still in hell, he questions a servant of Yama about the particular torments that result from particular sins. This is a part of the servant's reply:

Those base men who have gazed covetously with a sinful eye at the wives of other men, or who have had sinful, covetous thoughts about other men's possessions – birds with adamantine beaks tear out their eyes; and their eyes grow back again and again. And as many times as these evil men blinked their eyes, for that many thousands of years do they undergo the eye-torture. People who have taught false Shastras or advised that they be taught, with the purpose of destroying the proper vision even of their enemies, and people who have recited the Shastras improperly, or who have uttered false speech, or who have reviled the Vedas, the gods, and the twice-born, or their guru – cruel birds with adamantine beaks tear out their tongues, which are renewed again and again, for the same number of years.

And those base men who cause dissension between friends, between a father and a son or people of the same family, between a sacrificer and his priest, between a mother and the son who is her companion, between a wife and husband – they are torn apart with a saw. People who annoy others, and interfere with their fun, who take away their fans, breezy places, sandalwood paste, or bamboo screens; and base men who trouble dying people who have done no harm – these people who have parcelled out evil are stuck into gruel and sand. If a man has eaten the funeral offering of another man, when that man has invited him to a ritual for the gods or for the ancestors, he is torn in half by birds. A man who cuts at the vital spot of good men by speaking lies about them – these birds peck away at him ceaselessly. A man who slanders another, who dissembles in speech or thought – his tongue is split in half with sharp razors.

A proud person who looks down upon his mother, father, or guru – he hangs head-down in a pit full of pus, faeces, and urine. A man who eats when the gods, guests, other creatures, dependants or visitors still have not been fed, or when the ancestors, the fire, or the birds have not been fed, this bad person takes the form of a creature with a mouth as tiny as a needle and a stomach as big as a mountain, and in this form he eats pus and exudations. But a man who feeds different food to a Brahmin, or a man of another class, when he is in the same group as other men, this man eats faeces (in hell). And if a man has been in the company of a poor man who is involved in the same enterprise as he is, seeking money, and has eaten his own food after spurning the poor man – such a man eats phlegm (in hell).

A man who touches a cow, Brahmin, or fire before he has washed after eating – his hands are put into blazing fire pots. A man who looks at the sun, moon, or stars with desire, without washing his hands after eating – the servants of Yama place a fire in his eye and stoke it up. A man who allows his feet to touch cows, fire, his mother, a Brahmin, his eldest brother, father, or sister, or his daughter-in-law, gurus, or old people – his feet are bound with iron chains that have been heated in a fire, and he stands in the midst of a pile of hot coals that burn him up to his knees.

A man who has eaten milk, a dish of sesamum and grain, goat's flesh, or the food for the gods, without the proper ceremony – this evil man is thrown down on the ground, and as he stares with wide-open eyes, the servants of Yama tear his eyes out of his head with pincers. A base man who listens to blasphemy against gurus, gods, Brahmins, or the Vedas, taking pleasure in it – the servants of Yama thrust red-hot iron wedges again and again deep in the ears of such an evil man, ignoring his moans. A man who, under the power of anger or greed, breaks up and destroys a roadside reservoir or the home of a god or a Brahmin, or an auspicious assembly in a temple – the cruellest servants of Yama flay the skin from his body, using sharp instruments, over and over, as he screams.

If a man has urinated in the path of a cow, Brahmin, or the sun – crows drag his entrails out of his body through his rectum. If someone promises his daughter to one man but then gives her to a second man, he is chopped into many pieces and swept away in a river of acid. A man who is intent upon his own nourishment and abandons his son, servant, wife, or any other relatives, whoever they may be, in a time of famine or disturbance – the servants of Yama slice off pieces of his own flesh and put them in his own mouth, and he eats them hungrily. A man who through greed abandons those who come to him for protection, or a man who lives on bribes – the servants of Yama torment him by squeezing him in great vices. A man who has tried to prevent good deeds all his life long – he is ground up by grinding rocks, as are all men of evil karma.

A man who steals a deposit is bound with ropes on all his limbs and is bitten, day and night, by worms, scorpions, and ravens, while he grows thin from hunger, his tongue hangs out with thirst, and the back of his throat throbs with pain. An evil man who has sexual intercourse during the day, or with the wife of another man – he is made to mount a prickly silk-cotton tree; his limbs are pierced by its sharp, iron thorns and fouled by the streams of his blood as it flows out of him. Or a man who defiles the wives of other men may be put in a crucible called a 'female mouse' (a Sanskrit euphemism for the vagina) which the servants of Yama fan with bellows.

A man who in his stubborn pride puts down his teacher and goes on with his studies or his craft – he carries on his head a big rock that causes him anguish and he walks down the main street in pain, emaciated with hunger day and night, his skull throbbing with the pressure of his burden. A man who has emitted his urine, phlegm, or faeces in water – he goes to a foul-smelling hell of phlegm, faeces, and urine. People who did not feed their guests, with the proper ceremony, before they fed one another – these people now, starving, eat one another's flesh. A man who has discarded the Vedas and the sacred fire, once he has been given the sacred fire – he falls down from the tip of a high mountain, again and again. A man who marries a woman who was widowed as a virgin when he is already an old man – he becomes a worm and is eaten by ants.

A man who accepts favours from someone low, or who sacrifices for him or constantly serves him – he becomes a worm living in rocks. A man who eats sweets while he is watched by the group of his dependants, or his friend, or a guest – he eats piles of hot coals. A man who used to be a backbiter of people – the flesh of his back is constantly eaten by terrifying wolves. The lowest of all men, the man who is ungrateful to those who have done favours for him – he wanders around blind, deaf, and dumb, starving. A man who harms his friends and returns evil for good falls screaming into the Hot-pot hell and is burnt up; then into gruel and sand; then he is squeezed by the vice; then he goes to the Sword-leaf-forest and is cut up by the razor-sharp leaves; then he is cut by the thread of Time, and suffers many different torments. And I simply do not know how he will ever find a way to make restorations and get out of that place.

Wicked Brahmins who assemble at a funeral celebration and then argue with one another – they drink the froth that is exuded from (each other's) every limb. A man who steals gold, a man who kills a Brahmin, a man who drinks wine, and a man who sleeps with his guru's wife – these are burnt in a blazing fire, above them and below them and on all sides of them; they stay there for many thousands of years. Then they are born again as men marked by leprosy, consumption, diseases and other afflictions; they die again and go again to hells such as these. And they suffer from this sickness until the very end of the aeon. A man who kills a cow goes to hell for a shorter time, just for three births, and so does one who has committed one of the minor sins; this is a fixed rule.

When men who have committed major sins get out of hell, they go forth to be born in various different wombs. (*Markandeya Purana* 14.39–96)

5.5.3 How not to go to hell

This conversation takes place after a woman named Savitri has gone to the world of the dead to plead for the life of her dead husband, a story told a length in the Mahabharata *(3.277–83); she enters into a discussion with Yama, which ultimately results in the release of her husband. In the course of this discussion, she asks him about hell. For other ways of escaping from hell, compare the stories of the evil Brahmin Devaraja and king Vipashcit, above, sections 4.2.1 and 4.2.3.*

Savitri said, 'King of dharma, you who have gone to the far shore of the Vedas and the subsidiary Vedic texts, magnanimous and incomparable expounder of the various Puranas, histories, and Pancaratra texts, tell me: what action is it that is good for all creatures, desired by all, respected by all, the seminal action that cuts the chain of karma, that is praised by men and gives them happiness, that is conducive to good reputation and to dharma, the most auspicious of all that is auspicious? What action prevents people from being sent to experience the agonising torments of hell? What act keeps them from seeing the pits of hell, or falling into them, and keeps them from being reborn? What shape are those pits, and how big are they? And what form is assumed by the evil-doers who dwell in them? When a man's own body has been burnt to ashes, with what body does he go to another world and there experience his just deserts, good or bad? How is it that the body is not destroyed by suffering torture for such a long time? What sort of body is it? Tell me, please, good Brahmin.'

When the king of dharma heard what Savitri had said, he thought of Vishnu, bowed to his guru, and began to tell this story:

'My little calf, in the four Vedas, in the dharma compendia, in the Puranas and Epics, in the texts of the Pancaratras and so forth, and in all the other learned books, as well as in the subsidiary texts of the Vedas, what is essential, desired by everyone and most auspicious, is the worship of Krishna. This is what takes one across the anguish of birth, death, old age, disease, and sorrow; it is the very form of all things that are auspicious, the cause of supreme bliss. It is what causes all who achieve success in religion to cross over the ocean of hell; it causes the tree of devotion to sprout and cuts down the tree of karma. It is the staircase to the path of the world of the cows (Goloka, the heaven of Krishna), never failing, step after step; it is the primal place in which one comes into the presence of the very form of the creation of all the various worlds.

'The servants of the lord Krishna never see, even in a dream, the pits, or the messenger of Yama, or Yama himself, or the servants of Yama. Those house-holders, subject to the experience of their karma, who perform a vow to Hari, and those who bathe in the place of pilgrimage to Hari, or who fast on the day of Hari, who constantly bow to Hari and worship the image of Hari, they never go to my horrible city of destruction. And those Brahmins who are purified by the three twilight rituals, whose behaviour is pure, who take pleasure in their own dharma and are at peace, they do not go to the palace of Yama. They enjoy heaven. So do the other pure servants of other gods; but these go to heaven and come back again to the mortal world: they do not go there and obtain final release. No men attain final Release without worshipping Krishna, not even if they take pleasure in their own karma and in their own dharma.

'But when the servants of Yama, who are hard to combat, come to the mortal world, they recoil in fright from a worshipper of Krishna, just as a serpent recoils from an eagle. This is what I say to my messenger as he sets out with the noose in his hand: "Go everywhere, except to the hermitage of a devotee of Krishna." And Citragupta himself (the servant of Yama who records good and bad deeds), terrified, scribbles down with the tips of his nails the names of the worshippers who chant the mantras of Krishna. Brahma prepares milk and honey and so forth for those who pass through and go beyond the world of Brahma as they go to the world of cows. All evils are destroyed by their touch, just as dry wood and grass are destroyed in a blazing fire. Even Delusion is deluded with terror when it sees them; Lust becomes full of lust, and greed and anger full of greed and anger. Death flees, together with disease, old age, sorrow, fear, Time, good and bad karma, delight, and enjoyment. Thus I have described to you, good woman, the various people who do not go to Yama's hell.

'Now listen while I tell you how the body is transformed, according to the sacred texts. Earth, wind, space, fire and water – these are the seed of the body of all creatures who have bodies, in the creation of the Creator. Whatever body is made out of the five elements, earth and so forth, is artificial and perishable; it will become ashes. But the soul that has the form of a Person, the size of a large thumb, takes on a subtle body for the purpose of experiencing. That body does not become ashes in the blazing fire in my palace; that body is not destroyed in water, nor even in the course of a very long beating, nor under the blow of a sword or a knife or a very sharp thorn, nor when it is touched by a very hot object, or red-hot iron, or white-hot stones, or when it embraces an image that has been made very hot, or even when it falls from a very high place. That body is never burnt or broken when it suffers torment. Thus, my good lady, I have told you about the experience and its causes, according to the sacred texts.' (*Brahmavaivarta Purana* 2.32.1–33)

5.5.4 How to perform a funeral sacrifice

The funeral ritual, or shraddha, *is performed not only at the time of death but every month, to continue to nourish the spirit of the departed ancestor. This text cites several Rig Vedic funeral verses (similar to section 2.1.1.2, above) in which several different people are addressed: the mourners, as well as the dead man himself and the god of fire. But this text addresses only the descendants who are to perform the ritual.*

(Perform) the monthly (funeral ritual) on the day of the new moon, in the afternoon, or on the odd-numbered days of the dark fortnight. Prepare food for the ancestors and make seats by arranging blades of *darbha* grass pointing south; then invite an odd number of Brahmins who are pure, who know the (Rig Vedic) mantras, who have all their limbs intact, and who are not related to you by their mother, by their male ancestral line, or by having learnt the Vedas with you. Feed them without any regard for your own advantage.

Put fuel on the fire and scatter all around it blades of *darbha* grass pointing south and east; then prepare the clarified butter in a special pot for clarifying butter, a pot in which there is a single filter. Sprinkle water around the fire from right to left, and put a piece of fig-tree wood on it for kindling; then offer the oblation with a special spoon made of fig-tree wood. Perform the ritual that ends with the offering of the clarified butter; place your sacred thread over your right shoulder; then summon your ancestors with this verse: 'Come here, fathers, fond of Soma, on your hidden, ancient paths; bring us progeny, wealth, and a long life-span, one that lasts for a hundred autumns.'

Then sprinkle water in the same (southern) direction, while reciting this verse: 'Divine waters, send Agni forth. Let our ancestors take pleasure in this sacrifice. Let them enjoy their monthly nourishment and refreshment and give us wealth and (sons who are) all heroic.' Then put your sacred thread over the left shoulder and perform the ritual that ends with the utterance of the names of the seven worlds; put your sacred thread back on your right shoulder and offer the oblation while reciting these verses: 'Svadha! This drink and all honour to Soma with the ancestors! This drink and all honour to Yama with the Angiras sages and the ancestors! The waters that arise in the east, and those that arise in the north – by means of these waters, that support the entire universe, I place someone else between (myself and my) father. This drink and all honour! I place someone else between (myself and) my grandfather by means of the mountains; by means of the great earth; by means of the sky and the quarters of space; by means of infinite nourishments. This drink and all honour! I place someone else between (myself and) my great-grandfather by means of the seasons; by means of days and nights with beautiful twilights; by means of the half-months and the months. This drink and all honour!'

Then offer the oblation with their names: 'This drink and all honour to so-and-so! This drink and all honour to so-and-so! Whatever sexual mis-deameanor my mother has committed, lustfully violating her vows of chastity – let my father take that semen as his own; let the other man who is present go away. This drink and all honour!' And in the same way, make a second and third oblation, altering the verse to say, 'Whatever my grandmother . . .,' 'Whatever my great-grandmother . . .'

(Recite the Rig Vedic verses), 'The ancestors that are here, and those that are not here, those that we know and those that we do not know: Agni, you know them, if you are the knower of all creatures; let them rejoice in what is eaten with this sacrificial drink. This drink and all honour! Whatever limb of yours (addressing the dead man) the flesh-eating fire, the knower of all creatures, has burnt up while leading you to the worlds (of the ancestors) – I restore that limb to you again. Arise, uninjured, with all your limbs, O ancestors! This drink and all honour! Carry the clarified butter, Agni, knower of creatures, to the fathers where you know they are resting, far away. Let streams of butter flow to them; let all their wishes come true, and all their desires be fulfilled. This drink and all honour!'

And in the same way, make a second and third oblation, altering the verse to say, 'Carry the butter to the grandfathers . . .', '. . . to the great-grandfathers . . .' And in the same way, make an oblation of food, altering the verse to say, 'Carry the food . . .'

Then offer the oblation of the 'successful sacrifice', saying, 'This drink and all honour to Agni who carries the oblation of food and makes a successful sacrifice!' Then touch the food and say, 'The earth is your pot; the sky is its lid. I offer you as an oblation into the mouth of the Brahmin. I offer you as an oblation into the upward breath and outward breath of the Brahmins. You are unperishing; do not perish for the fathers over there, in the world beyond. The earth is just right; Agni watches over it so that there will be no careless errors in what is given.

'The earth is your pot; the sky is its lid. I offer you as an oblation into the mouth of the Brahmin. I offer you as an oblation into the upward breath and outward breath of the Brahmins. You are unperishing; do not perish for the grandfathers over there, in the world beyond. The middle realm of space is just right; Vayu, the wind, watches over it so that there will be no careless errors in what is given.

'The earth is your pot; the sky is its lid. I offer you as an oblation into the mouth of the Brahmin. I offer you as an oblation into the upward breath and outward breath of the Brahmins. You are unperishing; do not perish for the great-grandfathers over there, in the world beyond. The sky is just right; the sun watches over it so that there will be no careless errors in what is given.'

Then have the Brahmins touch the food while you say, 'I enter into the vital breath as I offer the oblation of ambrosial Soma.' Watch over them while they are eating, and say, 'My soul is in ultimate reality for the sake of immortality.' When they have eaten (and are leaving), follow after them and ask their permission for (you to make use of) their leftovers. Then take a water-pot and a fistful of *darbha* grass and go to a place midway between the south and the east; spread the *darbha* grass out with points to the south, hold your hands palms down, and pour out three handfuls of water, ending towards the south, while saying, 'Let the fathers, fond of Soma, wipe themselves! Let the grandfathers, fond of Soma, wipe themselves! Let the great-grandfathers, fond of Soma, wipe themselves!' And then, 'So-and-so, wash yourself!' 'So-and-so, wash yourself!'

Then turn your hands palms down and put down on those grasses three balls of rice (*pindas*), ending in the south; give the ball to your father, saying, 'This is for you, father'; give the ball to your grandfather, saying, 'This is for you, grandfather'; give the ball to your great-grandfather, saying, 'This is for you, great-grandfather.' You may give a fourth ball, in silence; but this is optional.

Now, if you don't know the names (of your ancestors), just give the ball to your father and say, 'This drink to the ancestors who dwell on the earth'; give the ball to your grandfather and say, 'This drink to the ancestors who dwell in the middle realm of space'; and give the ball to your great-grandfather and say, 'This drink to the ancestors who dwell in the sky.' And give, with each respective ball, collyrium, some other ointment, and a garment. When you give the collyrium, say, three times, 'So-and-so, anoint your eyes!' 'So-and-so, anoint your eyes!' When you give the other ointment, say three times,

'So-and-so, anoint yourself!' 'So-and-so, anoint yourself!' (When you give the garments, say,) 'These garments are for you, O ancestors. Do not grab anything else of ours.' Then tear off a piece of cloth or a wisp of wool and put that down, if you are in the first half of your life; tear out some of the hair on your own body if you are in the last half of your life.

Wash the pot and sprinkle that water all around, from right to left, while saying this verse: 'These honeyed waters, that refresh sons and grandsons, that milk themselves of the sacrificial drink and Soma for the ancestors, these divine waters that refresh both (the living and the dead), these rivers full of water, full of semen, with good places to cross over – let them flow up to you in that world beyond!' Then turn the pot upside down, and cross your hands so that the right hand is the left hand and the left hand is the right hand, and honour (your ancestors) with the words of greeting: 'I bow to you, my ancestors, for the sap.'

Then go to the brink of some body of water and pour out three handfuls of water and say, 'This is for you, father, this flowing wave of honey. As great as Agni is, and as great as the earth is, so great is its measure, so great is its power. I give this, that has become so great. And as Agni is unperishing and inexhaustible, may this drink be unperishing and inexhaustible for my father. So-and-so, live on that unperishing drink together with those (other ancestors). The verses (*rig*) are your power.

'This is for you, grandfather, this flowing wave of honey. As great as Vayu, the wind, is, and as great as the middle realm of space is, so great is its measure, so great is its power. I give this, that has become so great. And as Vayu is unperishing and inexhaustible, may this drink be unperishing and inexhaustible for my grandfather. So-and-so, live on that unperishing drink together with those (other ancestors). The formulas (*yajur*) are your power.

'This is for you, great-grandfather, this flowing wave of honey. As great as the sun is, and as great as heaven is, so great is its measure, so great is its power. I give this, that has become so great. And as the sun is unperishing and inexhaustible, may this drink be unperishing and inexhaustible for my great-grandfather. So-and-so, live on that unperishing drink together with those (other ancestors). The chants (*saman*) are your power.'

Then come back and pour out whatever is left in the water-pot, saying, 'Go away, my ancestors, fond of Soma, on your hidden, ancient paths. After a month, come back again to our house to eat our offerings – come back with good progeny, good heroic sons.'

That is the description of the funeral sacrifice that is performed in the middle of the rainy season. In that ritual, offerings of flesh are prescribed; but if there is no flesh, you can use vegetables. (*Hiranyakeshin Grihya Sutra* 20.4.1–26 (2.4.10.1–7, 2.4.11.1–5, 2.4.12.1–11, 2.4.13.1–5)

5.5.5 Who not to invite to the funeral

After he has performed the sacrifice to the ancestors, a Brahmin who keeps his sacred fire burning should offer every month on the new-moon day the funeral sacrifice (*shraddha*) with the offering of balls of rice (*pindas*) . . .

A man who knows dharma need not make a close inspection of a Brahmin for a ritual dedicated to the gods; but he should inspect him with great care when it comes to a ritual dedicated to the ancestors. Manu says that those Brahmins who are thieves, fallen from caste, eunuchs, or atheists are not worthy of the oblations to the gods and to the ancestors. One should not feed at a funeral an ascetic with matted hair, one who has not studied (the Veda), or who is a weakling or a gambler, or those who perform sacrifices for groups. One should avoid at sacrifices to the gods and to the ancestors physicians, temple priests, people who sell meat, and those who make their living in shops; a servant of a village or of the king; a man with bad nails or brown teeth, or who contradicts his guru, or who has abandoned his sacred fire, or a usurer; or a man who has consumption, or who lives by tending cattle; a man who marries before his older brother or who lets his younger brother marry before him; one who neglects his religious duties, or who hates Brahmins, or who belongs to a group; a wandering bard or actor, one who has violated his vows as a chaste student, the husband of a Shudra woman, or the son of a remarried woman; a one-eyed man or one in whose house his wife's lover lives; a man who teaches for a fee, or who is taught for a fee; who has Shudra pupils or a Shudra guru; a man who uses dirty talk; the son of an adulteress or the son of a widow; a man who has abandoned his mother, father, or guru without good reason, or who has joined, through ties of religion or sex, with those who have fallen from caste; a man who burns down houses, a poisoner, a man who eats food cooked by the son of an adulteress; a man who sells Soma, or who voyages on the ocean; a panegyrist, a man who deals in oil, a man who perjures himself; a man who argues with his father; a gambler, a drunk, a man who is sick as a result of having committed a sin, a man accused, a hypocrite, a man who sells liquors, a man who makes bows and arrows, or who takes as his first wife a woman who was married before (particularly if she was widowed by his older brother); one who betrays a friend or who lives by shooting dice, or who learns (the Vedas) from his son; an epileptic, one who suffers from scrofulous swellings of the glands, a man who has white leprosy, an informer, a madman, a blind man, a man who criticises the Vedas; a man who trains elephants, oxen, horses, or camels; a man who makes his living by astrology; a man who raises birds or who teaches the martial arts; a man who diverts streams or who takes pleasure in damming them up; a man who builds houses, a messenger, a man who plants trees; a man who plays with dogs or makes his living by falcons; one who defiles maidens; one who injures people, who lives off Shudras, or who offers sacrifice to goblins (*ganas*); who is devoid of good conduct, a eunuch, someone who is always asking for something; a man who is criticised by good men, a man who keeps sheep or buffaloes, the husband of a woman who has been married before, a man who carries dead bodies – all these must be carefully avoided.

A well-born and wise Brahmin should avoid at both sorts (of sacrifices, to gods or ancestors) those lowest of twice-born men, whose conduct is reprehensible and who are not fit to line up in rows with the others. A Brahmin who has no learning is extinguished like a grass-fire; sacrificial food should not be given to him, any more than one would make an oblation into ashes. I will tell you, leaving nothing out, what fruits come to the man who gives the oblation for the gods or the ancestors to a man who is not fit to sit in the rows (with the other Brahmins): the ogres are the ones who eat what is eaten by the Brahmins who have broken their vows, or by the man who marries before his younger brother, and so forth, and by all the other people unfit to sit in the rows. (Manu 3.122, 149–70)

5.5.6 How to perform a Tantric funeral

This is the prescription for a funeral sacrifice in a rather special community, the Kula or the Tantric 'family', the Tantric circle of a worshippers (who are called Kaulas or Kulikas). Though, like all Hindu rituals, it cites Vedic precedents, in many respects it differs dramatically, and intentionally, from the rite described by Hiranyakeshin and Manu; in particular, it includes people that are usually excluded. It also shows a special concern for the fate of a ghost (preta, *also called a* bhuta *or 'has-been'), a dead man whose first, transformative funeral has not yet been performed and who is therefore still in limbo, not yet having reached the world of the ancestors. Like most Tantric texts, it is spoken by Shiva to his wife, the Goddess, and pays far more respect to women than do parallel texts within the orthodox Hindu tradition; it even goes so far as to forbid suttee, or the immolation of the widow on her husband's funeral pyre, an act enjoined (though seldom carried out) upon conventional Hindu widows.*

O best of women, a man whose father, grandfather, and great-grandfather are still living should, if he is smart, offer the funeral offering to his great-great-grandfather. If the first three are alive, he really doesn't have to perform a funeral offering; if he satisfies them (with food), O queen of the gods, he obtains by that means the fruit that he would have had from a funeral sacrifice. If a man's father is alive, lovely one, he should not perform a funeral sacrifice for anyone else, other than his mother or his wife or the first triad of ancestors (father, grandfather, and great-grandfather).

When a man performs the funeral offering for someone other than an ancestor who has recently died, O queen of the Kula, he should not worship the All-gods but, rather, he should designate a single (god) and make the entreaty; then he should face south and give an offering of cooked rice and the ball of rice (*pinda*), and do everything as it is done in the usual funeral, except that sesamum seed should be used in place of barley.

In the funeral to a ghost, there is this peculiarity: the worship of the Ganges and so forth is omitted, and the dead man should be referred to as a ghost when the cooked rice and the ball of rice are offered to him. Since only one single god is designated, this funeral ceremony is known as the 'single-designation' ritual. One should offer meat and fish to a ghost, in addition to the cooked rice and the ball of rice. The ceremony is known as the funeral of a ghost, O leader of the Kula, when a man performs it on the second day after the end of the period of pollution.

If there is a miscarriage or a stillbirth, or if a child dies as soon as it is born, for some other reason, then a man remains polluted as long as the custom of his family reckons it. Among the twice-born, pollution is counted for ten days (for Brahmins), twelve days (for Kshatriyas), a fortnight (for Vaishyas), and a month for Shudras or the lower classes, O goddess. If a paternal relation who is not in one's direct male line dies, or if one only finds out about the death of a direct male relative when the period of pollution has already passed, the pollution lasts for three nights. A man within the period of pollution cannot perform any ritual for a god or an ancestor, except for a ritual which he has already begun or the Kula (Tantric) ritual, O primordial one.

One should burn in the funeral grounds anyone who dies over the age of five, but, O ruler of the Kula, one should not burn a lovely woman of the Kula along with her husband. Every charming woman is your very form, your body concealed within the universe; and so, if in her delusion a woman should mount her husband's pyre, she would go to hell.

The bodies of those who use the Brahma mantra, O dark godddess, should be thrown into water, buried, or burnt, according to their own instructions. Mother! The best death is the death in a holy place, or at a place of pilgrimage, or, especially, near the goddess or in the presence of the members of the Kula. He who at the moment of his death meditates on the one truth and forgets the three worlds, he is established forever in his true form. (*Mahanirvana Tantra* 10.67–83)

6 TANTRAS

As the reader will have noted from the previous selection, the Tantric funeral, attitudes to caste law are radically changed in the Tantras. But the belief that the Tantras are in any way hedonistic or even pornographic, though a belief that is shared by most Hindus as well as by Western scholars, is not justified; the Upanishads and Puranas – not to mention the Kamasutra – have far more respect for pleasure of all kinds, including sexual pleasure, than do the Tantras. Indeed, the Tantras seem sometimes to lean over backwards to be plus royaliste que le roi, *in hedging their sexual ceremonies with secrecy, euphemism, and warnings of danger.*

6.1 RITUAL

6.1.1 The five elements of Tantric ritual

The five elements, or tattvas, in orthodox Hindusim are the elements of earth, fire, water, wind, and space (to which some schools add a sixth, mind or soul). But Tantrism, which also accepts this schema, has, in addition, its own version of the five elements, the elements of the ritual, that are called the five 'm's, as all five words begin with 'm' in Sanskrit. In English, they might be called the five 'f's: madya (fermented grapes, wine), mansa (flesh, meat), matsya (fish), mudra (frumentum, parched grain), and maithuna (fornication).

The text elaborates upon each of these elements. It mentions three sorts of fish, that are apparently the Indian equivalent (in terms of delicacy) of salmon, trout, and sole. And it mentions several sorts of women. Officially, it states that there may be problems if any woman other than one's own wife is used as a partner for the Tantric ritual of fornication. It distinguishes between one's own wife (sva-kiya), who is permitted, in contrast both with another man's wife (parakiya) and with a woman used in common by the entire Kula (a sadharani woman). The latter two are permitted as partners by other Tantric texts from which the present author takes pains to distinguish himself. The ritual contact with one's own wife involves the use of her 'flower', that is probably a euphemism for menstrual blood, often called the 'flower' (pushpa) of a woman.

The other women present in the ritual are referred to as shaktis, a term that may designate the women who are the partners of the other men participating in the ritual. The shaktis are said to be 'beaten', and the commentator on this text says that 'beating' refers to sexual intercourse. An alternative reading of the text itself says that the women are to be worshipped, but are not to be used in the ceremony of 'beating'. Sir John George Woodroffe, the editor, uses this latter reading and argues that the women are divided into the women 'to be enjoyed' (bhogyas), on the left (the svakiya women), and the women 'to be worshipped' (pujyas), on the right (the parakiya women). If the worshipper yields to lust for the latter, says Woodroffe, he commits the sin of incest with his own mother. Against this argument it is to be noted that shakti, or 'power', also designates the female power of the god (that is, the Goddess) and the female power of the human worshipper (that is, his partner in the ritual, usually his wife).

(The Goddess said to Shiva, 'My lord, if you have compassion for me, tell me more about the five elements used in rituals such as worship, that you have mentioned.' Shiva said:)

There are three sorts of very good wine: made from sugar (or molasses), made from rice, and made from honey (or from the Mandhuka flower or grapes). There are also various sorts made from palm tree juice or from date palms, and these are further subdivided according to the locality and the various substances in them. All the various sorts are recommended for the worship of the deity. There is no distinction of caste with regard to whoever makes it, or whoever brings it; all of it is purified and bestows all powers.

Meat is also said to be of three sorts: from animals that come from the water, the land, or the sky. Wherever it comes from, and whoever kills it, all of it gives pleasure to the deity; this is certain. The wish of the worshipper is what has the power to determine what thing is to be given to the deity; whatever he likes, that substance should be made into a sacrificial offering. The male sacrificial animal is the one prescribed for the ritual of offering to the minor deities, O goddess; for Shiva has commanded that female animals of the species fit to be sacrificed are not to be killed.

There are three sorts of the best kind of fish: Shala, Pathina, and Rohita. The middling sort are the ones without bones, and the worst are the ones that have lots of bones – though these, too, may be offered to the Goddess if they are very well roasted or fried.

There are three sorts of parched grain: best, middle, and lowest. The kind made from Shali rice, white as a moonbeam, is very good, or the kind made from barley or 'cow-smoke' wheat, that is especially nice when fried in butter. This is the best parched grain. The middle variety is made from broken wheat and so forth. When other sorts of seeds are roasted, they are regarded as the inferior quality.

Meat, fish, parched grain, fruits and roots offered to the divinity when wine is offered are known as the purification (*shuddhi*). Without such purification, any offering for a particular purpose, or any puja or libation of water, will bear no fruit, O goddess; the divinity will take no pleasure in it. The drinking of wine without this purification, by itself, is like swallowing poison; the person who uses such a mantra becomes chronically ill and soon dies, after living only a short life-span.

O goddess, now that the destructive Dark Age has become impotent, seedless, a mere remnant, only one's own wife is ever to be regarded as a flawless partner. Beloved of my very life's breath, for this ritual, the (menstrual) flower that comes from the woman herself is prescribed, but one may use red sandalwood paste as a substitute for it. If the five elements of the ritual of the leaves, flowers, and fruits are not purified, they should not be given to the Great Goddess; if a man gives them (unpurified), he goes to hell. The worshipper should set the sacred goblet in place in company with his own good woman; then he should sprinkle her with the purified wine or the communal water. To begin, he should pronounce the mantras over the girl, and salute the Goddess of the Triple City; and when this mantra is over, he should utter the mantra, 'Hail! Drive this *shakti* upward! Purify her! Make her my *shakti*!' If the woman has not been initiated, he should speak the mantra of illusion ('Hrim!') into her ear. The other *shaktis* are to be worshipped with the ritual of 'beating'. (*Mahanirvana Tantra* 6.1–20)

6.1.2 A Tantric animal sacrifice
This text is particularly noteworthy for its attempt to assimilate the Vedic cult – in the form of the Gayatri hymn – the verse from the Rig Veda *(3.62.10) that every*

Hindu recites at dawn; it begins, 'tat savitur varenyam . . .' – while using non-Vedic sacrificial animals, and with a non-Vedic casualness (almost any animal will do, too) and a non-Vedic bluntness (calling a spade a spade when they kill the animal). This bluntness is in notable contrast with the great euphemism that this Tantric text, like most, uses in referring to anything sexual.

After the worshipper has worshipped (the Goddess) with all the offerings, he should sacrifice an animal to her. Deer, goat, sheep, buffalo, pig, porcupine, hare, lizard, tortoise, and rhinoceros are the ten prescribed animals; but one may offer other sacrificial animals, too, according to the particular wish of the worshipper. A man who knows the mantras should place a sacrificial animal – one that has all the right signs – in front of the Goddess and sprinkle it with specially consecrated water; he should use the cow-gesture to turn it into ambrosia. Then he should address the animal, saying, 'We bow to the sacrificial animal, the goat,' and honour it with perfume, vermilion, flowers, food, and water. Then he should whisper the Gayatri hymn into the right ear of the animal, for this releases the bonds (that make it a beast): after the words 'Let us pray' (from the Gayatri), he should add 'for the bond of the sacrificial animal' (from the Tantric mantra); and after the words 'let us meditate' (from the Gayatri), he should add 'on the Creator of All' (from the Tantric mantra). Then he should chant the mantra 'Let him drive forward' (from the Gayatri) and add 'our life' (from the Tantric mantra, where the Gayatri has 'our thoughts'). This is the Beast Gayatri that releases the bonds of the beast.

Then he should take the knife and honour it with the 'cluster' syllable ('Hum!'); and he should worship, in order, the Goddess of Speech (Sarasvati) and Brahma (her husband) at its tip: Lakshmi and Narayana at its blade; and Uma and Maheshvara at its handle. Immediately after, he should honour the knife by saying, 'We bow to the knife that is infused with Brahma, Vishnu, Shiva, and their *shaktis.*' After speaking this Great Speech, he should cup his hands in reverence and say, 'May this be offered to you with the ritual that has been properly ordained.'

When he has announced the sacrificial beast in this way, he should place it upon the ground. Then, keeping the love of the Goddess uppermost in his mind, he should kill it with a sharp blow. He may make the cut himself, or it may be made by the sons of his brother, or by his brother, or by a friend or any close kinsman; but he should never get an enemy to do it. When the blood is slightly warm, he should offer it as tribute to the young priests; then he should place a lamp on the head of the animal and offer the head to the Goddess, saying, 'We bow to the Goddess.' This is the sacrificial offering of an animal as it is prescribed for the members of the Kula in the Kula worship. If it is not done, there is never any pleasing the deity. (*Mahanirvana Tantra* 6.104–18)

6.1.3 Tantric sins of excess

The Tantras recognise three grades of human: men who are like beasts, capable only of conventional worship, such as image-worship; heroic men, who practise

Tantric rituals; and godlike men, who practise Tantric meditation, having transcended and internalised Tantric ritual. The first two grades are in danger of committing certain excesses in the course of the Tantric ritual as well as in the rest of their lives.

Even the Kula dharma leads only to evil rather than to Release and prosperity, if it is not followed according to the rules, and honestly. Wine is the liquid form of the Goddess Tara, who is the saviour of all living creatures, the mother of all enjoyment and Release, the destroyer of dangers and disease, who burns up all sins and purifies the worlds, O Beloved , who grants all success and increases knowledge, understanding, and learning. Those who have attained final Release, who strive for Release, who have mastered the techniques, who are engaged in using the techniques, kings, and gods always use wine to obtain success in whatever they want. Mortals who drink wine with the proper rituals and with a well-controlled mind are virtually immortals on earth. By partaking of any one of the five ritual elements at a time, with the proper ritual, a man becomes Shiva; who can know what fruit will arise from the use of all five elements?

But if this Goddess wine is drunk without the proper rituals, she destroys a man's entire intellect, life-span, reputation, and wealth. By excessive drinking of wine, people whose minds are intoxicated lose their intelligence, which is the means by which they achieve the four goals of a human life (release, dharma, profit, and pleasure). A man whose intelligence has been broken does not know what to do or what not to do; every step he takes results in something that he does not want and that other people do not want.

Therefore, the king or the lord of the wheel (the leader of the Tantric circle – *cakra*, wheel – or, possibly, a Buddhist king, in contrast with the [Hindu] king designated by the first term) should purify people who are excessively addicted to wine or to intoxicating substances, purify them by physical punishment or by fining them. The degree of destruction of the intellect of men who drink varies according to the type of wine, the nature of the individual, the quantity that is taken, and the time and place where it is used. Therefore, the degree of intoxication should be judged not by the amount of wine that has been drunk, but by the signs that reveal excessive drinking: slurred speech and unsteady hands, feet, and gaze. A man who is not in control of his senses because his mind is distracted by intoxication transgresses the moral bounds of gods and gurus and is terrible to see; he becomes involved in all sorts of unprofitable things, does bad deeds and opposes Shiva. The king should burn his tongue, confiscate his property, and beat him; the king should torture and confiscate the property of a man whom drink has made grotesque, with unsteady speech, feet, or hands, wandering in his wits and out of his mind. A king who wants to please his subjects should heavily fine a man whom drink has made foul-mouthed, crazy, or devoid of shame or fear.

Even if a man of the Kula sect has been initiated a hundred times, O empress of the Kula, if he drinks too much he should be regarded as a beast and expelled from the Kula. A man who drinks too much wine, whether or not it has been purified, should be abandoned by the members of the Kula and punished by the king, too. If a twice-born man gets drunk and makes his wife get drunk with him, a wife that he has married by the Brahma wedding, he should purify himself, together with her, by eating nothing but crumbs for five days. A man who has drunk unsanctified wine should purify himself by fasting for three days; if he eats unpurified meat, he should fast for two days. If he eats unsanctified fish or parched grain, he should fast for a day; but if he makes use of the fifth element (sex) without the proper ritual, he should be purified by being punished by the king.

Anyone who knowingly eats human flesh or the flesh of a cow, O gracious goddess, will be purified if he fasts for a fortnight; this is the prescribed restoration. My dear, a man who has eaten the flesh of an animal that has the form of a man, or a man who eats the flesh of an animal that eats flesh, may purify himself of this evil by a three-day fast. A man who has eaten food cooked by foreigners, Untouchables, men who are like beasts, or enemies of the Kula – he may become pure by fasting for a fortnight. If he should knowingly eat the leftovers of these people, O empress of the Kula, he should fast for a month to become pure; if he does it unknowingly, he should fast for a fortnight. If he eats food prepared by lower castes, even once, he should fast for three days to purify himself; this is my command.

But if food prepared by a beast-man or an Untouchable or a foreigner is placed within the circle (of Tantric worshippers) or in the hand of a (Tantric) adept, one can eat it without incurring any evil. Anyone who eats forbidden food to save his life in time of death or famine, in an emergency, or when it is a matter of life and death does not incur evil. No sins of improper eating count when food is eaten on the back of an elephant, on stones or logs so big that they can only be carried by several men, or where there is no one to notice anything reprehensible. My dear, one should not kill animals whose flesh is not to be eaten, or diseased animals, not even for the sake of a divinity; anyone who does this commits an evil act.

A man who knowingly kills a cow should perform the (following) 'difficult penance', according to Shiva's command; and he should not shave or cut his nails or wash his clothes until he has completed his vow. This is the 'difficult penance': he should fast for a month and then eat nothing but crumbs for a month; then for a (third) month he should eat only food that he has begged for, O gracious goddess. At the end of the penance, he should shave his head; and then, if he has knowingly killed a cow, he may free himself from that crime by feeding members of the Kula, distant relatives, and close relatives. If a cow is killed as a result of lack of care, (a Brahmin) is purified by fasting for eight days, a Kshatriya by six days, a Vaishya by four, and a Shudra by two, O gracious goddess.

O goddess of the Kula, if anyone willingly kills an elephant, camel, buffalo, or horse, he should fast for three days and then he is free of evil. If he kills a deer, ram, goat, or cat, he should fast for a day; for a peacock, parrot, or goose, he should fast as long as there is daylight (on the day of the killing). If he kills (any other) animals that have bones, he should eat no flesh for one night. If he kills living creatures that have no bones, he is purified merely by feeling sorry. Kings who, when they are hunting, kill beasts, fish, or birds do not commit evil, O goddess, for this is the eternal dharma of kings. But, my lady, one should always avoid injuring creatures except for the sake of the gods; a man who injures creatures according to the sacred rules is not smeared by evil. (*Mahanirvana Tantra* 11.104–43)

6.2 PHILOSOPHY

6.2.1 Tantric caste law

As the footprints of all living creatures disappear inside the footprint of an elephant, so, my dear, all dharmas merge into the Kula dharma. How full of merit are the Kaulas! They are themselves the very forms of places of pilgrimage, who by their mere contact purify foreigners, Untouchables, and the vilest people. As all the waters that flow into the Ganges become the Ganges, even so all who join in the Kula practice become Kaulas. As the water that flows into the sea is no longer separated (from the other waters in the sea), even so the people who plunge into the water of the Kula are no longer separated (from the other people in the Kula). All the two-footed creatures on the surface of the earth, beginning with Brahmins and ending with outcastes, all become masters in the Kula practice.

But those who, even when they are summoned to the Kula dharma, turn away from it, they fall from *all* dharma and go to the lowest place. And any members of the Kula who deceive men seeking the Kula ritual, no matter who they are, they go to the Terrible Hell (Raurava). Any member of the Kula who will not allow into the Kula an Untouchable or a Greek (a Yavana, literally an 'Ionian'), thinking them low, or a woman, despising her – he, being truly low, goes to the lowest place. The merit that is won by a hundred initiatory anointings, or by a hundred introductory rituals, ten million times that merit is won by initiating a single man into the Kula dharma. By becoming Kaulas, all the classes of men on the earth, whatever the different dharmas that they follow, are released from their bonds and go to the highest state. (*Mahanirvana Tantra* 14.180–9)

6.2.2 Tantric Release

This text provides an interesting variant of the Brihadaranyaka Upanishad *doctrine of kingdoms won in dreams; see above, 2.3.2.5.1. It also provides a more serious challenge to the conventional Hindu concepts of iconography, asceticism, and Release.*

All imagining of such things as name and form is like child's play; the man who abandons all this and dwells firm in the ultimate reality, he is Released; this is certain. If the shapes imagined by men in their minds could achieve Release for them, then surely men could become kings by means of the kingdom that they get in their dreams. Those who believe that the Lord lives in images made of clay, stone, metal, wood, or so forth, and wear themselves out with asceticism without true knowledge – they never find Release. Whether they waste themselves away by fasting, or get pot bellies by eating whatever they like, unless they have the knowledge of the ultimate reality – how could they be cured? If people could get Release by performing vows to eat nothing but air, leaves, crumbs, or water, then the serpents and cattle and birds and fish would be Released. (*Mahanirvana Tantra* 14.117–21)

7 THE HINDI TRADITION

Composed by unlettered poets and recited over highly diverse strata of Indian society, Hindi religious poetry developed as an oral tradition. From the fifteenth century into the eighteenth, devotional verse flowered in the North Indian vernaculars, penetrating peoples' lives in various ways: through witty, sometimes biting couplets punctuating ordinary conversation, as short lyrics sung communally at religious events, and in a highly polished literary epic often performed by professional specialists. Verses remained memorable through images at once familiar and striking, and with fairly simple metres and well-defined rhymes, many were kept alive as popular song.

Both devotees in the village and scholars of Hindi literature have traditionally seen devotional poems falling into two main categories: saguna *– those evoking the Lord with attributes – usually through a detail in the earthly sport of Krishna or Rama; and* nirguna *– those invoking the deity without attributes, the Formless Lord realised through humility, detachment, and yoga. Though the religious attitudes that the two types of poetry present need not be mutually exclusive, the* saguna *and* nirguna *styles typically draw out their imagery in opposite directions. Since most Hindus already understand abstractly that divinities like Rama or Krishna are incarnations of God, the poet in* saguna *tradition tries to elicit fervent devotion through vivid presentation of the deity's human image. Saguna verse thus concretises the particulars of the Lord's play, using detailed, sometimes mundane specifics to convey his immediate personal presence. Nirguna verse, on the other hand,* begins *with immediate mundane images – of catching fish, say, or of dealing with a merchant – and then uses these images figuratively to express more abstract messages of spiritual warning, yoga, and devotion to the formless divine.*

The two broad styles of Hindi devotional verse show their clearest differentiation in their origins. In the fifteenth century the nirguna *tradition found its greatest and most distinctive proponent in Kabir, the first major devotional poet in*

Hindi. Mocking Hindu and Islamic orthodoxies and invoking a Lord who transcended them both, Kabir set the tone for later nirguna poets, who are generally referred to as sants. *In the sixteenth century, as Krishna devotion took hold in North India,* saguna *verse found one of its greatest representatives in Sur Das. Many of the verses attributed to Sur Das were preserved in Krishnaite sectarian traditions, thus revealing a devotion to Krishna that is exclusive as well as intense. Not only are the sweet joys of Krishna's play described by Sur Das in every conceivable aspect, they are also contrasted to the arid meditations of yogis. The other major line of* saguna *worship – devotion to Ram – never produced as vital sectarian movements as did Krishna-devotion, but instead blossomed in Mughal India with the revival of the native Hindu tradition as a whole. The* Ramcharitmanas *of Tulsi Das, the literary masterpiece of Hindi devotion, thus presents a more catholic picture of the Hindu world than the one found in Sur: though Tulsi Das shows the great yogi Shiva adoring Lord Ram, Ram for his part is made to speak respectfully of Shiva.* Sants, *too, began to emerge from and contribute to the Hindu mainstream, often taking an attitude toward conventional deities more moderate than that of the iconoclastic Kabir; thus, by the eighteenth century Charandas of Delhi was able to integrate vivid aspects of Krishna worship into his sant's vision of inner life.*

In referring to mythological characters and religious concepts familiar in both Hindi and Sanskrit forms, Hindi poets did not worry much about consistency. Sanskrit and different Hindi renderings of the same word are frequently given together in one collection – the major consideration often apparently rhyme or meter. The following translations, which sometimes attempt to evoke the tone of an original as popular song, will take similar licence: in particular, final short a's – preserved in Sanskrit but not usually pronounced in Hindi – appear and disappear as metres demand.

7.1 KABIR

Kabir, although remembered as a Muslim, seems to have been born in a caste of weavers only recently converted and still conversant with popular Indic yogic traditions. While his dates of birth and death remain obscured by legend, recent critical estimates put his creative period in the first half of the fifteenth century.[1] Growing up on the lower margins of society, Kabir no doubt experienced both a hard life and abuses of traditional religion – factors inevitably contributing to his highly sceptical view of all orthodox ways, both Hindu and Islamic. Two major themes run through his verse: disgust with the hypocrisy and transitoriness of the world, and a corresponding devotion for the Lord beyond worldly forms, who may be known through the guru. Bridging these themes and adding to their religious persuasiveness are allusions to practical yogic experience, able to reveal at once the hollowness of outward ritual and a path toward the Formless Lord.

Though many longer lyrics bearing Kabir's name are extant, Kabir is *recognised throughout North India as the pre-eminent master of the trenchant couplet. He deliberately confounds us with striking, sometimes paradoxical language (1, 15:14) and bemuses us with insistent irony (15). Oral style remains visible in the repetition of phrases (3, 9:5, 9:35, 9:17, 9:36) as well as of images (3, 9:35, 9:36)². As is customary in collections of* sant *poetry, the selections below are ordered topically.*

Warnings

1 Couplets

Strive for one—you'll get the one; / Strive for all—lose all. / Turn within to water the root / And you'll get more than enough fruit.   *[15:14³*

Kabir says: don't puff up with pride, / Death's got you by the hair / And he can strike you anywhere— / abroad, at home inside.   *[15:44*

One night Kabir was dreaming, / His being seemed to break: / Two people when he's sleeping / But just one when awake.   *[15:47*

An unbaked jar, this body: / You took it on a trip; / It broke when it was hit; / Nothing remains of it.   *[15:59*

This body is the forest; / Your karmas are the axe. / Kabir has thought it out: it's you / who cut yourself down through your acts.   *[15:60*

So many different words there are— / Attend the word that's true. / The word through which you'll meet the Lord: / Grasp it close to you.   *[15:88*

The instrument remains unplayed, / with broken strings. / When the player's left – bereft, it can't / do anything.   *[16:1*

I'm living in a poisoned forest, / encircled by snakes. / Fear thus grasps my soul, / all night awake.   *[16:4*

You won't be overlooked, fish: / the fisherman is death. / Though you go round to all the ponds, / in each he's set his net.   *[16:7*

To a doll of five elements / a man's name they give; / It stays for four days / but needs such space to live!   *[16:14*

Shining now inside the shrine of the body, / like a lamp's light: the soul— / The wayfaring swan. When it leaves, though, they shout: / Drag that trash from the house!   *[16:22*

All the weepers are dead; / the corpse-burners have died. / The lamenters are dead: / so to whom can I cry?   *[16:23*

When they see the gardener come, / the buds make a loud fuss: / The flowers in bloom have all been picked— / tomorrow's time for us!   *[16:34*

Big deal, a son is born! / Why bang a plate to celebrate? / The souls that come and go all seem / like ants who're marching to and fro, in streams.   *[16:40*

Carrying on with another man's wife / is just like eating garlic: / You can hide in a corner to eat it / but finally can't keep it a secret.   *[30:1*

2

For you I live, O Allah-Ram / Show mercy to your slave, my lord.   *(refrain)*

If you draw blood and then call yourself mild, / hiding your guilt all the while

/ What will you get from then bathing in water / or hitting your head on the earth? / Why wash your hands and face, invoke the gods aloud, / or bow your head in mosques: / If your heart says crooked prayers, then what's it worth / to see the *kaaba*[4] in the pilgrims' crowd? / On the eleventh day of every month the Brahmin doesn't eat; / in Ramadan the *qazi*[5] fasts for twenty-four. / Pray tell me why eleven months are empty / and one month has so much more? / And if God only lives in mosques, / whose land lies in between? / Can Ram reside in images and pilgrims' stops? / In neither one has he been seen. / The east is the abode of Hari;[6] / Allah's station's in the West. / But Rama and Rahim[7] both lie within the heart, / and there alone is where to seek them.

As many women, men, that have been born: / they're all your forms. / Allah-Rama's little child, Kabir / knows that one as his guru and his *pir*.[8] [177

Experience

3 Couplets

When I existed, Hari didn't; / now Hari is—I'm not. / All darkness was destroyed just when / I saw the lamp that burns within.   [9:1

A flickering light, but no approach— / can't go there, cannot see it: / Where merit doesn't count, or sins, / Kabir is bound in adoration.   [9:5

The ice took shape from water / and then dissolved away. / Whatever was has become Him: / What more now can I say?   [9:9

Kabir has seen the impenetrable—one— / whose greatness can't be told: / Bright being, spouse, philosopher's stone, / how he absorbed my gaze! [9:12

No foundation for the temple there, / no body for the god— / Where Kabir lingers in service to / the one who can't be seen.   [9:13

Inside—a bright shining lotus / where Brahma makes his home. / The bee-mind is attracted there: / hardly anybody knows.   [9:17

There heavens are thundering, nectar drips down, / banana trees bloom, and the lotus shines bright: / Where just his few real slaves are found, / Kabir is bound in adoration.   [9:35

Kabir sees a bright shining lotus, / a spotless, risen sun. / Night's darkness disappears: he hears / the horn of unstruck sound.   [9:36

4

Who has died? Who has come into birth? / And who has found heaven and hell?   [refrain

The unchangeable gives rise to the five elements, / then lives in them itself. / When the elements slip off, it returns to what it was, / with no hope of a trace. / For the jug is in the water and the water's in the jug: / water within and without. / And the wise teach that when the jug breaks all the water / is one—one like the air. / Know: there's air at the start, and there's air at the end, / and, brother, all the air that's in between. / Kabir says: how can karma stick? / All plans and doubts are false.   [194

5

Kabir's gone bad;[9] / O help me, Ram— / Brother, you / don't go bad, too! [refrain

A tree that grows near sandalwood / goes bad: it turns to sandal. / Iron that's touched the philosopher's stone / goes bad: it turns to gold. / Water mixed into the Ganges / goes bad: it's Ganges' water. / Kabir says: he who's uttered 'Ram' / goes bad: he's turned to Ram. [166

Devotion

6 Couplets

The true guru's the true hero: / just one arrow he shot. / But how it struck! A wide wound in my heart, / I hit the ground. [1:9

The *satguru*,[10] with steady grip, / put an arrow in his bow, then let it go. / And I, exposed, was hit. My body / like a forest burst in flames. [1:23

The guru is the same as Govind: / the rest is all his forms. / To see him truly, worship Hari / and destroy your self. [1:28

He picks up dice of love, / and makes a game-board of his body. / The guru's taught him how to throw: / Kabir, the servant, plays. [1:33

The guru had been pleased with me, / and told me something true. / The cloud of love then burst, / and soaked me through and through. [1:34

I'll burn my body to ashes: with smoke / rising from the pyre; / perhaps Ram will show mercy, showering / rain to drown the fire. [2:20

Though his guru's in Banaras / and he lives by the sea, / if he's made of worthy stuff / they never will forget each other. [2:27

7

My guru's a great bumble-bee; / When bugs come near, that bee will / give them colours like himself.[11] [(refrain)

Their legs become different, their wings become different, / he colours them a different colour. / He doesn't look at rank or origins, / for the devotee is an outcaste. / When it flows into a crossing channel, / the Ganges water itself becomes a little stream. / But someone who has thus become the river / no longer has to jump across it. / He stopped the crooked / movements of my mind / To show that beyond the essence in essentials / and the companion in companionship. / He unbound my bonds / and tore through what was pressing me. / He gave Kabir an access to the Lord beyond all reach / and dyed him in Ram's colours. [1

7.2 SUR DAS

The historical Sur Das probably flourished sometime in the mid-sixteenth century but – like Kabir – he now presents a figure of legendary stature whose name adorns

a great corpus of verse. The pre-eminent poet of Krishna devotion in Hindi, Sur Das seems to have been particularly fascinated with the image of Krishna as a child. Sometimes knowingly (8), sometimes less so (9), Sur's helpless, mischievous infant was also the Lord, giving indescribable delight to his family: his father, Nanda, his mother, Yashoda, and brother Balram. But Sur revelled just as much in Krishna's later play in the pastures of Vraj country, showing us the Lord as beautiful cowherd teasing enraptured milkmaids (12–15), who in turn taunt his befuddled friend Uddhava (17–19). Uddhava for Sur Das presents both a philosophical foil and comic relief: when Krishna was away at Mathura, he had sent his friend to console the milkmaids in his absence, and in a long series of poems that explicitly contrast saguna *and* nirguna *paths, Sur Das depicts the scornful reactions of the milkmaids to Uddhava's misguided exhortations to yoga.*[12]

Frequent in the work of Sur Das are references to eyes and vision. Devotees are attracted to the sight of the Lord: He takes control of their eyes (14) which flow into him as into a sea (15), and which they do not want to close (18); indeed, even Uddhava's eyes, which had just come from gazing at Krishna, at first bring delight to the milkmaids (16). This play of inward and external vision in Sur's poetry makes the traditional representation of Sur as a blind poet particularly enigmatic.

The child-god

8

Krishna is coming outside from within.   *[(refrain)*

To walk in the courtyard was easy, indeed; / at the doorway he's caught, though: / He trips and falls down – he just can't pass the threshold; / what labour to get him beyond it! / In only three steps he traversed the whole world;[13] / but to move across his house takes him such time . . . / Deep within his soul Balram has understood: / Krishna's just pretending to be helpless. / The countless glories of Sur's Lord / delight devotees' hearts.   *[743*[14]

9

Watching Krishna walk gives joy to Mother Yashoda.   *[(refrain)*

On all fours now, close to the floor, Krishna flounders; / his mother sees the scene and points it out to all. / He makes it to the doorway then / comes back the other way again. / He trips and he falls, doesn't manage to cross— / which makes the sages wonder: / Ten millions of worlds he creates in a flash / and can destroy them just as fast; / But he's picked up by Nanda's wife, who sets him down, plays games with him, / then with her hand supports him while he steps outside the door. / When they see Sur's Lord, gods, men, and sages / lose track of their minds.   *[744*

10

Yashoda, his mother, is teaching him to walk.   *[(refrain)*

He stumbles and then grabs her hand, / Unsteady, his feet have found the floor. / At times she looks at his beautiful face / And prays for his well-being. / At times she beseeches her family gods: / 'Let my boy Krishna have long life.' / At times she gives a shout to Balram: / 'Come play here with your brother in the yard.' / Sur Das knows that this great glory of the Lord's play / Gives delight to Raja Nanda. *[733*

11

Kanha's[15] coming: crawling, crying joyfully. *[(refrain)*

In the courtyard of Nanda, golden and jewel-studded, / Hari hurries to catch his reflection. / Now and then Hari,[16] seeing his shadow, / gives it a grasp with his hands, / Then gleefully gurgles: two little teeth shine. / Hari repeatedly seizes his image. / Hand-shadows, foot-shadows, on the golden ground / Together all shine forth. / As if each hand and foot in every jewel on the earth / Had come together in a lotus-throne adorning Krishna. / Yashoda seeing the sweetness of childhood, / calls out to Nanda again and again. / Then hiding her son in the folds of her sari, / suckles Sur's Lord at her breast. *[728*

The milkmaids' fascination

12

In every house in Vraj they've started talking: *[(refrain)*

'Hari's stealing curds and butter, / Then eats it with his cowherd friends.' / The women of Vraj are delighted to hear this: / 'Maybe he'll come to *my* house; / I could creep up on him, as he eats butter, / And press him to my breast.' / This is their desire deep / within: the thought all their hearts keep. / Even if he were to take it away, says Sur Das, / They'd give the Lord butter to eat. *[890*

13

Young Kanha took away my heart. *(refrain)*

Since then I've been possessed, O Mother, / tell me what to do! / I've grown entangled in his twisted curls / and cannot come unloosed. / His pleasing glances, eyes seen from aside, / have settled in my body. / Grown shameless, I've destroyed our family pride: / What is his spell? / Time and time again I tell / him: 'I'm not entering your heart!' / But just as I said 'Hey, / you think I think like you,' / Oh, what a state he brought me to— / my body seemed to fade away. *[2517*

14

These eyes are sold to Hari— *[(refrain)*

A honeyed smile their price. / How could this happen? / Before, I controlled them so nicely, / but things have changed. / Now they're in Hari's camp, embarrassed when they see me. / They only come to leave again— / we meet as in a dream. / Says Sur: now that they flow toward Nanda's joy, / they trust in no one else. [3020

15

My eyes are mine no longer. *[(refrain)*
Gazing intently on beautiful Shyama, [17] / they've spilled out and flow like water. / My eyes behave like water / rushing downstream madly. / The water finally merges with the sea; / my eyes become attached to every part of Krishna. / The sea has no bottom, one cannot pass through it— / nor can one find the end of Krishna's beauty. / Says Sur, the milkmaids' eyes became converging sacred rivers / and mixed into the endless sea of Shyam. [2848

Songs to the bee[18]

16

Today we've been fortunate, Uddhav. *[(refrain)*
Those eyes of yours that come from Shyam / now fall on us. / Just as bees feel love when wind bears / flowers' scent / So bliss swells up in us today, / our limbs know joy. / Just as one's entranced when / looking in the mirror, / So when Hari's found, the pain / of longing leaves. [4151

17

Uddhav, consider our state here in Vraj. *[(refrain)*
Spread the word on yogic powers after that. / Think deeply of the reason Krishna sent you: / Can't you see how great a gap / lies between our longing and transcendent fact? / Since you live among the saints, they say you're smart, / and skilled in spiritual troubles. / Why, then, do you always tell the drowning to keep / grasping foamy bubbles? / How can we erase that smile from our hearts, / that glance that gives us pleasure? / Yogic means, release – the highest holy treasure— / we offer to his flute. / In what way can the *nirgun* come to live / in hearts that know those lotus eyes of his? / We'll let all adoration float away / that feels for something else. [4240

18

Uddhava, we are not worthy of yoga. *[(refrain)*
How can we weak women meditate? / How can we know the one truth? / How can you tell us to shut up these eyes / Where Hari's image glistens? / You're trying to trick us, bee, / and we won't listen! / Who can bear the yogi's pain: / split ears [19] and matted hair? / As we burn up with longing and despair / you'd trade our cooling sandal-paste for ashes. / The one for whom the yogi loses himself, wandering, / is there in us already. / Says Sur: not for a moment are they separate from him— / as if his body's shadows. [4543

19

What land does *nirgun* live in, bee?
We're serious, we swear it's not / a joke, so please explain! / Who's his dad and who's his mum? / His wife and maid are who? / If you try to tell us tales, / they'll come back to haunt you! / What's his colour? What does he wear? / What pleasures does he take? / Unbalanced, silent, Uddhav listens: / Sur thinks his brain might break.   *[4250*

7.3 TULSI DAS

If any one book can be singled out as the most influential devotional work in the Hindi-speaking areas, it is surely the Ramcharitmanas *of Tulsi Das (d. 1623). The basis of public commentary and dramatic performance, Tulsi Das' highly mellifluous verses are also chanted quietly by individuals in private acts of devotion. Historically, the* Ramcharitmanas *appears as a Hindu reaction to the increasingly attractive Indo-Muslim Mughal culture that had begun to take shape by Tulsi Das' time. Not only does it evoke a mythic past that presents the glories of Ram – the embodiment of traditional Hindu virtues – but it also attempts to reconcile deities that rivalled each other in contemporary sectarian versions of Hinduism. Thus, as the hero of the epic, Ram remains the focal point of devotion, but the other great deities are not demeaned by him.*

In the passage given here, Tulsi Das makes Ram instrumental in the Shiva mythology; but at the same time he presents Shiva as a powerful, omniscient yogi. The great ascetic Lord Shiva, having just heard of Ram's glory and longing to meet him, suddenly sees him in the forest. Ram, aided by his brother Lakshman, is in the midst of his long search for his abducted wife, Sita. Shiva is accompanied by his own first wife, Sati, who – by throwing herself into the sacrificial fire lit by her father Daksha – would achieve the dubious distinction of giving her name to the Hindu practice of widow-burning. According to Tulsi Das, Sati was led to her act of self-immolation through her doubts about her husband's devotion to Ram – the subject of the following extract.

20 Ramcharitmanas, Balakanda, 50–52

When Shiva then saw Ram, intense, uncommon joy grew in his heart. / Gazing at this beauty-sea, his eyes were filled. / Yet he did not reveal himself: / he knew it wasn't time / 'O truth, consciousness, and bliss, O world-redeemer – triumph' / —this was all that Shiva said, who once destroyed the god of love. / As he walked away with Sati, Shiva, the abode of grace, / kept shuddering with bliss. / When Sati saw her husband's state, uncommon doubt grew in her heart: / 'The world should worship Shiva, he's the ruler of the world. / To him all gods, all men and sages / bow their heads. / But *he* salutes that king's son – "O truth, consciousness, and bliss," he says, / "O other world!" How he was struck with rapture when he saw that form. / And love that can't be checked / keeps growing in his heart.

The all-pervading *brahman*, with no birth, no parts, no passion; / no wants and no distinctions – which the Vedas do not know / can it really take a body and become a man?   *[50*

Sure, Vishnu took a human form to benefit the gods, / but like my Shiva, he knows everything. / That home of knowledge, Lord of wealth, that one who kills the demons— / can he be searching for his wife just like a stupid man? / Yet Shambhu's[21] word cannot be false; / for everybody knows that he knows everything.' / This boundless doubt stayed in her mind; / her heart knew no enlightenment. / She said nothing of her state, but Shiva knew. / He knows all, who controls within: 'Listen, Sati, you've a woman's nature; / don't ever keep this doubt within your heart. / That's my Ram, my chosen deity, / the one of whom the jar-born *rishi* sang;[22] / in whom I have professed my faith, whom sages serve unceasingly, / the hero of the Raghavas.

Whom sages ever contemplate with spotless mind / —stern yogis, too, accomplished masters; / the *nigamas*, the *agamas*,[23] *puranas* all have sung his praises, / saying, "he's not this, not that": the indescribable; / Maya's Lord, the all-pervading *brahman* that rules all the worlds / —that's Ram. For the sake of his devotees he has manifest, / forever self-sufficient, the jewel of Raghu's race.'

This teaching did not sit within her heart, despite Lord Shiva's repetitions. / But deep within the great Lord knew the power of Hari's *maya* / and so he smiled and said: /   *[51*

'If so much doubt is in your mind, / then why not go and make a test? / I'll sit beneath this banyan's shade / till you come back to me. / Consider carefully, then do something to take away / this stupid, strong delusion.' Sati took Shiv's leave and went away; / 'Oh, brother,' she was thinking, / 'Just what am I to do?' / Shiva sitting there reflected: / 'Nothing good will come to Daksha's daughter. / If, with all I said to her, her doubt did not depart, / then the fates are against her, her fortune is bad. / Still, everything will come through Ram's arrangements; / no need to sit and think how matters could be worse.' / He muttered this, then took up Hari's name. / Sati went to where Ram was in person, the Lord, abode of joy.

She thought and thought within her heart / and took the form of Ram's wife Sita, / then walked along the road on which that king of men was coming. *[52*

Lakshman saw her in the guise of Sita. / Startled, he became confused within. / So grim he looked – he couldn't say a word. / Still, wise, he knew the power of the Lord. / That master of the gods saw through her pose / —all-seeing Ram, controlling all within. / Remember him and ignorance will cease; / Lord Ram knows all! / Yet Sati wanted to deceive him . . . / Behold – the power of woman's nature! / Admiring to himself the force of his illusions, / Ram smiled to speak sweet words. / His palms together, the Lord bowed; / and only

after giving out his own name and his father's, / inquired where Shiva was –
whose standard bears a bull. / And why was Sati wandering in the forest by
herself?

These words of Ram, so soft and deep, made her embarrassed. / Sati,
awestruck, walked toward Great Lord Shiva, / heavy-hearted, thinking: [53
'I disobeyed what Shiva said, / taking my ignorance to Ram. / What can I say to
Shiva now?' / An awful fire grew in her heart. / Ram knew the pain that Sati
felt, / so let her know some of his glory. / Walking down the road, she saw a
spectacle: / in front of her was Ram, with his brother and his wife; / She looked
around: behind she saw the Lord, / his brother, too, and Sita – beautifully
clothed. / Whichever way she looked, she saw the Lord enthroned; / wise
sages, adepts served him. / She saw many Shivas, Brahmas, Vishnus— / their
splendour boundless, one beyond the next. / All the gods she saw, in different
dress, / giving service to the Lord and bowing to his feet.

Satis, too, she saw, and Brahmas' wives and Vishnus' / —all limitless,
unequalled: their bodies fit to wear / the raiments of the gods.   [54

All the gods there, with their wives, / wherever she saw Ram; / all living and
all lifeless things in the created world / —she saw them there, all kinds. / In
many diverse guises, the gods worshipped the Lord. / But she saw Ram in just
one form. / However many Rams and Sitas she beheld, / they all looked just the
same. / Ram, Sita, Lakshman—all the same! / Sati was struck by mighty awe. /
With quivering heart and no awareness of her body, / she closed her eyes and
sat down by the road. / Then opening her eyes she looked again, / but Daksha's
daughter could see nothing there. / She bowed her head repeatedly down
toward the feet of Ram, / and went off to where Shiva had remained. / When
she approached him, Shiva smiled / and asked her how she was: 'I want to hear
the truth now, dear. / How did you test the Lord?'   [55

7.4 EIGHTEENTH–CENTURY SANTS

Though Kabir and most of the sants *who immediately succeeded him came from
some of the lowest strata of Indian society, by the eighteenth century important
poets in the* nirguna *tradition were coming from middle Hindu castes. Paltu
Sahib of Ayodhya – an important centre of Ram worship – was a* baniya, *a
member of a trading caste, and uses the imagery of the merchant to express both
spiritual problems (21) and spiritual potential (22–23).*[24] *Like Kabir at Banaras,
Paltu Sahib lived at a pilgrimage centre and denounced the practice of pilgrimage: more efficacious than empty rituals was devotion to the guru (24). Charandas Das of Delhi (1703–82), also from a merchant caste, was more open to Hindu
traditions of ritual and myth. He travelled to Vraj country, which he described
with a* sant's *insistence on its inner reality (25), and tells of the one divine that
transcends both* saguna *and* nirguna *truths (26).*

7.4.1 Paltu

21

A merchant is someone who measures his mind. *[(refrain)*

Inside the mind's a bazaar; / and the mind has itself become buyer. / In the mind is the giving and taking – for the mind is the store: / the mind lives out its life in the mind. / Loading, unloading take place in the mind – where else can they go? / For the mind must eat what the mind will grow. / In the mind is the measure, in the mind is the weight; / Paltu says it's all a circle in the mind. *[3:45*[25]

22

Look, there's a merchant gone mad— / he's running a knowledge
shop. *[(refrain)*
He's selling deathless nectar, but still it seems like poison: / no customers will buy it. / They ask for salty snacks, he shows them sugar in the raw; / he looks like he's confused. / He gives loans without conditions / and asks everyone to take them. / Those who do will leave him happy / and won't ever be asked to pay him back. / His scales forgive, his weights are full, / his words are sweet for all. / With gems of *nam*[26] just lying in piles about, / he weighs them out, and asks no price. / Of *surat* key and *shabda* lock, / he tells through yogic means. / Says Paltu: Truth's a constant bargain / offered always day and night. *[3:73*

23[27]

Who will keep my shop now, hey, who will keep the shop? *[(refrain)*
The goods are all at *trikuti, sushumna's* got a mattress on the floor; / my main store's at the tenth door; where sits the endless Lord. / *Ida, pingala* – my two scales, they hang from the soul's strings. / I'll grasp the cross-beam of true sound, and weigh out piles of pearls. / The sun and moon will keep up watch on heaps of primal stuff, / climb to *turiya*, set up shop; that's how I'll take charge. / The master *satguru's* interceded, I've met sweet-seller Ram. / He's sounded the drum at Paltu's house, / who keeps getting paid back a hundred and twenty-five per cent. *[3:38*

24

I'll give up all the rest to contemplate the guru. *[(refrain)*
I won't worship Brahma, Vishnu, or Mahesha,[28] / nor fix attention on a god of stone. / The object of my love resides within my body; / to Him alone I'll bow my head. / I won't take my final rest at Kashi, / or take the pilgrim's walk around the town. / Should I reach Prayag, I won't go to the bathing place, / nor will I sacrifice myself to Jagannath at Puri. / Sadhu, I won't mutter wordless phrases / or fix my gaze between my eyes. / Nor will I stretch to sit in yogic posture / and play myself internal sounds. / Sadhu, I'll abandon all God's names / to take the one my guru gave. / The guru's image overspreads my heart

/ and gets all my attention. / When he obliterates our separateness, / what's left I'll call the formless. / The world within the sky will be our kingdom / and with fanfare I will call out 'I'm that Truth.' / At my turn in the game of love, says Paltu, / I'll gamble with the guru. / I get the guru if I win, and if I lose, / then I can say I'm his.   *[3:2–3*

7.4.2 Charandas

25

Krishna always lives in Vraj / But doesn't meet me. / I feel his waves of mercy sometimes / as if he's grasped my arm.

In Vraj are twelve fortunate forests / and twelve enraptured groves / Where Hari plays his flute / and, wanton, sweetly sings.

The fourth state's[29] Lord, / who's deep inside us all, / He lives in Vraj for his devotees' sake, / concealed within Vrindavan— / Wandering over the glorious forest, / the place of play within.

Hari hides from worldly vision / but comes to those with fixed attention. / The sphere of Mathura is nowhere manifest; / if it's manifest it isn't Mathura. / To see the sphere of Mathura, / one needs the inner eye.   *[Bhaktisagar, p.3*[30]

26

In him there are countless forms, / profound and without bounds. / Look how he has manifest / in shapes and names and sounds.

I'll tell you the names of the seeds and the trees / and show all their manifestations: / For he who comprehends the seedless / knows the *nirgun* truth. / But when he understands the truth in all its forms, / he sees the marks of branches, roots, and fruit. / In this way is *brahm* complete, / not in formless *nirgun*. / Not *nirgun* and not *sagun*: / they're thought-up names – not him. / But what I say is nonsense, / for no one can tell the untellable tale. / When someone tries to tell it, pay attention, / but don't think what he's said the final truth. / Says Charandas: great *rishis*, *munis*, / heavy *pandits* – all have searched and failed.

He's *nirgun* and he's *sagun*, / He's different from them both. / Who he was I never knew / however much I pondered. / Endless power, endless play, / virtues of all kinds, / A spectacle of endless shapes / to which Charandas gives offerings. / Endless names, distinctions, actions, / endless *avatars*: / Of *avatars*, though, Shukdev thinks that / twenty-four stand out, / Then Ram and Krishna, both complete, / two in twenty-four: / From *nirgun* he is *sagun*/ for *bhaktas* to adore.   *[Bhaktisagar, pp. 176–7*

8 THE BENGALI TRADITION

Bengali religious texts have a continuous history reaching back to esoteric Budd-
hist poems (charya-padas) of the ninth or tenth century. Bengali verse (prose being
a development of the ninteenth century) experienced tremendous growth during the
fifteenth, sixteenth, and seventeenth centuries. The literature of this medieval
period consists of three major genres: (1) mahakavya *(great poetry), (2)* mangalakavya *(auspicious poetry), and (3) devotional literature.* Mahakavya *includes,*
most importantly, Bengali versions of the classical epics Ramayana *and* Mahabharata *(the best-known authors being Krittivasa and Kashirama Dasa*
respectively). These are not simply translations of the Sanskrit into Bengali, but
are original works that sometimes differ significantly from the classical Sanskrit
texts. Since selections from the classical epics have been translated in other
portions of this sourcebook, no translation of the Bengali epics is included here.
Mangalakavya *is a much more uniquely Bengali style of 'village poetry' that is*
concerned with the emergence of new deities, most frequently female, and the
establishment of their cults on earth. I have included the birth story of the goddess
Manasa as an example of this genre. The most popular among the Bengali
devotional movements is Vaishnavism. A Vaishnava revival took place in Bengal
during the sixteenth century which produced a wealth of religious texts including
biographies, philosophical works, and devotional poetry. I include a selection
from the Chaitanya-Charitamrita, *the most influential of the biographies written*
about the fascinating saint Chaitanya; the first chapter of the Bhaktirasamritasindhu, *a work (written in Sanskrit) which defines the way of devotion in*
aesthetic terminology; a poem (also in Sanskrit) produced for meditation on the
playful activities of Radha and Krishna; and three poems addressed to Krishna by
Narottama Dasa Thakura. I conclude this section with two poems by Ramapra-
sada Sen addressed to the goddess Kali and two poems by the famous Baul singer
Lalan.

Those interested in learning more about the history of Bengali literature would
do well to consult either D. C. Sen, History of Bengali Language and Literature, *second ed., Calcutta, 1954, or S. Sen,* A History of Bengali Literature,
New Delhi, 1960.

8.1 THE BIRTH OF MANASA[1]

Devi, or the Goddess, assumes a vast variety of manifestations throughout the
South Asian subcontinent. Here is the story of the birth of Manasa, one of the
forms she assumes in Bengal. Manasa is the goddess of snakes. A complex cult is
associated with the worship of Manasa, which commonly involved the use of a
sacred pot. The goddess Manasa is worshipped in Bengal to secure a host of

blessings ranging from granting fertility to curing diseases. As snakes are the guardians of treasure, Manasa is also worshipped to obtain welath.

The Manasa-mangala *of Ketakadasa is representative of Bengali* mangala kavya, *a type of poetry which eulogises one of the gods or goddesses. Though few of the remaining poems seems to be earlier than the fifteenth century, many of the stories are much older and appear to have had a long oral history before being written down by a particular author. Dozens of poems about Manasa have been written; Ketakadasa's poem dates from the seventeenth century.* Mangala *poems contain much that is outside the 'great Sanskritic tradition' of Indian thought. The Shiva we meet in the following story, for example, is not the austere ascetic of the Puranas, but is rather a lusty character fond of chasing after young and beautiful women. The* mangala kavyas *typically relate the greatness and power of a particular deity, the benefits to be gained from worshipping that deity, and the suffering to be incurred by denying it. The real gem of the* Manasa-mangala *is the story of the trials of Chando, a defiant merchant marked by Manasa to perform her worship; it also tells of the moving love of Chando's daughter-in-law Behula for his son Lakhindar, a love which brought Lakhindar back from death. Readers are strongly encouraged to read the translation of this story in* The Thief of Love: Bengali Tales from Court and Village, *edited and translated by E. C. Dimock, Jr., Chicago, 1963, pp. 195–294. Those further interested in the cult of Manasa, see: P. K. Maity,* Historical Studies in the Cult of Manasa, *Calcutta, 1966.*

Lord Shiva, Ruler of the Animals (Pashupati), arose one morning and said lovingly to Durga: 'Dear, I am going out to fetch flowers to use in worship. Take (our sons) Karttika and Ganesha inside the house and play dice.' The Destroyer (Hara) then took a basket and knife in his hand, sounded his drum and horn, and mounted his bull. Telling the lords Karttika and Ganesha to remain in the house, the Lord with Beautiful Hair (Ramakesha) went away. The Destroyer set out for the peak of the mountain to gather flowers.

About this time Gauri (Durga) had an idea: 'I will play a trick on Shiva by turning myself into a passionate ferrywoman, and I will see how the Bearer of the Trident (Shulapani) picks flowers.' Durga remained in the house and said to her two sons: 'This morning I will go out to bathe, and then I will come back and cook our meal.' Having said this, with much affection in her heart she gave her two sons sweet candies to eat. After securing her two sons in the house, the Destroyer's wife transformed herself into a very attractive young ferrywoman.

Her beautiful body was a cannon of sex loaded with the god of Love, and her eyes and mouth were armed with ten arrows of passion. Her nose was lovely as a flower, and oh, how beautiful her lips; her bright teeth were as brilliant as a flash of lightning. And oh, how gorgeous were her two breasts, like two sumptuously soft fruits, and how graceful her hair, which hung all the way down to her waist. The vermilion beauty mark on her forehead was like the rays of the sun, and so enchanting was the glance of her eyes that it snatched away one's breath.

Chandika (Durga), Daughter of the Mountain, arrived at the top of the mountain before Shiva and caused a great river of grand illusion to flow. Then she fashioned a boat out of a palm tree, took an oar, and sat waiting near the edge of that river. In the meantime, Shiva came to that place, and when he saw the beauty of the ferrywoman, he was overcome by an arrow of passion. Ketakadasa composed this at the feet of the Goddess.[2] Mother will skilfully protect the best of her devotees.

The Goddess rowed the enchanting boat on the water; seeing her beauty, the Destroyer fell completely into delusion. The sensuous ferrywoman heard him say, moved by her beauty: 'Take your boat and ferry me to the other side of the river.' To this married woman who sat all alone on the water, (Shiva said): 'You are like a doll made out of fine cream; your body is so soft and tender. Seeing your complexion, even the moon becomes humbled. Again and again the arrows from your eyes strike me. When I see your beauty, my heart is ruptured. Why don't you just row us about anywhere you like?'

The sensuous ferrywoman replied to the Great God (Mahesha): 'Come, I will take you to the other shore. This is an opportune moment.' With these words, the ferrywoman placed the boat near him. Shiva then took the hand of the ferrywoman into his own. The sensuous ferrywoman chided him: 'Oh, how disgraceful! How can there be such lust in an ascetic? My husband's name is Shiva and he is at home, but if he were suddenly to come what would he say to me? My intention was simply to take you to the other shore! You old man, why did you take hold of my hand?' The Destroyer said: 'It is useless to depend on your husband. How can he protect your heart after sending you here?' The ferrywoman replied: 'If my husband catches sight of this he will grab hold of your torn rags and kill you. You keep your dignity! I will take you to the other shore, old man, and will not even charge you any money.' Shiva pressed on: 'Hey woman, I am your slave; hug me and give me bliss.' But when she heard this, the ferrywoman said: 'We should never do such a thing.'

About that time, a male and a female heron came together to make love, and a bee was drinking honey from a clump of lotuses. There was much drinking of honey and much love-making. The Destroyer spoke: 'Dear ferrywoman, lift up your eyes and look at this love-play. I am unable to speak any more; my body is shaking. (If you don't submit) my rage will be upon you.' The ferrywoman said: 'This boat is my dharma. If it is violated, my boat will sink. If it becomes heavy with sin it will sink into the water. A wave will then come into my boat and wash me completely away.' Shiva assured her: 'I will do no such thing to your boat, O Lotus-Woman; I will hold you on my lap and just play with you a bit.' Having placed her on his lap, the old man's mind went wild, and Shiva remarked: 'Promise me more O Moon-Faced Lady.' The beautiful lady replied boastfully: 'I will take you out and dump this confident old man in the water.' The Destroyer declared: 'You will not shove me in the water, for I am the God of Gods; satisfy me!'

The ferrywoman said: 'Listen, O Three-Eyed (Trilochana) God, a group of sages sits and meditates at this place. If anyone sees this, a scandal will spread across the country. I will take your tigerskin and spread it out to make a bed.' Shiva declared: 'By means of a mantra I can make it dark. Even if I die, I will not leave this tigerskin.' The ferrywoman said: 'You don't want this love-play; come to my home and I will embrace you completely.' When he heard this, God, the Ruler of the Universe (Jagannatha), turned day into night and spread out his tigerskin. With a voice choked by passion Shiva muttered: 'Come, sit close to my heart and satisfy me, O Moon-Faced Lady.' Trembling, the old man waited with his arms outstretched. Alone, he got ready and finally began to express himself.

Having released his powerful sperm, Shiva laid back and said: 'I have made love with a beautiful lady.' After making love Shiva turned around to find that the Lady of Grand Illusion (Mahamaya) had suddenly vanished from that place. Chandi (Durga) was thinking: 'What have I done? The sperm will now pass into my body, and if this sperm passes into my body I will carry a baby in my womb. And if I give birth to a child at this old age, the gods will ridicule me. I would then be very miserable in the presence of the gods.' Thinking this she placed the sperm on a lotus leaf.

The blood and sperm had come together and were united, and the resulting egg fell near Vasuki, king of the snakes. The Imperishable Vasuki saw it, and by means of his meditative insight determined that it was very powerful. 'This sperm of the Great God has tumbled down to the underworld.' Carefully he placed it in a copper shell. The Imperishable Vasuki placed it in a copper shell; so writes Ketakadasa, who has become very happy.

Paduma (Manasa) was born on a lotus leaf in the underworld and was unequalled in beauty. Seeing her beauty, Vasuki evaluated her in his own mind: 'You will be famous throughout the world and will be regarded as auspicious for the world. This child of Shiva's desire will be successful throughout the three worlds and the whole world will worship her. This will result from the churning of the ocean. The Three-Eyed God will churn the ocean and will drink the poison; he will then whirl around and fall to the surface of the earth. You will rescue that lifeless corpse and bring it back to life, giving honour to my name. He will travel by waterways and will float on the ocean, and then you will revive him.' At this thought, Vasuki felt very happy and gave instructions to many snakes to adorn her body with various ornaments. They made her body very graceful by providing her with a snake throne, snake ornaments, snake poison, a snake's conch for her hand, and a bodice for her breasts. It was as if hundreds of moons were drinking from the circle of her lips, and oh, how beautiful was her curly hair arranged in the chignon of a young girl. It was wonderful. She had pearls in her ears, a bright diamond in her nose, a necklace between her breasts, bracelets of snakes on her arms, and special ornaments on her clothing. There was no one to equal her. Dressed in this manner and riding on a snake, she bid them a joyful farewell.

The Princess Manasa bowed to them and happily mounted the lotus throne. In this way she sat on the lotus throne revealing her smiling face. Kshemananda says: It was at this time that Shiva stopped by to pick flowers.

When he saw the fine and beautiful girl in his path, the Destroyer became enchanted with her physical charm. 'Whose nymphet is this and why is she on a lotus leaf?' The girl bowed to the Forgetful Lord (Bholanatha). Shiva said: 'Tell me quickly: who are you?' Overcome with desire he took her by the hand. Greatly surprised, the Goddess replied, turning aside: 'What are you doing? You are my father! I am your daughter! This is disgraceful! As my father, how can you disgrace your daughter? There will be a scandal in the world of the gods!' When he heard this, the Destroyer was amazed: 'How can you be my daughter?' The daughter of the Lord (Ishana) answered: 'Listen to the reason. You made love with a certain woman. The sperm was not absorbed into her womb. She took the blood and sperm and placed it on a lotus leaf. This blood and sperm was so heavy that it broke the lotus leaf and tumbled to the house of Vasuki. Vasuki nurtured this sperm, and that is how, O Father, I was born.' When the Princess of the Underworld provided this information, the Destroyer of course realised that this was his daughter.

8.2 THE BIOGRAPHY OF THE SAINT CHAITANYA[3]

Chaitanya (b. 1486 C.E.) was a famous Bengali saint and inspirational founder of the devotional movement known as Gaudiya Vaishnavism. Chaitanya was perceived by his followers in a variety of ways, but over the course of time the interpretation of Krishnadasa Kaviraja came to dominate the community's understanding of the true identity of Chaitanya. The central teaching of Krishnadasa's biography of Chaitanya, the Chaitanya-charitamrita, *is that Chaitanya was an incarnation of both Radha and Krishna in the same body. In their previous incarnation Radha and Krishna were considered to be essentially one (Radha was Krishna's own essential energy [svarupa-shakti] or power of pleasure [hladini-shakti]), but were incarnated in two bodies. According to Krishnadasa Kaviraja, Krishna decided to take this unique dual form for two major reasons: one exoteric, one esoteric. Exoterically Krishna assumed the incarnation of Chaitanya to promulgate the form of religious devotion most conducive to the present age. Esoterically Krishna took the dual incarnation to experience Radha's love for himself. I have translated two short passages from the* Chaitanya-charitamrita. *The first presents Krishna's reflections leading up to his decision to embody the dual incarnation. The second describes a devotee's encounter with this dual form. This incident is similar to Krishna's revelation of his true form to his devotee Arjuna in the eleventh chapter of the* Bhagavad Gita. *In the text translated below the devotee Ramananda Raya asks Chaitanya: 'Who are you really?'; with a smile Chaitanya shows him the dual form of*

Radha-Krishna, and like the revelation of the Gita, *this proves overwhelming.*

Two English translations of Krishnadasa Kaviraja's Chaitanya-charitamrita are available and a third, the best, will soon be available:

Sri Sri Caitanya caritamrta, translated by N. K. Ray and revised by S. C. Ray, second edition, 6 vols., Calcutta, 1959.

Sri Caitanya caritamrta, translated with commentary by A. C. Bhaktivedanta Swami Prabhupada, 17 vols., New York, 1974–5.

Caitanya caritamrta, translated by E. C. Dimock, Jr., Harvard Oriental Series, Cambridge, Mass., forthcoming.

Good sources for further information about Gaudiya Vaishnavism include:

S. K. De, *The Early History of the Vaishnava Faith and Movement in Bengal*, second ed., Calcutta, 1960.

E. C. Dimock, Jr., *The Place of the Hidden Moon*, Chicago, 1966.

8.2.1 Krishna's decision to take birth as Chaitanya (*Adi-lila*, chapter 4, verses 238–72)

Once Krishna pondered within his own mind: They say that I appear full of bliss and full of all *rasas*.[4] All three worlds are joyful because of me, but is there anyone who can give me joy? Only one who has hundreds more qualities than I have is able to delight my heart, but it is impossible to find anywhere in the world anyone with qualities greater than mine. Only in Radha can I experience this delight. Even though my beauty surpasses millions of love-gods, even though my sweetness is greater than all other sweetness, and even though the three worlds are delighted by my beauty, my eyes are satisfied only by the sight of Radha. The three worlds are attracted by the call of my flute, but my ear is captured by the voice of Radha. Even though the world is perfumed by my sweet fragrance, my heart and mind are captivated by the fragrance of Radha's limbs. Even though the world is flavoured by my nectar, I am overcome by the nectar from the lips of Radha. Even though my touch is as cool as a million moons, the touch of Radha cools me. For these reasons, I am the source of all happiness in the world, but the beauty and qualities of Radha are the fountain of my life.

My experience may be understood in this way, but when I examine it everything appears in the reverse manner. My eyes are satisfied at the sight of Radha, and Radha faints in ecstacy at the sight of me. She loses her mind at the call of my flute and embraces the Tamala tree, mistaking it for me. 'I have embraced Krishna; my life is fulfilled.' Holding the tree to her bosom, she remains absorbed in the bliss of Krishna. When she smells my fragrance on a pleasant breeze, blinded by love she struggles to fly up to it. When she tastes betel which I have chewed, she plunges into the ocean of joy and is aware of nothing whatsoever. Even with a hundred mouths I cannot describe the joy that Radha experiences in union with me, for it has no end. Seeing the sweetness of her body in bliss at the end of our love-play, I forget myself in that bliss.

The sage Bharata[5] believes that the *rasa* of both (lover and beloved) is equal, but he knows nothing of my Vraja-*rasa*[6] The bliss that Radha experiences is a hundred times greater than the bliss that I experienced in union with another. I said this in the *Lalitamadhava*:[7]

O Fortunate One, your succulent lips surpass the sweetness of nectar, your face is as fragrant as a lotus, your voice puts an end to the proud boasting of the cuckoo's song, your limbs are as cool as sandalwood, and your body shares in all beauty. Tasting you, O Radha, all my senses are suddenly delighted.

Also, Shri Rupa Gosvamin has written this verse:

Her eyes long for the beautiful body of Kamsa's slayer (Krishna); her skin is most anxious for his touch; her ears are eager for his voice; her nostrils are thrilled with his fragrance; her tongue thirsts for his lips; her lotus-like face is cast downward feigning great patience, but also gives outward signs of agitation.

Therefore, I know that within me there is a particular *rasa* which is controlled by my enchanting Radha. I am ever eager to taste that special kind of bliss which Radha experiences from me. I have made many attempts, but I was unable to taste it. At the slightest hint of the sweetness of that bliss, the desire for it grows in my heart. I have descended into the world to taste *rasa*, and I will taste the *rasa* of love in a variety of ways. By the activities of my love-play I will teach the kind of devotion (*raganuga-bhakti*) performed by a devotee who follows the path of passion. My three desires[8] have not been satisfied, for they cannot be truly tasted in the emotions of another. Without taking on the radiance and emotional state of Radha, the three blisses can never be experienced. Thus, having taken on the emotional state of Radha as well as her complexion, I will descend also to experience the three blisses.

In this manner, Krishna made a decision to assume all these emotional states, and at that very moment the time came for the incarnation of the present age. For at that time Shri Advaita[9] was praying and attracted Krishna with his loud petitions. His mother, father, and teachers descended first; then he descended taking on the emotional state and complexion of Radha. Krishna, the full moon, manifested himself in Navadvipa in the pure milk ocean of Shachi's[10] womb.

8.2.2 An encounter with the dual form (*Madhya-lila*, chapter 8, verses 267–91)

The devotee Ramananda Raya is speaking with Chaitanya: 'A confusion still remains within my heart; please be gracious and explain it to me with certainty. First I saw you in the form of a renouncer; now I see you in the form of the dark blue cowherd (Krishna). I see a golden image appearing before you, and its golden radiance is concealing your body. Within it I see a flute raised to your mouth and lotus eyes which are trembling with various emotions.[11] Seeing you in this manner is astonishing. Tell me directly, O Lord, what is the cause of this?'

The Lord replied: 'You have an intense love for Krishna, and this is the nature of love; know this for certain! When a great devotee of the Lord looks at both animate and inanimate objects, Shri Krishna appears to him to be everywhere. He looks at animate and inanimate objects, but does not see their form. Instead, his own cherished deity appears everywhere. As it says in the *Bhagavata Purana*:[12]

The greatest devotee of the Lord is one who sees his own Lord in all beings and all beings in his own Lord. The trees and creepers of the forest, as if manifesting Vishnu in themselves, are richly laden with flowers and fruits and bow their branches under their burden; their bodies thrilled with love verily pour forth streams of honey.

You have a great love for Radha and Krishna; thus Radha and Krishna appear everywhere to you.'

Raya said: 'You are the Lord. Give up this pretence! Do not conceal your true form from me! Having assumed the complexion and emotional state of Radha you descended to taste your own *rasa*. Your secret task is to taste your own love; simultaneously you infuse the three worlds with love. You came to rescue me, and now you trick me. What is the meaning of your behaviour?'

The Lord smiled, and then revealed his true form: the Prince of Rasa (Krishna) – the Container of Profound Emotions (Radha), the two in one body. Seeing this, Ramanda became faint with ecstasy, was unable to control his body, and fell to the ground. The Lord touched him with his hand and thereby caused him to regain consciousness. Seeing the Lord once again in the guise of a renouncer, he was amazed. The Lord embraced him and consoled him: 'I have never showed this form to anyone except you. I have showed this form to you because of your knowledge of the essential truth of my love-play and *rasa*. Actually my body is not golden, but appears so because of the touch of Radha. She touches no one except the cowherd-king's son (Krishna). Having transferred my own heart into her emotional state, I taste my own sweetness.

'Now nothing concerning my activities is unknown to you. Even though I concealed it, you learned the inner truth of everything by the power of love. Guard it in secret! Do not reveal it to anyone! The world will only ridicule my mad activity. I am a madman; you also are a madman. Therefore, you and I are in the same position.'

8.3 RUPA GOSVAMIN

The Bhaktirasamritasindhu *is 'an ocean filled with the nectar of the aesthetics of devotion'. This text was written in the sixteenth century by Rupa Gosvamin, one of the chief theologians of the Gaudiya Vaishnava movement inspired by the saint Chaitanya. Chaitanya had sent six prominent figures to establish the North Indian town of Vrindavana as the major scholastic and pilgrimage centre of Vaishnavism. The* Bhaktirasamritasindhu *is one of the products of the Six Gosvamins of Vrindavana. In this text Rupa Gosvamin sets out to define the religious life of* bhakti *(generally translated as 'devotion') in terms of the aesthetic theory of classical drama. Here the goal of religious activity is to experience* rasa. Rasa *literally means 'sap', 'essence', or 'taste'. Though it retains this original meaning, in the context of aesthetics it can perhaps best be translated as 'dramatic sentiment' or 'aesthetic enjoyment'. Under the pen of Rupa Gosvamin rasa came to mean the supreme bliss that comes from a loving relationship with God.*

Below is the opening chapter of the Bhaktirasamritasindhu *in which Rupa defines the general characteristics of* bhakti, *or devotion. The remaining chapters outline the dramatic world of Krishna's play, as well as the techniques for assuming a part in that cosmic drama. A quarter of this text has been translated into English:* Bhaktirasamritasindhu, *I, translation and notes on the commentaries of Jiva Gosvamin, Mukundadasa Gosvamin, and Vishvanatha Chakravartin by H. H. Bon Maharaj, Vrindaban, 1965. Those who wish to read more will have to await my own forthcoming translation.*

8.3.1 The general characteristics of devotion

Glory be to the Moon (Krishna), whose form is the essence of all *rasas*, who subdued Taraka and Pali with his radiant beauty, excited Shyama and Lalita,[13] and is the beloved of Radha. Even though I am unworthy I praise the lotus-feet of Hari, compelled in my heart by the command of Chaitanya.[14] May this Ocean of Nectar of Devotional Rasa always delight the Lord of Delight whose form is eternal, and be a temple for his rest. And . . . May this Ocean of Nectar of Devotional Rasa ever satisfy my spiritual master, Sanatana, and be a temple for his rest.[15] I pay homage to the porpoise-like devotees swimming in the Ocean of Nectar of Devotional Rasa, who have overcome the fear of the fishnets of time, and have left behind the rivers of liberation.[16] O Sanatana, may your Ocean of Nectar of Devotional Rasa outshine even the Mimamsaka[17] fire, dulling its cruel tongue for all time. Though I am ignorant, I undertake this praise of Devotional Rasa which makes all worlds joyful, for the delight of sensitive people.

Four divisions of the Lord's Ocean of Nectar of Devotional Rasa will now be described in order, beginning with the Eastern.[18] Within this Eastern Division, which explains the distinctions of devotion, four waves will be discussed in due order. The first wave involves the general characteristics of devotion, the second relates to the means of realisation (*sadhana*), the third concerns the foundational emotions (*bhava*), and the fourth considers supreme love (*prema*).[19] The distinguishing characteristic of the highest devotion, fully known by the sages, is clearly explained in this First Wave.

The highest devotion is defined as devoted service to Krishna which is agreeably rendered, is devoid of desire for another, and is not dependent on intellectual knowledge or sacrificial action.[20] As the *Shri Narada Pancaratra*[21] says:

Service with the senses to the Lord of Senses, a service which is pure, and being devoted to Him and free from all restrictions, is called devotion.

And the third canto of the *Bhagavata Purana*[22] says:

Devotion to the Supreme Lord is motiveless and ceaseless. Even if the five kinds of liberation are offered, namely, residence in the same world, equality in power, proximity, similarity in form, and even oneness, my people do not accept them unless they can serve me. This yoga of devotion is the highest goal.

The explanation of the superiority of the devotee mentioned in the previous verses illustrates that quality of devotion which is a manifestation of supreme purity.[23] Devotion: (a) destroys suffering, (b) bestows auspiciousness, (c) easily accomplishes liberation, (d) is very difficult to obtain, (e) consists of a special concentrated joy, and (f) attracts Shri Krishna.

(a) The destruction of suffering

This suffering is of three kinds: sin, the seeds of sin, and ignorance. Sin is of two kinds: that which has not yet begun to yield effects, and that which has already begun to yield effects. Concerning the destruction of sin which has not yet begun to yield effects, the eleventh canto of the *Bhagavata Purana*[24] says:

Just as a blazing fire turns all fuel into ashes, O Uddhava, so devotion focused on me completely consumes all sins.

Concerning the destruction of sin which has already begun to yield effects, the third canto of the *Bhagavata Purana*[25] says:

Even a lowly dog-eater is immediately made fit for the Soma sacrifice by singing, hearing, and meditating on your name, and also by bowing to you and remembering you. How much more so is this true of a direct vision of you, O Lord.

A bad birth is known to be the reason for one's ineligibility for the Soma sacrifice, and that sin which has already begun to yield effects is the cause of a bad birth. The *Padma Purana* says:

Sins which have not yet begun to yield effects, the highest sins, the seeds of sins, and sins which are about to yield effects are gradually dissolved for those intent upon devotion to Vishnu.

Concerning the destruction of the seed of sin, the sixth canto of the *Bhagavata Purana*[26] says:

Such practices as asceticism, charity, vows, etc. cleanse these sins, but not the heart of one born wicked. Yet even such a heart is purified by means of service to the feet of the Lord.[27]

Concerning the destruction of ignorance, the fourth canto of the *Bhagavata Purana*[28] says:

The wise loosen the knots of accumulated karma by means of devotion which delights in the lotus-blossom feet of Vasudeva; while the ascetics who have emptied their minds (i.e. do not bear Vasudeva in mind) and have suppressed the senses are not able to accomplish this. Therefore, take refuge in Vasudeva.

The *Padma Purana* says:

The highest devotion for Hari, which is attended by knowledge, quickly burns up ignorance as a forest fire burns up serpents.

(b) The bestowal of auspiciousness

The wise speak of such auspicious things as these: the pleasing of the whole world, the endearing of the whole world, good qualities, and happiness. Concerning the two-fold pleasing and endearing of the world, the *Padma Purana* says:

The whole world is pleased by him who worships Hari; all animate and even inanimate creatures become enamoured of him.

Concerning the bestowal of good qualities, the fifth canto of the *Bhagavata Purana*[29] says:

The gods who are accompanied by all good qualities abide in him in whom there exists a pure devotion for the Lord; but where are these great qualities for the one who lacks devotion for Hari and whose mind is rushing outward toward the unreal?

Happiness is of three kinds: ordinary, that relating to ultimate reality, and that relating to Ishvara.[30] As the Tantra says:

The most marvellous powers, ordinary enjoyment, eternal liberation (i.e. the enjoyment of ultimate reality), and the never-ending highest joy (i.e the enjoyment of Ishvara) are all obtained from devotion to Govinda.

The *Haribhaktisudhodaya* says:

O God of gods, I pray again and again that firm devotion to you be mine, a devotion which like a creeper bears happiness and the fruit of the four goals which end in liberation.[31]

(c) Easily accomplishes liberation

When the heart is filled with even a little love for the Lord, the four goals of life (which culminate in liberation) become completely like straw.

The *Narada Pancaratra* says:

All powers, liberation, and so forth, and all marvellous enjoyments, accompany the Great Goddess of Devotion to Hari like her servants.

(d) Difficult to obtain

It is difficult to obtain for two reasons: it is not obtainable through even long periods of much practice which is devoid of attachment, and is not given immediately by Hari. Concerning the former, the Tantra says:

Freedom is easily obtained from knowledge, and ordinary enjoyment is easily obtained from the merit of sacrifices, but devotion to Hari is very difficult to obtain even by means of a thousand practices.

Concerning the latter, the fifth canto of the *Bhagavata Purana*[32] says:

O King, the Lord is the protector, the teacher, the deity, the dear friend, the family guardian, and sometimes even the servant of you Yadus. So be it! The Lord Mukunda grants liberation to his worshippers any time, but he certainly does not always grant the yoga of devotion.

(e) Consists of a special concentrated joy

The joy of ultimate reality, which is accomplished over millions of years, does not approach even a drop of the ocean of the happiness of devotion. The *Haribhaktisudhodaya* says:

Even the happiness of ultimate reality is like the water contained in the hoof-print of a cow for one situated in the ocean of pure bliss which comes from the direct perception of you, O Lord of the Universe.

And the *Bhavarthadipika*[33] says:

Skilful people, who are extremely joyful, wander about in the ocean of the nectar of your stories and easily accomplish the four goals, the highest of which seems like straw.

(f) The attraction of Shri Krishna

Having made Hari, who is surrounded by dear friends, the receptacle of its love, devotion subdues Him. For this reason, devotion is known as the attractor of Shri Krishna. The eleventh canto of the *Bhagavata Purana*[34] says:

Neither yoga, nor Sankhya philosophy, nor righteous duty, nor study of the Vedas, nor asceticism, nor renunciation accomplish me, O Uddhava, as does powerful devotion to me.

And in the seventh canto of the *Bhagavata Purana*[35] Narada says (to King Yudhishthira):

Ah! You are the most fortunate in the world of humans; sages who sanctify the world visit your houses because the highest, ultimate reality disguised in the form of a man clearly dwells there.

The three types of devotion (*Sadhana*, *Bhava*, and *Prema Bhakti*) have first been described in due order, as the magnanimity of devotion has been proclaimed by means of six phrases arranged in corresponding hierarchical pairs.[36] Even a tiny taste of devotion involves an understanding of the essence of devotion, while mere argumentative reasoning does not, since it lacks a solid basis for such understanding. Thus it has been said by the ancient teachers: A position which is asserted with even meticulous effort by clever logicians is proven to be otherwise by those who are even more clever.[37]

8.3.2 Remembering the eightfold activities of Radha and Krishna

The Ashta-kaliya-lila-smarana-mangala-stotram[38] *('Auspicious Praise of the Remembrance of the Divine Play Divided into Eight Time Periods') is a poem composed by Rupa Gosvamin which provides a skeletal script for a meditation called* lila-smarana *('remembering the divine play'). This meditative technique involves withdrawing the mind from the illusory activities of the ordinary world and visualising the ultimate world of Radha and Krishna's divine play. This poem establishes the eight time periods of the meditative cycle of the Gaudiya Vaishnavas. The daily cycle commences with the beginning of night's end, a point in time that coincides with a moment called* brahma-muhurta. *Brahma-muhurta occurs three* muhurtas *before sunrise (a* muhurta *is a period of forty-eight minutes) and is held to be the most auspicious time of the day. It is accordingly the time most serious practitioners rise from bed and begin their meditations, following the activities of the eight time periods in due order. The poem also briefly indicates the cycle of service performed for the temple's images of Vrindavana.*

I praise Krishna's eternal activities in Vraja in order now to explain the mental worship to be performed by those travelling on the path of passion.[39] This mental worship achieves the service of love at the lotus-feet of the dear friend of Shri Radha (i.e. Krishna), a service which is attained by those absorbed in the activities of Vraja with eager desire, but is inaccessible to Kesha, Shesha, and Adi (Brahma, Shiva, and Ananta-Shesha i.e. those following the path of 'liberation' [*mukti*]).

May we be protected by Krishna, who at night's end leaves the bower and returns to the cowhered village, in the morning and at sunset milks the cows and enjoys his meals, at midday roams about playing with his friends and tending cattle, in the afternoon returns to the cowherd village, in the late evening amuses his dear ones, and at night makes love in the forest with Radha.

At night's end, I remember Radha and Krishna who are awakened by the songs of parrots and cuckoo birds, both pleasing and displeasing, and by many other noises sent by a concerned Vrinda (goddess of the forest). Arising from their bed of joy, these two are looked upon and pleased by their female friends (*sakhis*), and though filled with desire and trembling from the passion that occurs at that time, they return to the beds of their own homes, fearful of the crowing cock.

In the morning, I take refuge with Radha who, bathed and decorated, is summoned with her friends by Yashoda to his house (Krishna's house at Nandagrama) where she cooks the prescribed food and enjoys Krishna's remnants. And I take refuge with Krishna who awakens and goes to the cowshed to milk the cows; he is then well-bathed and fed in the company of his friends.

In the forenoon, I remember Krishna who goes to the forest accompanied by his friends and cows, and is followed by the cowherds. Desiring to possess Radha, he goes to the bank of her pond (Radhakunda) at the time of their secret rendezvous. And I remember Radha, who having observed Krishna leaves the house for the purpose of performing the sun-worship as instructed by an ascetic. She keeps her eye on the path for her own girl friend who had been sent to make arrangements with Krishna.

At midday, I remember Radha and Krishna who are full of desire and are decorated and made lovely by the various changes brought about by their mutual union. They are served by a host of attendants, are delighted by the jokes of their girl friends such as Lalita, which arouse the god of Love, are trembling with passion and coyness, and are engaged in such playful activities as swinging, playing in the forest, splashing in the water, stealing the flute, making love, drinking honey wine, worshipping the sun, and so forth.

In the afternoon, I remember Radha who returns home, prepares various gifts for her lover, is bathed and beautifully dressed, and is then filled with pleasure at the sight of the lotus-face of her lover. And I remember Krishna who is accompanied back to Vraja by his friends and the herd of cattle, is pleased by the sight of Shri Radha, is greeted by the face of his father, and is bathed and dressed by his mother.

At sunset, I remember Radha who by means of a girl friend sends many kinds of foods which she prepared for her lover, and whose heart is delighted upon eating the remnants brought back by her friend. And I remember the Moon of Vraja (Krishna) who is well-bathed, beautifully dressed, and caressed by his mother. He goes to the cowshed and milks the cows, then returns to his house and enjoys his meal.

In the late evening, I remember Radha, who is dressed appropriately for either a light or dark night and accompanied by her group of girl friends, and who by means of a female messenger makes plans, according to Vrinda's instructions, to rendezvous at a bower consisting of trees of desire located on the bank of the Yamuna. And I remember Krishna who, after watching the performance of skilful arts with the assembly of cowherds, is carefully taken home and put to bed by his affectionate mother. Later, he secretly arrives at the bower.

At night, I remember Radha and Krishna who, being full of desire, have possessed one another. They are worshipped by Vrinda and the many attendants, and they play with their dear friends with songs, jokes, riddles, and sweet speech, which are all associated with the circle dance and the love dance. The minds of these two are on love and they drink prepared honey wine. Masters of love, their hearts expand by the acts performed in the bower, and they experience the various *rasas* of love.

These two are delighted by the company of their girl friends and are lovingly served with betel nut, fragrant garlands, fans, cold water, foot massages, and so forth. After their girl friends have fallen asleep, they too drift off to sleep on their bed of flowers, murmuring the utterances of lovers full of the *rasa* of a secret love.

8.4 POEMS TO RADHA AND KRISHNA

Narottama Dasa Thakura was a Gaudiya Vaishnava poet who lived in the seventeenth century. Narottama was centrally involved in a religious practice known as Manjari Sadhana. After visualising Radha and Krishna's love-play in the forest of Vrindavana, the practitioner of Manjari Sadhana serves the divine couple by assuming the identity of one of the female servants (manjaris) mentioned in the previous poem of Rupa Gosvamin. The first of these poems expresses the desire to give up all for the enchanting world of Vrindavana; the last two express the desire for the loving service of Radha and Krishna in the body of a manjari.

Older Bengali poems describing the love-play of Radha and Krishna are also plentiful. For a delightful collection, see In Praise of Krishna: Songs from the Bengali, *translated by E. C. Dimock, Jr., and D. Levertov, Chicago, 1967.*

Hari! O Hari! When shall I be transformed into such a state that having become indifferent to everything I will go to the land of Vrindavana? This is the desire I hold in my heart.

Renouncing family, wealth, sons, and wife, and becoming all alone, when shall I go? Casting off all sorrows, I will dwell in the town of Vraja. Begging from door to door, I will eat what is offered.

When shall I fill my stomach with the water of the Yamuna River, the immortal nectar? When shall I fall into and bathe in the waters of Radha's pond, delightfully known also as Krishna's pond?

I will roam through and play love games in the twelve forests, all of which cause one to welter in supreme love. Having touched their feet, I will humbly petition the residents of Vraja dwelling in those places.

When shall I set eyes on the feasting place? And how much longer until I see the secret bower? The desire of Narottama Dasa's heart is the feet of the divine couple in the middle of this bower of Vrindavana.

Hari! O Hari! When shall I attain such a state in which I will serve the feet of the divine couple?

Becoming a bumble-bee, I will forever reside at your feet and ceaselessly drink the blessed nectar from these feet.

Fulfil this hope of all the female friends. All that is desired is fulfilled by your grace.

Day after day I wish for this fulfilment. After all have assembled, be merciful and show your grace.

Day and night Narottama weeps for the hope of your service. By your kindness, makes me a faithful female servant.

Hari! O Hari! When shall I attain such a state? When shall I, abandoning this male body, assume the body of a female and apply sandalwood paste to the bodies of the divine couple?

Having drawn up your topknot of hair, when shall I bind and encircle it with fresh *gunja* seeds, string various flowers and offer them to you as a necklace, assist your female friends in dressing your body with yellow cloth, and place betel nut in your mouth?

When shall my eyes be filled with the sight of the two forms which steal away the mind? This is my heart's desire. Glory be to Rupa and Sanatana (Gosvamin). This female body is my treasure. Humbly, Narottama Dasa.

no.28, no.35, no.45 of the *Prarthana Padavali* of Narottama Dasa Thakura in N. P. Nath, *Narottama Dasa o Tahar Racanavali*, Calcutta, 1975, pp. 307–53.)

8.5 POEMS TO MOTHER KALI

The Mother Goddess, known frequently as Durga or Kali, is extremely popular in Bengal. Ramprasad Sen was a famous eighteenth-century devotee of the Goddess and was very influential in her rise to popularity. His poems reflect the attitude of the cult of Shaktism, where the feminine aspect of divinity (shakti) is supreme. Worship of the divine as Mother made new forms of devotion possible; in the poems of Ramprasad the unpredictable other is petitioned as a child would petition its mother. Ramprasad typically addresses his poems to the mysterious mother who appears in the fierce and naked form of Kali, the mistress of a world rushing uncontrollably toward death.

Two English translations of Ramprasad's poetry are available: L. Nathan and C. Seely, Grace and Mercy in Her Wild Hair, *Boulder, 1982; J. Sinha,* Ramaprasad's Devotional Songs, *Calcutta, 1966.*

Who can comprehend your cosmic play, Ma? What you take and what you return?

You give and you take, my dear, and don't keep anything from morning till evening. Your unbounded activity is unavoidable; you determine the fate of everyone.

Even the Forgetful Lord (Shiva), bound by your feet, has forgotten your ensnaring design.

Whatever you reveal is exactly what I see; you float rocks on the surface of the water.

Your tactics won't work any longer on me, Ma. Ramprasad is your son who knows the secret of all your tricks.

Kali, why are you naked again? Come on, where is your modesty?

You wear no splendid apparel, Ma, yet you boast of being a king's daughter. And Ma, is this standing on your husband a demonstration of your aristocracy?

You are naked, and your husband is naked; You wander about the cremation grounds.

Ma, we are dying of shame. Put your clothes back on.

You have cast aside your necklace of jewels, Ma; a garland of human skulls glistens at your throat.

Prasad says: Even the Naked Lord (Shiva) fears you in this form, Ma.

No. 132 and no. 79 of Yogendranath Gupta, *Sadhak Kavi Ramprasad*, Calcutta, 1954, pp. 323–4 and 306.)

8.6 SONGS OF THE BAULS

The Bauls are a group of wandering singers from village Bengal. The word Baul is generally accepted to be a derivation from the Sanskrit vatul, meaning mad, crazy, affected by the wind. Most Baul songs involve inquiry into one's ultimate nature and one's relationship with the Infinite. The following two songs are attributed to Fakir Lalan Shah, a famous Baul of the late eighteenth century. The image of the bird and cage (soul and body) is a favourite among the Bauls. Since Lalan's songs draw from Muslim as well as Hindu imagery his songs remain popular in Bangladesh as well as the Indian state of West Bengal.

Two readily available works containing further translations of Baul songs are: The Mirror of the Sky: Songs of the Bards of Bengal, translated by D. Bhattacharya, London, 1969), and Roots in the Void: Baul Songs of Bengal, translated by A. and M. A. Dasgupta, Calcutta, 1977.

This bird may fly away any time now; a bad wind has struck its cage.

The resting post suspended in the cage has fallen down; how then will the bird remain? Now I sit and worry, and endure a feverish terror in my body.

Whose cage is this? And who is this bird? Which do I consider my own; and which as stranger? Which is my eye most eager for? This bird wants to charm me.

If I had only known earlier that this wild thing could never be tamed, I wouldn't have fallen in love with it, but now I see no way out.

On the day my beloved bird flys away, the cage will suddenly be empty. On that day there will be no companion to console me. So mourns the wanderer Lalan.

A certain flower contains four colours; and oh, what beauty exists in the city of love within this flower!

The flower floats in the middle of the primordial waters, drifting from shore to shore. An anxious white bumble-bee buzzes around in hopeful expectation of the flower's nectar.

The flower's creeper is without roots and its leaves without branches. All this is quite true, but who can I talk to about the existence of this flower?

Dive deep into the waters and explore with an open heart, O mind. A saint is born in that flower, and that flower is certainly no ordinary flower. Lalan says: It has no roots in this world.

No. 32 and n. 128 of the songs of Fakir Lalan Shah in U. Bhattacharya, *Banglar Baul O Baul Gan*, Calcutta, 1981, pp. 566 and 623.)

9 THE TAMIL TRADITION[1]

The literary languages of southern India – Tamil, Telugu, Kannada, and Malayalam – belong to the Dravidian family, which has no inherent relationship to Sanskrit or Indo-Aryan, although each of these languages has borrowed Sanskritic vocabulary and concepts to a greater or lesser degree. Tamil is the earliest Dravidian language attested (there are Tamil loan-words in the Hebrew Bible), and the Tamil country, Tamil Nadu, can fairly claim to have been, from its beginnings, one of the most creative, formative areas of Hindu culture. Tamil civilisation as we know it goes back to the last centuries B.C.E. and early centuries C.E., when the three small-scale kingdoms of the Cholas, Pantiyas, and Ceras emerged as political and cultural centres, linked by trade to the outside world (including the Mediterranean basin). This early stage of Tamil history is often referred to as the Sangam Age, after three legendary 'academies' (sangam) which are said to have supervised the work of the classical poets and scholars. And, indeed, one of the great legacies of this period is a body of poetic works (dating roughly from the first to the fourth centuries C.E.) devoted to the subjects of love (the 'inner' poetry, akam) and the heroic themes of battle and panegyric (the 'outer' poetry, puram). Both because of the largely 'secular' nature of this poetry, and because it has become much better known in the West in recent years through extensive translations,[2] no selections from Sangam poetry are presented here.

Beginning approximately in the sixth century C.E., in the period known as Pallava-Pantiya and marked by a powerful synthesis of northern Sanskritic culture and local Tamil elements, a new wave of religious thought and feeling swept through South India: this is the movement of devotion (bhakti) in its passionate mode, which eventually spread through the entire subcontinent and coloured much of the subsequent history of Hinduism. We can observe three main stages in the evolution of the bhakti movement in its southern birthplace: a first, rhapsodic period, when the wandering poets and saints of Shiva (the nayanmar, 63 in the traditional numbering) and of Krishna-Vishnu (the twelve Alvars) created a corpus of devotional poetry that was to constitute the sacred texts of each respective current (sixth to ninth centuries); a second stage of establishing the limits of this Tamil canon, of crystallising hagiographical traditions, and of initial Sanskritisation (ninth to twelfth centuries); and a third stage of philosophical elaboration and explication in terms of the pan-Indian Vedanta (the creation of the Shaiva Siddhanta corpus in Tamil and the Shrivaishnava Vishishtadvaita writings, from the eleventh century on). The Shaiva canonical literature is represented here by one central figure, Cuntaramurtti, whose poems may be said to exemplify Tamil Shaiva devotionalism in its more extreme and dramatic form. Devotion to Vishnu is illustrated not from the Alvar corpus but from Kampan's lyrical narative on Rama.

In later medieval times, Tamil poets continued to produce devotional poetry, often of innovative types and, in some cases (such as the Tamil Siddhas or Cittar), with an antinomian twist. One development, that of satirical poems of 'worship through insult,' is illustrated in the verses of the fifteenth-century poet Kalame-kam. The mutts (Tamil matam, Sanskrit matha), centres of teaching and study mostly concentrated in Tanjore District, produced scholar-poets active in many genres – commentaries on canonical texts and Sanskrit philosophical treaties, devotional 'romances,' lyrics, and, later, dance-dramas, ethical works, local Puranas, and so on.

Tamil bhakti also had a profound impact on the development of Telugu in Andhra, to the north of the Tamil country (attested in literary form from the eleventh century onwards; the earliest major work to survive is the Telugu Mahabharata produced by three successive poets, Nannaya, Tikkana, and Erra Pragada, which is, however, essentially independent of the southern, Tamil tradition). Telugu bhakti-poetry also absorbed other influences, including those of the iconoclastic Virashaiva poets from neighbouring Karnataka and of the highly developed models of Sanskrit court poetry (kavya). In some poets, such as the sixteenth-century Dhurjati, these different sources and visions combined to produce a uniquely complex and engaging blend. Others pursued the southern predilection for passionate devotionalism in various creative modes (such as the seventeenth-century poet Kshetrayya's erotic hymns to Krishna, composed in the Tamil south). We cite in conclusion two very distinct examples of this medieval Telugu poetic world.

9.1 CUNTARAMURTTI: THE HARSH DEVOTEE

Cuntaramurttinayanar, or simply Cuntarar, or Nampi Aruran (as he calls himself), is the third and last of the Tamil poets of the Tevaram, *which forms the basis of the Tamil Shaiva canon. He differs from his predecessors, Tirunanacampantar and Tirunavukkaracucuvamikal or Appar, mainly in the angry tones that predominate in his verse; he sometimes calls himself* van tontan, *the harsh devotee, although the Shaiva tradition knows him as* tampiran tolan, *the friend of god. The hagiographical tradition tells us that Shiva blinded this devotee after Cuntarar deserted his second wife, Cankiliyar, from the shrine of Tiruvorriyur in the north of the Tamil country; but the poet's vision was restored when he reached his home, and the home of that form of Shiva he chose to worship, in Tiruvarur. Many of Cuntarar's finest poems, in which he quarrels bitterly with the god he loves, are ascribed to this period of his blindness. The poems translated here illustrate both the tensions and the sense of intimacy between Cuntarar and Shiva; the poet threatens to abandon the god in revenge for the latter's maddening silence and withdrawal, even hurls ironic curses at him (in poem 95), although he also blames himself for forgetfulness, stubbornness, and sensuality (especially in poem 60).*

The characteristic poetic form of the Tevaram *is the* patikam, *a set of ten or eleven verses addressed to the god of a single shrine (with his local name and mythology) and loosely unified in tone and themes. Puranic myths and iconic traits of the god are also usually mentioned, as are the poet's powerful and often conflicting emotions. The final, signatory verse, called the* tirukkataikkappu *or 'the closing of the doors', frequently spells out the rewards to be gained by reciting the* patikam.

1 *Patikam* 14, on Tiruppaccilacciramam[3]

1. I placed before him my head and my tongue; I even offered him my heart. I didn't try to cheat him. But whenever I talk of being the servant of his feet, I'm just a man of metaphors to him,
   our supreme lord of Paccilacciramam, that madman who ties his loin-cloth with a hooded serpent:
   if *he* doesn't want us, can't we find some other god?

2. I don't call to him as my mother. I don't call to him as my father. I thought it would be enough to call him my lord—
   but he pretends I don't exist, doesn't show an ounce of mercy.
   If that lord who dwells in Paccilacciramam, surrounded by pools filled with geese, postpones the mercies meant for his devotees—
   can't we find some other god?

3. Except when I'm in trouble, I don't realise how much I need him. I used to think my heart would be enough.
   He destroyed by fire the Triple City of his enemies,[4]
   the lord of Paccilacciramam with his red matted hair and neck soaked with

poison[5], who has mercy on those who have nothing—
  say what you will, we can rejoice when he gives to us or curse him when he doesn't,
  but can't we find some other god?
4. He holds his tongue, that lord of Pacilacciramam with its ponds full of raucous birds and its fields yielding gold—
  he fails even to distinguish *our* people from the others, never says 'good' or 'bad', won't plaster over anything.
  Listen to me, my heart: he will enslave many, yet never say one loving word or give them anything, so
  can't we find some other god?
5. Although it was his nature to harm the city in the sky[6] with his fierce, bound bow,
  the day that he blesses us is a time of service, worthy of praise.
  But when he goes away, it is a day of dying, of disaster:
  if our lord of Paccilacciramam, who has mercy for those who love, departs from us in a flash and disappears, no matter what we say—
  can't we find some other god?
6. I won't follow in the path of those who torture their bodies; his feet are my only way, I know no one else, no other way to annihilate evil deeds—
  and *he* knows *that*, our lord who holds the trident, best of weapons, supreme god of Paccilacciramam:
  if he just smears himself with white ash, as he likes to do,
  can't we find some other god?
7. Skull clinging to one hand,[7] he lives his life in the wilderness; another hand holds high the club; his body bears the sacred thread; the white moon crowns the sleek, glistening hair
  of the disfigured[8] supreme god of Paccilacciramam, where women bathe, their mounds of Venus like hooded serpents—
  if he appears to be faithful and yet plays us false,
  can't we find some other god?
8. I never thought the body covered with flesh could survive. I used to think my heart alone could support me.
  Immersed in the crowd, I worship him night and day in my mind, with my hands—
  while in *his* hands he grips a hooded serpent,
  our supreme lord of Paccilacciramam:
  if he *must* dance in the burning-ground littered with corpses,
  can't we find some other god?
9. You melt yourself down, my heart— you run to join him, to perform his smallest service.
  There are those without love who won't escape their appointed day, yet when they call him as their lord, he finds mercy for *them*,
  our lord of Paccilacciramam: but if he won't forgive *our* mistakes or give us

anything, no matter what we say,
  can't we find some other god?
10. Ragged clothes, lime-white ash—
  if I see them, if I concentrate, my mind turns to the god with the sapphire
neck, and I call to him as his servant with my voice.
  He grasps a hooded serpent in his hand, our supreme god of Paccilacciramam—
  if he won't bind us, master us, command us,
  can't we find some other god?
11. Not just once am I yours, but in all the seven kinds of birth I am your
servant and your servants' servant.
  I belong to you by right; even my heart melts in love—
  yet you still won't show me your feet decked with flowers.
  If our lord of Paccilacciramam, who has mercy on those blessed with
precious fame, talks big and then acts low,
  can't we find some other god?
12. I'm not abusing him or showing contempt; all the time I know him as our
lord.
  For many days, I, famous Aruran from Naval(ur) with its rich fields, have
sought to worship the feet of the lord of Paccilacciramam,
  calling to him with my voice, thinking of him with my mind—
  but if he won't put up with the things that I have said, can't we find some
other god?

2 *Patikam* 3, on Tirunelvayil Aratturai[9]

1. Aloe-wood from the mountains and luminous jewels are cast forth by the
Niva River in its course:
  here, on its shore, at Nelvayil Aratturai, you dwell as of old, flawless lord
crowned with the white crescent moon.
  I know how in the world life passes like a word: 'Their birth was celebrated,
they lived their life, dressed up, grew old, and died.'
  I have followed you as your servant; now tell me— by what ruse can I
survive?
2. Women with long, curled hair look on as you do your dance on the bank of
the Niva River which casts up spicy pepper and hardwood trees in its course,
  flawless lord of Nelvayil Aratturai:
  you made me a man on this poor earth, impermanent,
  where I, too, will not endure.
  Show me some secret ruse that I may fight to curb my senses and take refuge
at your feet.
3. In joy, you bound the serpent that dances in the anthill to your waist. Holy
one! Your mount is the martial white bull.
  Why am I without an eye, flawless lord of Nelvayil Aratturai? I cling to no
one but you, great lord who shares his body with the Woman, whose curls are

covered with bees:[10]
    tell me some secret ruse that I, your servant, can cross the sea of death
    and still survive.
4. Flawless lord of Nelvayil Aratturai, where tall groves rise on the banks of
the Niva flowing with flowers of the *venkai* and *konku* with its high branches—
    you are in the mind of those who think of you:
    youth is the bank of a flowing river; birth is like waking after sleep.[11]
Show me some secret ruse that I, your servant, can survive, no longer
withering in sorrow.
5. Here, when the clouds' rain soaks the stony mountain, the Niva overflows
and washes away the tall bamboos, while women, like bright peacocks, practise their dance on its banks.
    Flawless one of Nelvayil Aratturai: before my five senses grow confused and
my heart melts in pain; before the henchmen of Death with his sharp spear
torment me and I grow weary in confusion and in fear—
    tell me, your servant, some secret way to survive.
6. Cardamom and cinnamon and brilliant gold are cast up by the rushing Niva
on its banks:
    you who are here, in Nelvayil Aratturai, where geese flock to the pools filled
with dark blue lotuses—
    my body aches at the touch of the tip of a grain of paddy; I take no joy in it; I
have suffered enough,
    lovely god sitting in the banyan's shade, immortal: tell me, your servant,
some secret way to survive.
7. Heavy logs of aloe-wood carried down from the mountain-peaks are cast up
by the Niva on its banks, where matchless women, like peacocks, practise their
dance.
    Flawless lord of Nelvayil Aratturai with the *makara* earrings[12]—
    the body dressed up for a wedding becomes a corpse to be burnt. So much
for life!
    You who are First as the sound 'a' among syllables[13]—
    show me, your servant, some secret way to survive.
8. You crushed, in your mercy, the twenty strong arms of the king of Lanka,[14]
where heavy chariots rumble through the long streets,
    flawless lord of Nelvayil Aratturai in the pasture-lands where crabs crawl
through the wide paddy fields:
    through my good fortune achieved long ago, I have won the boon of uttering
your name,
    supreme light, cowherd,[15] immortal lord to the immortals—
    show me, your servant, some secret way to survive.
9. That god who assumed an ignoble form and then measured the world[16] and
the one who sits upon a flower[17] failed to see you, for all their long searching,[18]
    flawless lord of Nelvayil Aratturai worshipped by the gods with their high
crowns—

before I am caught in a net of women with radiant foreheads, like a fly fallen into a ripe jacket-fruit,

show me some secret way, lord with the form both of man and of woman, that I, your servant, can survive.

10. Aruran, the devotee, king of Naval(ur) in the south crowded with fine buildings and long streets where the chariots pass, sang this garland of ten verses, in good Tamil, to the flawless lord of Nelvayil Aratturai in the uplands, surrounded by well-watered fields.

Those who can learn these verses will become kings with elephants that attract dark, drunken bees; they will rule the whole heavenly world.

3 *Patikam* 60, on Tiruvitaimarutur[19]

1. Like a donkey laden with a burden of saffron, harried through a wasteland,[20]

half-dead, I stumble, father— trapped in a whirling vortex.

And you, my heart— why go on weeping? I am too much a fool to call to Hara[21] of the lovely eyes.

Show me in your mercy some way to be saved,
father, lord, dwelling in Itaimarutu.

2. Now the grey miseries of age will be upon me: intent upon ungrateful deeds, I have worn myself thin, seen fine-ground turmeric grow stale.

Death frightens me.

Grating and grinding my way to your bright feet, I wheeze and sputter, confused, knowing nothing of the life of feeling.

Show me in your mercy some way to be saved,
father, lord, dwelling in Itaimarutu.

3. Like a dew drop on the tip of a blade of grass as the sun grows warm— such is life, without substance:

each day I wonder what today or tomorrow will bring. I have suffered, father— for I was the fool who failed to reach your feet long ago. So much time has been lost! Is it too late to show me some way to be saved,
father, lord, dwelling in Itaimarutu?

4. My former deeds torment me here and now. I have wasted so much time being stubborn. I don't think of you, can't keep you in my mind. To those who seek my help, I give nothing, however small.

In red twilight the white crescent crowns you, our lord, chief of the immortals who resides in Arur:[22]

It is up to you to show me some way to be saved,
father, lord, dwelling in Itaimarutu.

5. Five vicious officers[23] ruled me entirely, until they rejected me, trampled me underfoot—

and, in the end, I became a burden on *you*, my last resort.

I have awakened to the truth: if this is human life, I want no part of it— I despise it.

Show me in your mercy some way to be saved,
father, lord, dwelling in Itaimarutu.

6. Overflowing with flaws— but with a few good features, too— I have lost myself in lovely, slim-waisted women, learned none of the arts, gained no wisdom,
accomplished harsh, cruel deeds.
There is nothing else to cling to: evil as I am, my works, too, are evil. Why am I still alive?
Have mercy, show me some way to be saved,
father, lord, dwelling in Itaimarutu.

7. I cannot offer anything of fine substance, cannot abandon flaws such as rancour, lust, anger, could not control my five senses even if I wanted to.
I am miserable, afraid that as old age approaches with its tremors Yama's henchmen will throw me into hell.
Show me in your mercy some way to be saved,
father, lord, dwelling in Itaimarutu.

8. These five[24] rule me like five rival kings: they never leave me alone. I rush about, conforming to their various demands.
I know not what to do, lord of Shiva's world, fire-hued fire-dancer—
somehow you must show me some way to be saved,
father, lord, dwelling in Itaimarutu.

9. Seeking foolish human joys, I let myself be snared by beautiful young women. Thinking that 'for us, the plantain will always bear fruit!'[25] I was trapped in a net of deceitful, harsh deeds.
I sided with dullards, followed their way.
I am a fool, innocent of wisdom and of meaning.
Have mercy, show me some way to be saved,
father, lord, dwelling in Itaimarutu.

10. Here, in Itaimarutu, on the south bank of the raging Kaviri, which casts upon both banks its rich burden of sandal to be ground into paste, aloe-wood, and wild mountain-rice,
dwells our father, our lord, put to the test by Uran[26] with his brilliant garland of verses. Those who can praise him thus with joy, with all their hearts, will be free from grey old age and its tremors;
they shall surely approach the bright feet of the lord.

4 *Patikam* 95, on Tiruvarur[27]

1. Those who have become your servants in irrevocable bondage need no others;
yet their hearts go on smouldering within them like a fire contained. Their faces grow thin.
For though they *are* your own servants, whenever they speak of their sorrow, you just sit there, impassive, O lord of Tiruvarur—
we wish you luck; go away![28]

2. You can sell me off, but I am nobody's pawn— I *chose* to be mastered by you!

I did nothing wrong, yet you blinded me— why, lord, did you take my eye? The disgrace is wholly yours.

If you won't restore my other eye— then I wish you luck; go away!

3. You who are in Arur, where the *anril* birds constantly gather in the groves: like cows that give milk when the calves butt against their udders, your devotees are always pouring forth their songs— and still their eyes cannot see! What if they stumble against the high places or fall into a pit? But never mind— we wish you luck; go away!

4. You live in Turutti, have Palanam as your place, rule over Corrutturai; but your real home is Tiruvarur.

You have no need to take up residence in our minds.

If, when your loving servants speak of their sorrow, you make them suffer more and offer blessings in *future* births—

then I wish you well: go away!

5. Is this Tiruvarur, its gardens radiant as cool coral?[29]

Master, is this any way to treat your slaves? The devotees who sing to you in many metres see nothing with their eyes, but if they come to complain to you, 'Lord, is this right?'—

Never mind; just be well and go away.

6. Herons, their legs bright as millet stalks, come to Tiruvarur where *you* are, with your fine twisted hair and your gold-like garland of thick *konrai* from the pasturelands.

Your devotees grow more emaciated each day, though not for want of money! They cannot see you with their eyes. If they should become dejected at heart—

we wish you luck; go away!

7. You are in Arur, where birds gather in the groves; hey, great lord of ours— is this any way to treat your slaves?

You played your tricks, gave us birth, gave us minds which can't forget, gave us bodies, too; now if you take away our tears—

we wish you luck; go away!

8. Our words mix the salt-marsh with the ocean, ships and dry earth as we praise you; we're not insulting you— *we* were born in good families!

But as for you, our master— you know nothing of shame.

Don't mind us: if we, your singing servants, can't even see the road, even if we stumble and get lost—

We wish you luck; go away!

9. Separation, even from a demon, is horrible—

as anyone can tell you.

'Even an unripe fruit turns ripe, if you care for it'— that's what they are thinking, your slaves who follow you like a dog, clinging to the middle;[30] yet you won't open your mouth to give them even one word, O lord of Tiruvarur—

we wish you luck; go away!

10. Is this Tiruvarur, with the *cerunti* flowering into gold in the groves?

O you who have chosen for your own place the Tirumulattanam:[31] sitting, standing, or lying down, we praise you; we won't insult you. But if, in our sorrow, we come to say to you a single word—

we wish you luck; go away!

11. A neck drenched in darkness; eight arms; three eyes; the form of many arts— I, Aruran, bear the name of that lord in the Tirumulattanam of Arur.

You took away my eye, and all the villages of the world know about it; still, *yours* is the disgrace.

You have taken into your body the Woman whose breasts are tightly bound. Congratulations! Go away.

9.2 KAMPAN: THE SIGHT OF SITA'S JEWELS

Kampan's Iramavataram, *a Chola-period work belonging perhaps to the twelfth century, is one of the masterpieces of Tamil literature. Although basing himself on Valmiki's Sanskrit* Ramayana, *Kampan has in fact produced a text imbued with the unique spirit of medieval South India and reflecting, above all, its devotional ethos. Rama, here, is simply God – or rather, since there is nothing simple about this identification, he is God embodied in the profoundly problematic and often painful state of being human, with all the rich complexities of emotion and perception that accompany this state.*

In the short passage translated here, the kalan kan patalam *from Book IV, Rama, wandering in the forest with his brother Lakshmana in search of Rama's kidnapped wife Sita, encounters Sugriva, former king of the monkeys in Kishkindha. Sugriva displays before the eyes of his new-found friend the jewels that Sita had torn from her body while being carried off to Lanka by the demon Ravana; the monkeys had found these ornaments and saved them. Identifying them at once as Sita's, Rama is overcome with longing, sorrow, remorse, and self-castigation at his helplessness and passivity. The speech he addresses to Sugriva and the latter's minister, Hanuman, presents us with a succinct and moving picture of the Tamil* bhakti-*god, embroiled in the world, astonishingly close in his heart to his worshippers' own inner state.*[32]

As the passage opens, Sugriva is speaking to Rama.

1. 'Some time ago, while we were somewhere here, a woman far away – was it your wife?— looking straight at us screamed in sorrow as a cruel demon carried her away.

2. We couldn't understand what was in her mind— perhaps she thought these jewels could serve as messengers. She cast them off together with a flood of tears from her eyes, dark as a raincloud, and we found them here.

3. We have kept them, generous lord— let us bring them to you now, and you will know them.' Thus, with a heart full of love— like ghee mixed with milk—

Sugriva brought forth the jewels and held them out in his hand.

4. Rama looked at the jewels that had graced his wife's body and understood. We cannot say that his body melted, like wax in a burning flame. Nor can we say that he drank in sustenance for his spirit. What, then, can words convey?

5. What more could those jewels have given him than this: those that had adorned her breasts took the form of those breasts; those that had graced her mound of Venus *became* that mound of Venus; each of the ornaments reshaped her body before his eyes.

6. What can I say?— that these jewels called up his forgotten understanding? that they attacked his spirit? that they cooled him like the soothing touch of sandal-paste, or, rather, burned him like flames?

7. He sniffed at the lady's jewels, and they were flowers in his arms, or fine cloth, a cloak of light that covered his limbs like gleaming sandal-paste as he held them in his embrace.

8. The flood from his red eyes swept all before it. Bristling hairs covered his entire body. Did he break out in a drenching sweat? Did he rage within? What can I say about that pure lord?

9. Like poison spreading through his system, heat overcame him; for a long while, he lost consciousness and ceased to breathe— but he[33] supported him, touching his body with his heavy hairs.

10. He[34] steadied him, but his own heart, unable to bear such suffering, moaned within him as he said in sorrow; 'Mighty lord, it is I with my evil deeds who have taken your life by bringing you these jewels.

11. I shall search tirelessly through the whole world fashioned as Brahma's egg[35] and then go beyond it; I will reveal my power and bring back your queen. Why wear yourself out in anguish, master of the Vedic texts?

12. Could all the seven worlds together survive one arrow shot from your bow, let alone that cruel demon with his twenty arms and ten heads who terrified this divine and devoted woman, so like the goddess Shri?[36]

13. Please stay here and watch the service I perform: I shall search through all the fourteen great worlds, wring that demon's neck, and bring back your queen.

14. We are your friends, ready to serve you; here is your brother, of perfect strength; this, prince, is your true power! Why abase yourself here when the three parts of the universe[37] obey your every word?

15. The truly great never speak of greatness. Their deeds alone bear witness. Does *dharma* exist apart from you? What is too difficult for you to do? Why stand here in such pain?

16. Tell me, you whose word cannot be doubted: even if the god who dwells on a lotus[38] and Murukan's father, who has a gentle woman as half his body,[39] and the bearer of the discus in his great hands[40] were to join together, could they equal you, to say nothing of each of them alone?

17. Forget, for now, my minor problems[41]; they can wait—first let me free the sorrowing Janaki[42] with her waist thin as a streak of lightning and return in

haste, O master of the golden bow!'

18. As the son of the brilliant sun[43] spoke thus, the god with Shri upon his breast[44] opened his flooded eyes and looked at Sugriva with love; and, as consciousness returned and, with it, a sort of understanding, he began to speak.

19. 'It is I who am loaded down with deeds: she tore off her jewels while I was still alive, holding a bow in my hand— what other chaste woman would do that?[45]

20. She is waiting for me to come, watching for me with her eyes long as swords— while I have passed the time weeping on mountain-tops, beside forest pools, and now here, with her jewels. I have not even been ashamed to go on carrying this bow with its long string.

21. There are those who would give their lives defending soft-spoken women who are perfect strangers, molested by others on the roads— but I am unable to allay the sorrow of that one woman who relied on me.

22. In my lineage of worthy kings, there are those who dug the sea,[46] who brought down the Ganges to earth,[47] who made the deer drink with the tiger;[48] and after them came I, who failed to save my wife from sorrow.

23. My father did away with Indra's distress and wiped out the fierce demon[49] whom even Death could not combat. Here am I, who came from him: my bow has brought nothing but cruel suffering and disgrace.

24. I thought that if my great father's word were to fail, there would be a disgrace— so I rejected the crown.[50] But when the enemy seized my wife whose words are sweeter than sugar-cane, disgrace itself became my crown. Now there is no escape.'

25. Sobbing, exhausted, he spoke these words from the unfathomable depths of his grief; but the son of the splendid sun, seeing his pain, lifted him out of that ocean of sorrow.

26. Again Raghava[51] spoke: 'My lord, could I go on living without your words of comfort? What other power do I have? To wipe out this disgrace in the world I must die— but not before I carry out my promise to you.'

27. At that moment, the mighty son of the wind[52] bowed low and said, 'O you whose shoulders are tall mountains, there is something I must say— please listen to me and understand.

28. Commanding lord— unless, after killing mighty Valin and crowning the sun's son, we assemble a mighty army, we shall never find the hiding-place of the demon with his murderous host.

29. Is it in heaven, or on earth, or on a mountain-top, or in the great serpents' world?— we do not know, lord of the garland swarming with bees, because we are embodied in this human state.

30. Those demons rage through all the worlds in the blinking of an eye, happily preying on whatever they find in their way; like the inevitable fruit of one's deeds, they suddenly appear and then depart. Can anyone know where they live?

31. We must spread through the entire universe at a single moment to seek Tirumakal;[53] and we must search each and every spot in this world which has no limit— for this difficult task we need endless years!

32. But our army of seventy furious hordes will cover the whole world like the doomsday sea— even if we must drink up the ocean or take hold of Brahma's egg from below and carry it away, we shall do what must be done.

33. This is what lies before us, in my view, O righteous lord'— so he spoke, and the master of the bow just replied, 'Good, let us go to find Valin'— and moved away.

34. One *ali*[54] of fearsome eyes, two wild tigers, two swift elephants, and two lions[55]— that was the group that set off over the slopes dense with *sal*, deep-rooted areca, cardamon and plantain, and flourishing *punnaga* trees.

36. As the heroes, their bodies redolent of goodness, went up and down those mountains together with the monkey herds, their anklets chimed in endless, joyful song, waking the clouds that had closed their eyes to sleep upon the peaks, sending them back into the skies.

38. The slopes of that bewildering mountain became slippery beneath their feet as maddened elephants, blind with passion, hurled themselves at the black aloe and sandal trees, which shattered, fell, and rolled downhill, spilling viscous streams of honey from the broken honeycombs.

9.3 KALAMEKAPPULAVAR: WORSHIP BY INSULT (*NINDASTUTI*)

The antagonistic tones of Cuntaramurtti's devotion became formalised in the ironic genre of nindastuti, *with its deliberate double entendres, paronomasia, and playful irreverence towards the gods. One of the masters of this genre was the peripatetic fifteenth-century poet and satirist Kalamekappulavar. Although his verbal pyrotechnics are largely untranslatable, the following three short, annotated stanzas can perhaps suggest something of the flavour of the games he played.*[56]

1 To Vishnu (Mal) at Kannapuram

Listen, Mal of Kannapuram: you are greater than God,[57] and I am greater still than you! Your births number ten;[58] he has none at all; and there is simply no counting mine.

2 On Shiva at Tiruccenkattankuti

The Butter-eater has locked up the temple at Kannapuram and taken to eating earth

now that the god of Cenkatu has taken a skull in his hand and set off to beg for alms.[59]

3 On Shiva at Cidambaram

He has been hit by a bow, kicked by a leather sandal, stoned by an angry man, struck by a staff; what is more, this lord of the shrine in Tillai[60] with its dark groves doesn't even have a mother or father. How low can you sink! Is it any wonder the world despises him?[61]

9.4 THE PIRATE OF TIRUCCENTUR

The vast literature of the Tamil talapuranam *(Sanskrit* sthalapurana), *which dates mostly from the sixteenth to the eighteenth centuries, celebrates the hundreds of local shrines spread throughout the Tamil country. Each such shrine has its own, unique embodiment of the god (usually Shiva or Vishnu, but sometimes Murukan-Skanda or Ganesha) and the goddess, who are invariably said to have been married at this site; each claims to be the centre of the universe, the one truly effective point of transition to heaven, as well as the source of much-sought earthly benefits such as health, fertility, longevity, and wealth.*

The following story, from the Tiruccenturttalapuranam *by the seventeenth-century poet Venrimalaikkavirayar, is a fairly typical example of the claims made for a shrine by its Purana. We should note the realism and immediacy of the opening description and the humour with which the anti-hero is depicted (and the accuracy with which even his manner of speaking is recorded). This is a literature which expresses deeply felt human needs and emotions, including the love that a local village bears for its landscapes, its familiar, everyday figures, and its god. At the same time, the story is linked to popular pan-regional and, indeed, pan-Indian themes – for example, that of the power of devotion, even unconscious devotion, to defeat death. Although this theme cuts across another basic notion of Tamil Shaivism – that the 'magical' effects of* bhakti *are definitely inferior to the desired state of cultivated awareness – the pirate's experience does exemplify the equally powerful and widespread pattern of 'contrary salvation' – for, very often, it is the god's crude antagonist and rival who arrives most quickly and directly at the goal sought by all.*

The story is narrated by Vyasa, archetypal teller of tales, to his son, the sage Shuka.[62].

There was once a *mleccha*[63] without learning or understanding, who sought riches in the conch-filled sea; he sailed in boats in search of wealth, went night and day without sleep, happily lived on fish and foul raw meat. With his tireless band of retainers, he would prey upon merchants plying their trade in boats; mercilessly, he would plunder their goods and then order their heads to be cut off. He harmed the Brahmins who follow the Vedic way of sacrifice; he would slaughter pregnant cows, make curries from their flesh, and, after greedily enjoying this repast himself, would also feed his relatives on these dainties. He was, moreover, proud of the evil and vicious way he had chosen; in his arrogance, he would hack off the heads of those good people who followed better ways. Thus, for a long time he bore the heavy burden of a body loaded down with evil.

One day, after wandering about for some time, he came to Sindhupuram[64] and stood before the golden shrine where great ascetics worship. 'What place is this?' he asked, angry at heart; then he entered the shrine that Indra had built up and worshipped. Inside, he stared at the Brahmins who take all the three worlds for their home[65], who had worshipped Arumukan[66] and were silently reciting Veda, and asked: 'Hey, what's that there image?'

They answered: 'He is Shanmukha,[67] born from Shankara's forehead eye,[68] who conquered the demon with an elephant's head[69] and received the high title of king of all our gods; he is the Swami, our lord. He does away with the sorrows of those poor creatures who praise him, gives true knowledge, permanent splendour, and all one's earthly wishes. He is the true Being, united with his power'[70] – but before the Brahmins could finish their speech, he interrupted them and said, 'Just who is that Hara,[71] anyway? and who is Murukan,[72] who carries a spear, supposedly born from Hara?' Furious, he took his long-bladed sword and advanced upon the bearer of the blazing spear. But as he drew near, he fell, his life departed, and all the seven worlds trembled – for that hopeless criminal fell before the feet of the First, six-headed lord just like those who serve him truly.

Noose in hand, Yama's[73] messengers came to carry him away; but the lords of Shiva's hosts, who worship Shiva's son, turned them back, saying, 'You lowly creatures, release this man who has won life at the feet of flawless Kumara!'[74] They returned and bowed to the king who rules the southern quarter.[75] 'Tell me what happened', he said; and, as they told him, in proper order, he shuddered – like a cloud caught in a whirlwind – and headed for Sindhupuram.

When he arrived there, Vel,[76] who carries the spear, was sitting in state with his seal of wisdom: on one side was the innocent girl born from a deer,[77] and on the other the lady of the elephant,[78] her black eyes bright as the spear given by the king of the gods; the Tiricutantirar Brahmins, who live with love, were praising him, and all-knowing Agastya,[79] born from a pot, and other silent sages such as learned Sanaka were worshipping in joy. Gratefully, the lord who guards the southern quarter came before the fragrant lotus-feet, bowed low, and, standing directly before him, praised lord Kumara.

He was filled with amazement: 'Unknown even in great Vedic speech are these lotus-like feet of the six-headed god who removed the gods' distress and tore the ornaments of the demons' wives from their necks.[80] Son of the Mountain lady[81] – if someone, no matter how ignorant, bows at our father's feet, then you, Peacock-Rider,[82] make even Brahmins ripe with Vedic knowledge worship that person.' Thus great Death praised the lord.

Kumara looked at Yama tenderly and said, 'Our heart rejoices in your praise; tell me why you have come here today.' The king of the south took heart and dared to say, 'By virtue of the great compassion of the god crowned with the crescent moon,[83] I perform my work, allotting the fullness of heaven or the miseries of hell to each, according to his deeds, with the fourteen Manus[84] as my witnesses. This is the way I pursue, with my heart in awe of the god who is garlanded with the moon, beside the Brahmins and the royal Manus who know the wisdom of the ancient books. My concern is only to do what is right, aware of each person's actions. Thus, when I learned of all the evil wrought by that unregenerate criminal, I sent my messengers to hurt him and to call him to me. But before they could touch him, the lords of hosts who stand beside you struck out at them. How can you offer a *mleccha* the gift of *moksha* which is the embrace of your lotus-feet?'

Hearing Yama's soft words, Arumuka Velan[85] replied: 'They may be wise or ignorant, confused by lust for women with eyes like the deer's, or intent on other impure ways; they may have forsaken the duties proper to their birth, or be condemned by fate to carry out predestined sins – but if they come to Sindhupuram to see our radiant face, worshipped by the Tiricutantirar of the lovely Veda, they shall wipe out all the evil they have done and remain, luminous, pure, avid with love, in the shade of our lotus-like feet. As for this man, he collapsed and died right after staring steadily at our six faces; he spoke freely with the Tiricutantirar; he looked at us quickly, with desire – and thus he rid himself of disgrace and achieved release at our feet, worshipped by Vedic rite. This I swear to you' – and Sthanu's[86] son looked with sweet compassion on the face of mighty Death, and his cool mercy flowed forth like a spring.

9.5 THE STORY OF NILANAKKANAR[87]

In the mid-twelfth century, Cekkilar, court poet of the Chola king Kulottunga II, composed a monumental narrative poem on the lives of the sixty three saints of Shiva (the nayanmar*), called the* Periya Puranam. *Cekkilar's work became the twelfth and final volume of the Tamil Shaiva canon (the* tirumurai) *and the standard version of these tales, as one can see from the temple sculptures at Daracuram, from the end of the twelfth century, which follow Cekkilar very closely. Shaiva hagiography, as we find it in Cekkilar, has a rather grisly and fanatical cast; devotion to Shiva has become an absolute value which often extracts a near-absolute price from the devotee and his family. In the story translated below, the protagonist is a learned, traditional Brahmin, wholly absorbed into the sphere of Shaiva piety; the setting is the classic milieu of the South Indian* agraharam *or Brahmin village in the rich, paddy-growing terrain of the Kaveri Delta. The Brahmin with his Vedic heritage is here deliberately subordinated to the* bhakti *order, with its extreme vision. But the real hero of the tale comes, as so often in* bhakti *literature, from the lower limits of the social and family hierarchy – in the form of the Brahmin's wife, who nevertheless receives amazingly short shrift both from her husband and from Cekkilar.*

There is a village called Cattamankai[88] in the Kaviri land where the bright paddy grows thick as a jungle and *kayal*-fish leap on to the pericarps of the flowering lotuses – a village fit to be praised by all the world, a beautiful first home to auspicious Brahmins. At this place permeated by goodness, geese bathe in the ponds together with innocent young women whose foreheads emit sweet fragrance, while the mynah birds in the groves sing Saman chants[89] and correct the mistakes of young Brahmin boys studying the Veda. Imbued with the protective knowledge that 'ash is the final truth to be discovered'[90], twice-born Brahmins tend the three fires;[91] and women tend them too, as a way to swim across the ocean of birth, along with a fourth – the fire of their chastity.

In this prosperous, ancient village of Brahmins trained to good character lived Nilanakkanar, who had the gift of explaining the meaning of the hidden Veda celebrated by the whole world; he was slave and lover to the god who placed poison in his neck.[92] Driven by desire, he concentrated on accomplishing the two tasks he had defined: 'The inner meaning[93] of the Veda is to worship with longing the feet of the lord with water flowing through his hair,[94] and of his servants – that is our work, our service.' He performed both the daily worship of the Source of the Vedas[95] according to the true rites prescribed by the Agamas[96] as well as additional occasional rites.[97] He also took upon himself various kinds of other services, such as feeding the devotees of the god.

One Atirai day,[98] after completing the standard *puja* according to rule, this pure devotee, motivated by love, decided to worship the Nayanar[99] who resides in the ancient, tall shrine of Ayavanti.[100] Taking all that he needed for a ritual performed with single-minded love, that man of limitless devotion left home, together with his wife, and came to the temple of the lord. He drew near, bowed to the anklets of that ambrosial god who dwells in Ayavanti, and began the *puja*; standing beside him, his wife held out to him everything that he needed for the rite while he, overcome with feeling, conducted the great ceremony. But even when the lengthy ritual was complete, his love was still not sated; so they circumambulated the whole shrine, worshipping and praising – and, looking straight, with clear vision, at that Truth for which even the great Veda searches, he recited, with feeling and understanding, the five syllables[101] that everyone desires.

Just then, while that indefatigable devotee was concentrating on the five syllables that contain the truth of *shruti*[102] and all other sciences, a spider slipped from its place and fell on to the body of the god who made Mount Meru into his long, golden bow.[103] As it fell, the devotee's wife, who was standing near-by, quickly blew it away, in alarm and with overflowing love, just as one would hastily blow away a spider that had fallen on a young child. The ascetic Brahmin, who was destroying all ties that bound him to the world, saw her anxious action and hid his eyes in horror. 'What have you done, you fool!' he cried. She replied, 'A spider fell on him, and I shooed it away with my breath.'

He paid no heed to the love that was manifest in his wife's deed; his only thought was that such an act was most inappropriate[104] in the context of serving the lord who wears the sacred thead. So he drove her away with the words, 'You couldn't find any way to remove the spider that had fallen on to the pure god whose long hair glistens like lightning except by blowing on him in close contact, thus defiling him with your saliva; from now on, I will have nothing to do with you'.

The sun set over the mountain; the woman, following her husband's command, went off to one side; and the devotee of the god with thick matted hair, after finishing to perfection all the necessary parts of his *puja*, returned home.

His wife, still frightened, could hardly approach his side – so she remained in the temple of the god who had eaten poison. As for Tirunilanakkanar, proficient in the four Vedas with their fine words, he went to sleep that night on his bed made of a soft cotton mattress. While he was sleeping, the supreme lord of Ayavanti came to his dream, showed him his body along with his long hair flooded by water, and said: 'Except for that part of us where your wife blew and splattered us, after placing us in her heart, the entire surface of our body is covered with blisters from that spider!'[105]

The devotee realised that this great dream was a waking reality; alarmed, he cupped his hands in reverence – and woke at once. He worshipped, danced, sang, offered praises, and wept at this show of mercy by the master of the whole world. As night turned to dawn, he went to the temple and fell at the feet of the Primeval Lord, god of Ayavanti, with his lovely eyes; and, as he rose, he extolled him, took his wife, too, and went home.[106]

9.6 TWO TELUGU POETS[107]

Tallapaka Annamacarya, from the first half of the sixteenth century, was a temple poet serving the god Venkateshvara-Vishnu at the famous pilgrimage site of Tirupati, on the border between the Tamil and Telugu countries. He is credited with 32,000 kirtanas, relatively short musical compositions expressive of the poet's imaginative engagement with the deity and with all conceivable aspects of the latter's daily existence at his shrine (as well as with his mythological propensities and powers). The following example gives voice to the banter between the god's consort at Tirupati, Padmavati, and her close female friends and servants, who have been waiting for her to emerge from her bedroom after a night of love.[108]

1. Pallavi-refrain:
What are these black marks of musk on her lips, red as buds, if not letters of love sent by our Lady to her lord?

Caranamulu-verses:
1. Her eyes are beautiful as the *cakora* bird's— but what is this redness in their corners?
Think it over, my friends— isn't that the blood left to stain the sidelong

glances with which she pierced her beloved after she drew them from his body,
back to her eyes?

2. How is it that this woman's breasts glimmer so clearly through the sari she
wears?

Can't you guess, my friends? Those are just the brilliant moon-marks left by
the nails of her lover who clawed her in his passion, now luminous as the
moonlight of a summer night.

3. It looks almost as if delicate pearls were pouring down this woman's cheeks!

Can't you imagine what they are, my friends— the lovely drops of sweat left
on my lotus-face by Tiruvenkatapati, when he pressed against me, wildly
making love.

*Radically different in tone from Annamacarya's voluptuous fantasies are the
often sarcastic verses of the* Venkatacala vihara satakamu, *by an unknown
seventeenth-century poet, also, no doubt, from Tirupati. This is a period which
witnessed Muslim attacks on several of the great temples of Andhra and Tamil
Nadu; the poet excoriates Venkateshvara-Vishnu for not defending himself or his
shrine. Loving vituperation of this sort became, roughly from this time, a conventional feature of the Telugu* satakamu *genre; but the sense of a real threat from
violent, alien foes is nevertheless palpably present in these verses.*[109]

1. I have seen the radiance of the gentle smile playing upon the graceful lines
of your face; and, as I served you, I beheld your image that promises all that is
good, all that belongs to love; and your arms, graced by the five great weapons
you hold, gentle signs of your valour, became visible to me and I stared at your
twin lotus-feet that are worshipped in order to purify the whole world—

all this wonder, and more, was mine! I was freed from sin by your mercy.
Protect me now, make me intent upon reaching your feet, you who give refuge
to all who seek you, showering compassion like rain,

you who delight in Venkata hill.

2. By now they have broken the serving vessels into pieces, shattered the great
doors to your temple, robbed the *nambi* preists, thrown away the gods'
vehicles,[110] peeled the gold off the *garuda*-pillars, demolished the entrance-
towers, made off with the fine cakes of the offerings, tormented the *jiyar*,[111]
and even dared to strip the ornaments off *your* body—

and up to now you have lied, haven't you, boasting that you would stab all
the Turks to death with your dagger – tucked in your waist! That's the fighting
spirit,

you who annihilate your enemies, who delight in Venkata hill!

3. Don't you have any manliness left? Aren't you still young enough to fight?
They call you Vairidanda, 'Death to your Foes!' Why this sudden weakness? If
I, though I'm but a Brahmin, had a weapon like that discus you carry in your
hand, I would stick a horse's head on the trunk of a warrior's body and a
soldier's head on a horse's body— I would chop them all to pieces, happily
hack away at them and pursue them, yelling furiously at the top of my lungs all
the way back to Golconda,[112]

you who annihilate your enemies, who delight in Venkata hill!
4. Did you think that the fiery blows of the *ghulam*[113] are like being grazed by the long, soft hair of a woman? Or that the abuse hurled by the warriors would be like the playful insults of a loving, moon-faced maiden? Or that the Muslim fighter's fist in your face feels like being rubbed by the breasts of your young, graceful lover? Or that the harsh battle-cries of the mercenaries would sound like the soft moanings of a woman making love?

Forget it, lord! Better run away now, while life is still in your body. You'll still be able to chew the cheap leaves you like – these Turks are simply fearless,
    you who annihilate your enemies, who delight in Venkata hill!
5. What's left for you now of the sacred Dravida poems? Only the harsh *mantra* that starts, 'Khoda . . .'[114] Do they call you with the proper invocations of the Vaikhanasa texts?[115] No— you are surrounded by the graceless noises of a foreign tongue. The delicious cakes once offered you in worship have been replaced by Muslim feasts with their foul odours, and instead of the delicate fragrance of aloe burned as incense before you, you inhale the stifling fumes of the taverns. Hey! You're becoming a Turk! And losing your power, but what's it to us? Our only worry is that your Tamil ears will be clogged,
    you who annihilate your enemies, who delight in Venkata hill!

BIBLIOGRAPHY

For a general introduction, see *The Literatures of India: an Introduction*, by E. C. Dimock, E. Gerow, C. M. Naim, A. K. Ramanujan, G. Roadarmel, and J. A. B. van Buitenen, Chicago, University of Chicago Press, 1974. See also J. A. B. van Buitenen, 'Hindu sacred literature' and 'Hindusim' in *Encyclopaedia Britannica*, Macropaedia, viii, 1974; the updated 'Hinduism' article in the 1985 edition; and my forthcoming revision in the 1988 edition. A useful outline is provided by J. N. Farquhar's *An Outline of the Religious Literature of India*, first published by Oxford University Press in 1920 and reprinted by Motilal Banarsidass in Delhi in 1967. More detailed summaries are provided by M. Winternitz's three-volume *A History of Indian Literature*, translated by Mrs. S. Ketkar, University of Calcutta, 1963, and by the two multi-volume series edited by J. Gonda, of which several volumes

have already appeared: *A History of Indian Literature*, Wiesbaden, Otto Harrassowitz; and the *Handbuch der Orientalistik, Zweite Abteilung: Indien*, Leiden, E. J. Brill; most volumes are in English. Information on individual topics may always be found in M. L. P. Patterson's mammoth *South Asian Civilizations, a Bibliographic Synthesis*, published by the University of Chicago Press in 1981.

There are also several useful sourcebooks that complement the present work. For mythology, there is my own *Hindu Myths*, Harmondsworth, Penguin, 1975, and J. A. B. van Buitenen's and C. Dimmitt's *Classical Hindu Mythology*, Philadelphia, Temple University Press, 1978; for philosophy, there is the *Sourcebook in Indian Philosophy* by S. Radhakrishnan and C. A. Moore, Princeton, 1957. A fine set of translations and commentaries is found in R. C.

Zaehner's *Hindu Scriptures*, London, 1966, often reprinted. More general collections are provided by the indispensable *Sources of Indian Tradition*, first compiled under W. T. de Bary at Columbia University in 1958, and recently updated by A. T. Embree and Stephen Hay; and by A. T. Embree's own *The Hindu Tradition*, New York, Vintage, 1966.

In addition to these sourcebooks, there are several useful overviews of Hinduism, such as R. C. Zaehner's *Hinduism*, London, 1962; D. Kinsley's *Hinduism*, Englewood, New Jersey, 1982; L.

Renou's *Hinduism*, New York, 1963, and *Religions of Ancient India*, New York, 1968; T. J. Hopkins's *The Hindu Religious Tradition*, Encino, California, 1971; and J. R. Hinnells and Eric J. Sharpe, *Hinduism*, in *World Religions in Education*, Newcastle upon Tyne, 1972. A more comprehensive coverage is provided by J. Gonda's three-volume survey, available not in English but in German, *Die Religionen Indiens*, Stuttgart, 1963, and in French, *Les Religions de l'Inde*, Paris, 1962. Further bibliographic information is given in the notes to each individual section.

1. INTRODUCTION

For the notion of scripture in India, see B. K. Smith, *Reflections on Resemblance, Ritual, and Religion*, Oxford and New York, 1988; F. Staal, 'The concept of scripture in the Indian tradition', in *Sikh Studies: Comparative Perspectives on a Changing Tradition*, edited by M. Juergensmeyer and N. Gerald Barrier, Berkeley, 1979, pp. 121–4; and J. C. Heesterman, 'Veda and dharma', in *The Concept of Duty in South Asia*, edited by W. D. O'Flaherty and J. D. M. Derrett, Columbia, Missouri, 1978, pp. 80–95

2. VEDAS

For the Vedas in general, see J. Gonda, *Vedic Literature (Samhitas and Brahmanas)*, I, 1, in Gonda's series, *A History of Indian Literature*, Wiesbaden, Otto Harrassowitz, 1975; M. Winternitz, *A History of Indian Literature*, I, translated by Mrs. S. Ketkar, University of Calcutta, 1963; and A. B. Keith, *The Religion and Philosophy of the Vedas and Upanishads*, Harvard Oriental Series, xxxi–xxxii, Cambridge, Mass., 1925. A

useful bibliography is provided by L. Renou (*Bibliographie vedique*, Paris, 1931), updated by R. N. Dandekar (*Vedic Bibliography, since 1930*, Bombay, 1946).

2.1.1 There are complete translations of the *Rig Veda* into German, by K. F. Geldner (*Der Rig-Veda*, 4 vols., Harvard Oriental Series, 33–6, Cambridge, Mass., 1951–7), H. Grassmann (*Rig-Veda*, 2 vols., Leipzig, 1876–9), and A. Ludwig (*Der Rigveda*, 6 vols., Prag, Leipzig, 1876–88); into French, by A. Langlois (*Rig Veda*, 4 vols., Paris 1848–51) and (not quite complete) L. Renou (*Etudes vediques et panineennes*, 17 fasc., Paris, 1955–69); and English, by H. H. Wilson (*Rig-Veda Sanhita*, 6 vols., London, 1850–88). With the exception of Geldner and Renou, none of these translations is very reliable. There are, however, several better translations of selections from the *Rig Veda*. Into Russian: by T. Elizarenkova (*Rigveda*, Moscow, 1972). Into English: by F. Edgerton (*The Beginnings of Indian Philosophy*, London, 1965); by C. R. Lanman (*Sanskrit Reader*, Cambridge, Mass., 1884); by A. A. Macdonell (*A Vedic Reader for Students*, Oxford, 1917, and *Hymns from the Rigveda*, Calcutta, London, 1922); by F. M. Mueller (*Vedic Hymns*, Oxford, 1891);

by R. Panikkar (*The Vedic Experience*, Berkeley and Los Angeles, 1977); and my own *The Rig Veda* (Penguin, Harmondsworth, 1981) – which also has an extensive bibliography.

For the *Atharva Veda*, see the edition with the commentary of Sayana (Bombay, 1895) and the translations by M. Bloomfield (Sacred Books of the East, XLII, Oxford, 1897; reprinted Delhi, 1964) and by W. D. Witney (Harvard Oriental Series, VII–VIII Cambridge, Mass., 1905).

2.1.1.1 Invocation of Agni. RV 1.1.1–9. For discussions of this hymn, see my *Rig Veda*, pp. 97–99; cf. Sri Aurobindo, *Hymns to the Mystic Fire*, Pondicherry, 1952.

2.1.1.2 Hymn to the funeral fire. RV 10.16.1–14. See my *Rig Veda*, 43–58, which also discusses several other related hymns: 10.14, 10.18, 10.154, 10.135, and 10.58. Cf. also M. Bloomfield, 'On Vedic Agni Kravyavahana and Agni Kavyavahana', *Streitberg-Festgabe*, Leipzig, 1924; and B. Lincoln, 'Death and resurrection in Indo-European thought', *Journal of Indo-European Studies*, V, 1977, 247–64, and 'The Lord of the Dead', *History of Religions*, XX, 3, 1981.

2.1.1.3 The horse sacrifice. RV 1.162.1–22. This hymn is discussed in my *Rig Veda*, pp. 87–95, together with other closely related hymns (RV 1.163 and 10.56). See also A. Hillebrandt, 'Zu Rgveda 1.162', *Zeitschrift der Deutschen Morgenlaendischen Gesellschaft* XXXVII, 1883, pp. 521–4.

2.1.2 Brahmanas. Many of the Brahmanas have been translated into English, and still others into German. The most important and most accessible of these are: *Aitareya Brahmana*, with the commentary of Sayana, Calcutta, 1896; translated by A. B. Keith (in *Rigveda Brahmanas*, Harvard Oriental Series, XXV, Cambridge, Mass., Press, 1920; reprinted Delhi, 1971). *Gopatha Brahmana*, edited by R. Mitra and H. Vidyabhusana, Calcutta, Bibliotheca Indica, 1872; reprinted Delhi, 1972. *Jaiminiya Brahmana*, edited by R. Vira and L. Chandra, Nagpur, Sarasvati Vihara Series, 1954; translated by H. Bodewitz (incomplete), Leiden, 1973; translated into German by W. Caland (incomplete), Amsterdam, 1919; reprinted Wiesbaden, 1970; translated by H. Oertel (incomplete), 'Contributions from the *Jaiminiya Brahmana*', *Journal of the American Oriental Society*, 1897, 1898, 1899, 1902, 1905, 1907, and 1909. *Kaushitaki Brahmana*, edited by H. Bhattacharya, Calcutta, 1970; translated by A. B. Keith (in *Rigveda Brahmanas*, Harvard Oriental Series, XXV, Cambridge, Mass., 1920; reprinted Delhi, 1971). *Panchavimsha [Tandya-maha-] Brahmana*, with the commentary of Sayana, Calcutta, 1869–74; translated by W. Caland, Bibliotheca Indica, Calcutta, 1931. *Shatapatha Brahmana*, edited by A. Weber, Calcutta, 1903; reprinted Chowkhamba Sanskrit Series, 96, Benares, 1964; translated by J. Eggeling, Sacred Books of the East, XII, XXVI, XLI, XLIII, XLIV, Oxford, 1882. *Taittiriya Brahmana*, with the commentary of Sayana, Calcutta, 1859.

For general studies of the Brahmanas, see A. C. Banerjea, *Studies in the Brahmanas*, New Delhi, 1963; J. Basu, *India in the Age of the Brahmanas*, Calcutta, 1969; M. Biardeau and C. Malamoud, *Le sacrifice dans l'Inde ancienne*, Bibliotheque de l'Ecole des Hautes Etudes, Sciences religieuses, LXXIX, Paris, 1976; G. V. Devasthali, *Religion and Mythology of the Brahmanas*, Poona, 1965; N. Drury, *The Sacrificial Ritual in the Satapatha Brahmana*, Delhi, 1981; J. Gonda, 'Bandhu in the Brahmanas', *Adyar Library Bulletin*, XXIX 1965, pp. 1–29; J. Gonda, 'Etymologies in the Ancient Indian Brahmanas', *Lingua*, V, 1955, pp. 61–85; J. C. Heesterman, *The Inner Conflict of Tradition*, Chicago, 1985; H. R. Karnik, 'Morals in the Brahmanas', *Journal of Bombay University*, XXVII, 1958, pp.

95–127; S. Levi, *La doctrine du sacrifice dans les Brahmanas*, Bibliotheque de l'Ecole des Hautes Etudes, Sciences religieuses, xl, Paris, 1898; W. D. O'Flaherty, *Tales of Sex and Violence: Folklore, Sacrifice, and Danger in the Jaiminiya Brahmana*, Chicago, 1985; B. K. Smith, *Reflections on Resemblance, Ritual and Religion*, Oxford, 1988; G. U. Thite, *Sacrifice in the Brahmana-Texts*, Poona, 1975.

2.1.2.1 The offering into the fire. For the Agnihotra, see H. W. Bodewitz, *The Daily Evening and Morning Offering (Agnihotra) According to the Brahmanas*, Leiden, 1976; W. Caland and V. Henry, *L'Agnistoma: description complete de la forme normale du sacrifice de Soma dans le cult vedique*, 2 vols., Paris, 1906; H. S. Converse, 'The Agnicayana rite: indigenous origin', *History of Religions*, XIV, 1974, pp. 81–95; P.–E. Dumont, *L'Agnihotra: description de l'Agnihotra dans le rituel vedique d'apres les Shrautasutras*, Baltimore, 1939; D. M. Knipe, *In the Image of Fire: The Vedic Experience of Heat*, Delhi, 1975; D. M. Knipe, 'One fire, three fires, five fires: Vedic symbols in transition', *History of Religions*, XII, 1972, pp. 28–41; H. Kirck, *Das Ritual des Feuer (Agnyadheya)*, Wien, 1982; B. K. Smith, 'Gods and men in Vedic ritualism: toward a hierarchy of resemblance', *History of Religions*, XXIV, 1985, pp. 291–307; F. Staal, *Agni: The Vedic Ritual of the Fire Altar*, 2 vols., Berkeley, Asian Humanities Press, 1983.

2.1.2.1.1–2 The creation of fire and the origins of death. *Shatapatha Brahmana* 2.2.4.1–8 and 10.4.3.1–10. I have used the standard Weber edition of the *Shatapatha Brahmana*, the Madhyandina recension of the White *Yajur Veda*. For death in the Brahmanas, see my *The Origins of Evil in Hindu Mythology*, Berkley, 1976, pp. 212–21. See also W. O. Kaelber, 'The "dramatic" element in Brahmanic initiation: symbols of death, danger, and difficult passage', *History of Religions*, XVIII 1978, pp. 54–76. For discussion of the first of these passages,

see my *Hindu Myths*, pp. 28–33. See also the parallel passages in the *Shatapatha Brahmana* 2.5.1, 3.9.11, 10.4.2.2; 10.4.4.1; and *Taittiriya Brahmana* 1.1.10.1; 1.2.6.1; 1.6.2.1; 1.6.4.1; 2.3.6.1; 2.7.9.1; 3.10.9.1

2.1.2.1.3 Prajapati dismembered and remembered. *Shatapatha Brahmana* 1.6.3.35–37. Compare the parallel texts: *Shatapatha Brahmana* 7.5.2.6; 14.4.2.1; *Taittiriya Aranyaka* 1.23. 1–9; *Taittiriya Brahmana* 2.2.9.1; *Brihadaranyaka Upanishad* 1.4.1–6. See the discussion in my *Hindu Myths*, pp. 33–5, and B. K. Smith, 'Sacrifice and being: Prajapati's cosmic emission and its consequences', *Numen*, XXII, 1985, pp. 71–87.

2.1.2.2 The horse sacrifice. The classical study of the horse sacrifice is P.–E. Dumont, *L'Asvamedha: description du sacrifice solennel du cheval dans le culte vedique d'apres les textes du Yajurveda blanc*, Paris, 1927. See also Dumont's 'The horse-sacrifice in the Taittiriya-Brahmana', *Proceedings of the American Philosophical Society*, XCII, 1948, pp. 447–503; 'The animal sacrifices in the Taittiriya-Brahmana', *Proceedings of the American Philosophical Society*, CVII 1962, pp. 246–63. See also the analysis of the horse sacrifice in my *Women, Androgynes, and Other Mythical Beasts*, Chicago, 1980, pp. 149–65.

2.1.2.2.1 Seed as rice. *Shatapatha Brahmana* 13.1.1.1–4. For seed as rice, see D. M. Knipe, 'Sapindikarana: the Hindu rite of entry into heaven', in *Religious Encounters with Death: Insights from the History and Anthropology of Religions*, edited by F. E. Reynolds and E. H. Waugh, University Park, Pa., 1977, pp. 111–24.

2.1.2.2.2 Killing the dog. *Taittiriya Brahmana* 3.8.4.2. The parallel text is at *Shatapatha Brahmana* 13.1.2.9. The connection between the eyes and the dice was suggested by David White in a paper presented at Madison, Wisconsin, on 7 November 1986.

2.1.2.2.3–7 Killing the horse; the mockery of the women; the king copulates with the people; dismembering the horse; the restorations. *Shatapatha Brahmana* 13.2.8.1–4; 13.5.2.1–10; 13.2.9.6–9; 13.3.1.1–4; 13.3.8.1–6.

2.1.2.3 The human sacrifice of Shunahshepa. *Aitareya Brahmana* 7.13–18. A parallel text is the *Shankhayana Shrauta Sutra* 15.17–27. For discussions of the text, see G. Dumezil, *Flamen-Brahman*, Paris, 1935, pp. 13–42, 97–112; J. C. Heesterman, 'Recitation of the Shunahshepa legend,' in his *The Ancient Indian Royal Consecration*, 's-Gravenage, 1957, pp. 158–66; A. B. Keith, *Rg-Veda Brahmanas*, pp. 299 ff.; F. M. Mueller, *History of Ancient Sanskrit Literature*, London, 1859, pp. 408 ff., 573 ff.; W. H. Robinson, *The Golden Legend of India, or Story of India's God-given Cynosure Shunahshepha-Devarata*, London, 1911; R. Roth, 'Die Sage von Shunahshepa', *Indische Studien*, I, 1850, pp. 457–64; II, 1853, pp. 112–23; A. Weber, 'Ueber Menschenopfer bei den Indien der Vedische Zeit', *Zeitschrift der Deutschen Morgenlaendischen Gesellschaft* XVIII, 1864, pp. 262–87; F. Weller, 'Die Legende von Shunahshepa', *Verhandlungen der Saechsichen Akademie der Wissenschaften* C11, 2, 1956.

2.1.3 Upanishads. The standard translation remains that of R. Hume (*Thirteen Principal Upanishads*' Oxford, 1921), which also has excellent bibliographies and notes, but there are other good translations, particularly the one by S. Radhakrishnan (*The Principal Upanishads*, London 1953). The Sanskrit edition that I have used is *One Hundred and Eight Upanishads*, Bombay, 1913. Among the hundreds of studies of the Upanishads, P. Deussen's *The Philosophy of the Upanishads*, New York, 1966, and M. Eliade's *Yoga: Immortality and Freedom*, New York, 1958, remain exciting and useful. As for this particular passage, *Brihadaranyaka Upanishad* 1.1.1–2, 1.2.1–7, relevant parallels occur throughout the ritual literature of the horse sacrifice, above section 2.1.2.2.

2.2.1.1. The dismemberment of the cosmic Person. RV 10.90.1–16. See my *Rig Veda*, pp. 29–32, and my *Hindu Myths*, pp. 27–8. Cf. also, among the many discussions of this hymn, W. N. Brown, 'The sources and nature of the Purusa in the Purusasukta,' *Journal of the American Oriental Society*, L1, 1931, pp. 108–18; 'Theories of creation in the Rg Veda', *JAOS*, LXXXV, 1965, pp. 23–34; A. K. Coomaraswamy, 'Rgveda 10.90.1', *JAOS*, LXVI, 1946, pp. 145–61.

2.2.1.2 The three strides of Vishnu. RV 1.154.1–16. See my *Rig Veda*, pp. 225–27, and my *Hindu Myths*, pp. 175–9. Cf. also F. B. J. Kuiper, 'The three strides of Visnu', in *Indological Studies in Honor of W. Norman Brown*, New Haven, Conn., 1962, pp. 137–51; and G. C. Tripathi, *Der Ursprung und die Entwicklung der Vamana-legende in der Indischen Literatur*, Wiesbaden, 1968.

2.2.1.3 Rudra. RV 1.114.1–11. See my *Rig Veda*, pp. 223–5; my *Hindu Myths*, pp. 116–25; and my *Siva: the Erotic Ascetic*, Oxford, 1973; 1981.

2.2.2 Brahmanas: the creation of gods and demons. *Shatapatha Brahmana* 11.1.6.6–11. See my *Hindu Myths*, pp. 270–3, and my *The Origins of Evil in Hindu Mythology*, Berkeley, 1976, pp. 57–93; and cf. S. Levi, *La doctrine du sacrifice*, pp. 12–62. Among the many Brahmana myths on this theme, cf. *Shatapatha Brahmana* 1.2.26; 1.4.1.35; 1.7.2.22; 5.1.1.1; 5.5.5.1; 6.6.2.11; 6.6.3.2; 9.5.1.12–27; 11.5.1.12; *Aitareya Brahmana* 3.45; *Taittiriya Brahmana* 1.4.11; 2.3.8.1–3; 3.2.9.6; *Taittiriya Samhita* 2.5.1; *Tandya Mahabrahmana* 8.6.5 and 8.9.15.

2.2.3.1. Indra and the demons. *Maitri Upanishad* 7.9–10. There is a close parallel in *Chandogya Upanishad* 8.7–12. For discussions, see M. Eliade, *Mephistopheles and the Androgyne (The Two and the One)*, New York, 1965, pp. 78–124; and my *The Origins of Evil*, pp. 174–211 and 272–320.

2.2.3.2 Satyakama and the animals. *Chandogya Upanishad* 3.3.1–5; 4.5.1–3;

4.6.1–4; 4.7.1–4, 4.8.1–14; 4.9.1–2.

2.3.1. *Rig Veda*: creation. RV 10.129.1–7. See my *Rig Veda*, pp. 25–6. Cf. also W. N. Brown, 'Theories of creation in the Rg Veda', *Journal of the American Oriental Society*, LXXXV, 1965, pp. 23–34; F. B. J. Kuiper, 'The basic concept of Vedic religion', *History of Religions*, XV, 1975, pp. 107–20; W. D. Whitney, 'The cosmogonic hymn, Rig-Veda X.129', *Procedings of the American Oriental Society*, 1882, p. 109.

2.3.2.1 The self. *Brihadaranyaka Upanishad* 1.4.7. Cf. A. K. Coomaraswamy, 'Atmayajna: self-sacrifice', *Harvard Journal of Asiatic Studies*, VI, 1941, pp. 358–98; T. Goman and R. Laura, 'A logical treatment of some Upanishadic puzzles', *Numen*, XIX, 1972, pp. 52–67; J. C. Heesterman, 'Brahmin, ritual, and renouncer', *Wiener Zeitschrift fur die Kunde Sud- und Ostasiens*, VIII, 1964, pp. 1–31.

2.3.2.2. The ultimate reality and the two birds. *Shvetashvatara Upanishad* 4.1–10. This text is best read in conjunction with *Rig Veda* 1.164 (see my *Rig Veda*, pp. 71–84). See also W. Johnson, 'On the Rg Vedic riddle of the two birds in the fig tree', *Journal of the American Oriental Society*, XCVI, 1976, pp. 248–58.

2.3.2.3 Rebirth. *Chandogya Upanishad* 5.3.1–7, 5.4.1–2, 5.5.1–2, 5.6.1–2, 5.7.1–2, 5.8.1–2, 5.9.1–2, 5.10.1–10. There is a closely parallel text at *Brihadaranyaka Upanishad* 6.2.1–16. For the theory of karma, see. W. D. O'Flaherty (ed.), *Karma and Rebirth in Classical Indian Traditions*, Berkeley, 1980, with an extensive bibliography. See also U. Arya, 'Hindu contradictions of the doctrine of karma', *East and West*, XXII, 1972, pp. 93–100; and N. R. Reat, 'Karma and rebirth in the Upanishads and Buddhism', *Numen*, XXIV, 1977, pp. 163–85.

2.3.2.4 The Person in the eye and in sleep. *Maitri Upanishad* 7.11b.1–8. For the theory of dreams expressed in this and the following two passages, see my *Dreams, Illusion, and Other Realities*, Chicago, 1984.

2.3.2.5 The self in sleep. *Brihadaranyaka Upanishad* 2.1.17–20 and 4.3.9–14, 18.

2.3.3 Vedanta. For this and other Indian philosophical texts, the standard works are S. Dasgupta's five-volume *A History of Indian Philosophy*, Cambridge, 1922–55, and K. Potter's on-going series, *Encyclopedia of Indian Philosophies*, of which his own volume on *Indian Metaphysics and Epistemology: the Tradition of Nyaya-Vaishesika up to Gangesha*, Princeton, 1977, is highly relevant to the present text. For Shankara's theory of dreams, see also my discussion in *Dreams, Illusion, and Other Realities*. The standard translations of the commentaries of Shankara and Ramanuja are G. Thibaut's (in Sacred Books of the East, XXXIV, XXXVIII, XLVIII, Oxford, 1890–1904).

2.3.3.1 Shankara dreams. *Vedanta Sutras* of Badarayana, with the commentary of Shankara. *Brahmasutrashankarabhashya*, Varanasi, 1917; commentary on 3.2.2–4.

2.3.3.2 Ramanuja dreams. *Vedanta Sutras* of Badarayana, with the commentary of Ramanuja. *Shribhashya* of Ramanujacharya, edited with notes in Sanskrit by V. S. Abhyankar, Bombay Sanskrit and Prakrit Series, 68, Poona, 1914, 1.1.1 (pp. 96–8 and 100–1 of the Sanskrit text).

2.3.3.3 Illusion: the man who built a house of air. *Yogavasishthamaharamayana* of Valmiki, with commentary, ed. W. L. S. Pansikar, 2 vols., Bombay, 1918, 6.1.112.16–35. For more stories from the *Yogavasishtha*, see my *Dreams, Illusion*.

3. EPICS

3.1 *Mahabharata*. I have used the critical edition, 21 vols., Poona, 1933–60, but I have also incorporated several lines and passages that are rejected by that edition. There is one fairly accurate but

NOTES 193

hardly readable complete translation of the *Mahabharata*, the so-called P. C. Roy edition, actually a translation by K. M. Ganguli that was published by P. C. Roy, 11 vols., Calcutta, 1927–32; and another by M. N. Dutt, 7 vols., Calcutta, 1895–1905. Far better, but only completed as far as the first six books, is the translation by J. A. B. van Buitenen for the University of Chicago Press (1974–) that is being finished by other scholars. A readable translation, but only of a rather banal selection of passages dealing with the central plot, is C. V. Narasimhan's version, Columbia University Press, 1965; a far more imaginative, but hardly reliable, translation is W. Buck's, Berkeley, 1973.

The scholarship on the *Mahabharata* is great in size, if not always in quality; among the most exciting analyses are G. Dumezil's studies of the Indo-European epics, particularly his *Mythe et epopee*, Paris, 1968; 1971; M. Biardeau's *Etudes de mythologie Hindoue*, published through the Ecole des Hautes Etudes of the Sorbonne, beginning in 1969; and A. Hiltebeitel's *The Ritual of Battle*, Ithaca, N. Y., 1976.

3.1.1 The birth of the Epic heroes. *Mahabharata* 1.99.1–49, 1.100.1–30, with additional lines omitted by the critical edition: in chapter 1.99, 5 lines after verse 5, 6 after 10, 7 after 12, 1 after 43, 1 after 47; in chapter 1.100, 1 after 3, 4 after 5, 5 after 12, 4 after 14. See I. Karve, *Yuganta*, New Delhi, 1974, pp. 7–18.

3.1.2 The karma of Dharma. *Mahabharata* 1.101.1–27, plus 2 lines after verse 21ab and 2 after 24. For an interesting Freudian analysis of this passage, see R. P. Goldman, 'Karma, guilt, and buried memories: public fantasy and private reality in traditional India', *Journal of the American Oriental Society*, CV, 1985, pp. 413–25.

3.1.3 Yudhishthira approaches heaven with his dog. *Mahabharata* 17.2.1–26, 17.3.1–36. A fine discussion of the character of Yudhishthira appears in R. C. Zaehner's *Concordant Discord*, Oxford,

1970.

3.1.4 Salvation and damnation in the *Bhagavad Gita*. 16.1–24. There are as many translations of the *Gita* as there are scholars who think they understand the essence of Hinduism – and believe that they see that essence in the *Gita*. F. Edgerton's translation, 2 vols., Harvard, 1952, remains the most lucid; and R. C. Zaehner's translation, Oxford, 1966, has the best scholarly apparatus.

3.2 *Ramayana* of Valmiki. I have used the critical edition, 7 vols., Baroda, 1960–75, re-inserting several verses that they have cast out. There is a quite serviceable translation of the *Ramayana* by H. Shastri, 3 vols., London, 1962. A new translation, under the editorship of R. P. Goldman, is now being published by Princeton University Press; two volumes have already appeared. For analyses of the *Ramayana*, see H. Jacobi, *Das Ramayana*, Bonn, 1893, and C. V. Vaidya, *The Riddle of the Ramayana*, Bombay and London, 1906.

3.2.1 The birth of Sita and the bending of the bow. *Ramayana* 1.65.1–27, including 5 lines inserted after verse 13ab, and using for lines 11–27 the alternative lines rejected by the critical edition; and 1.66.1–27. See C. Dimmitt, 'Sita: fertility goddess and shakti', in *The Divine Consort*, edited by J. S. Hawley and D. M. Wulff, Berkeley, 1982, pp. 210–23.

3.2.2 The song of Kusha and Lava. *Ramayana* 7.84.1–16; 7.85.1–23; 7.86.1–2a; appendix 1, no. 13, 56 lines, after 7.88; and 7.89.1–15. For the intermediate passage, the disappearance of Sita, see my *Hindu Myths*, pp. 197–204.

4 PURANAS

The classic studies of the Puranas are R. C. Hazra's *Studies in the Puranic Records on Hindu Rites and Customs*, Dacca, 1948, and *Studies in the Upapuranas*, 2 vols., Calcutta, 1958 and 1963; W. Kirfel's *Die Kosmographie der Inder*, Bonn and Leipzig, 1920, and

Purana Panchalakshana, Leiden, 1937; and A. D. Pusalker's *Studies in the Epics and Puranas*, Bombay, 1955. See also T. B. Coburn, 'The study of the Puranas and the study of religion', *Religious Studies*, XVI, 1980, pp. 341–52. The All-India Kashiraj Trust in Benares has begun to publish a series of critical editions and English translations of the Puranas and a journal, *Purana*. Another ongoing series of English translations, entitled *Ancient Indian Tradition and Mythology (AITM)*, is published in Delhi.

4.1.1 How Brahma created the universe. *Brahmanda Purana*, Delhi, 1973, 1.2.8.1–61. English translation in *AITM*. For other Puranic creation myths, see my *Hindu Myths*, pp. 43–55. Parallel texts include *Shatapatha Brahmana* 6.1.1.1–15; 6.1.2.1–13; 11.1.6.1–11; *Mahabharata* 1.60; 12.160; *Bhagavata Purana* 2.5–6; 3.12; 3.20; *Brahma Purana* 2; *Brahmavaivarta Purana* 1.5.8; *Brihaddharma Purana* 3.12.1–50; *Garuda Purana* 4; *Kurma Purana* 1.8; *Linga Purana* 1.41; *Markandeya Purana* 50–51; *Padma Purana* 5.3; 5.6; 6.620; *Vayu Purana* 2.16; *Vishnu Purana* 1.5.

4.1.2 The four Ages. *Linga Purana*, Calcutta, 1812, 1.39.5–34, 48–70; 1.40.1–3, 66cd–76. English translation *AITM*. For discussions of this and parallel texts, see my *The Origins of Evil*, pp. 14–45, and *Hindu Myths*, pp. 235–7. For the Kali Age, see F. E. Pargiter, *The Purana Text of the Dynasties of the Kali Age*, Oxford, 1913, second ed., Varanasi, 1962, and D. Pocock, 'The anthropology of time-reckoning', *Contributions to Indian Sociology*, VII, 1964, pp. 18–29.

4.1.3 How Rudra destroys the universe. *Vishnu Purana*, with the commentary of Shridhara, Calcutta, 1972, 6.3.11–40, 6.4.1–7. Translated by H. H. Wilson, London, 1840, Calcutta, 1961. For parallel texts see my *Hindu Myths*, pp. 125–41.

4.2.1 The fruits of hearing a Purana. *Shiva Purana*, Benares, 1964, 1.2.15–40. For a discussion of this and parallel texts, see *The Origins of Evil*, pp. 232–43.

4.2.2. The *Mahabharata* expiated. *Kurma Purana*, Varanasi, 1972, 1.34.5–18. Translated by A. S. Gupta, Varanasi, 1972.

4.2.3 Karma transferred in hell. *Markandeya Purana*, Bombay, 1890, 14.1–7, 15.47–80. Translated by F. E. Pargiter, Calcutta, 1888–1904; reprinted Delhi, 1969. For a discussion of this text, and of its relationship with the story of Yudhishthira in hell (*Mahabharata* 18.2, which follows the story of the dog in heaven, section 3.1.3 above), see my 'Karma and rebirth in the Vedas and the Puranas', in my (ed.) *Karma and Rebirth* (above, 2.3.2.3).

4.2.4 Ethics: how to stay out of trouble. *Garuda Purana*, Benares, 1969, 114.1–75, 115.39–83. Translated by M. N. Dutt, Calcutta, 1908; Delhi, 1968.

4.3.1 An animal sacrifice. *Agni Purana*, Poona, 1957, 27.17–28. Translated by M. N. Dutt, Calcutta, 1901; reprinted Varanasi, 1967. Cf. J. Schwab, *Das altindische Thieropfer*, Erlangen, 1886.

4.3.2 The origin of the lingam. *Brahmanda Purana*, Delhi, 1973 1.2.26.10–61. Translated in *AITM* series. For a discussion of this myth and the following myth, see my *Shiva: the Erotic Ascetic*, *passim*, and my *Hindu Myths*, pp. 137–54.

4.3.3 The origin of the shrine of the lingam. *Vamana Purana, Saromahatmya*, Varanasi, 1968 23.1–36, 24.1–31. Translated by A. S. Gupta, Varanasi, 1968. In addition to the sources cited for 4.3.2 above, see also the discussion of the themes of the overcrowding of heaven and the corruption of the Pine Forest sages in my *The Origins of Evil*, pp. 248–60 and 291–320.

5 SHASTRAS

5.1 The body. The two basic Sanskrit texts on medicine are the *Carakasamhita*, 2 vols., Delhi, 1963 and the *Sushrutasamhita*, Delhi, 1968. The standard Western study of Indian medicine remains *La doctrine classique de la medecine indienne*, Paris, 1949, of J. Filliozat, whose work is now being carried on and advanced by his student, Francis Zimmerman. See also G. U. Thite, *Medicine: Its Magico-Religious Aspects according to the Vedic and Later Literature*, Poona, 1982.

5.1.1 Second opinions. *Carakasamhita*, 2 vols., Delhi, 1963, 1.1.15.3–34. See M. Weiss, 'Caraka Samhita on the doctrine of karma', in my (ed.) *Karma and Rebirth*, pp. 90–115.

5.1.2 The humours of the mind and body. *Carakasamhita* 1.1.1.54–62a.

5.1.3 How not to get sick. *Carakasamhita* 1.1.8.17b–24a.

5.2.1 Embryology. *Markandeya Purana* 10.1–7, 11.1–21. For a discussion of the mechanics of conception, see my *Women, Androgynes, and Other Mythical Beasts*, pp. 17–65, and my (ed.) *Karma and Rebirth, passim*.

5.2.2 A strange birth. *The Svarga Khanda of the Padma Purana*, edited by A. C. Shastri, Varanasi, 1972, 16.6–24. See my 'Karma and rebirth in the Vedas and Puranas', in my *Karma and Rebirth*, pp. 3–10.

5.2.3 The perils of growing up. *Vishnu Purana* 6.5.9–35. This is a set-piece that occurs in almost all of the Puranas, though each tells it differently.

5.3 Marriage. The rules for marriage are laid down in the Dharma Shastras. The great source of information on all Dharma Shastra topics is P. V. Kane's *History of Dharmasastra*, 5 vols., second ed., Poona, 1968–75. See also R. Lingat, *The Classical Law of India*, translated by J. D. M. Derrett, Berkeley, 1973; G. Jha, *Hindu Law in its Sources*, Allahabad, 1930–1; J. Jolly, *Recht und Sitte*, Strasburg, 1896; translated as *Hindu Law and Custom*, Calcutta, 1928. For the mythology of marriage, see J. J. Meyer, *Sexual Life in Ancient India*, New York, 1930.

5.3.1 Women to marry. *Manusmriti*, with the commentary of Kulluka Bhatta (Varanasi, 1970) 3.4–34, 45–50. There are many translations of Manu available, none of them satisfactory. The best are G. Buehler, *The Laws of Manu*, Sacred Books of the East XXV, Oxford, 1886, reprinted New York, 1969; Sir William Jones, *Manava Dharma Sastra, or the Ordinances of Manu*, Calcutta, 1974; A. C. Burnell and E. W. Hopkins, *The Ordinances of Manu*, London, 1884, reprinted 1971; G. Jha, *Manusmrti*, 5 vols., with a translation of the commentary of Medhatithi, Calcutta, 1920–9. See also L. Dumont, *Homo Hierarchicus: the Caste System and its Implications*, Chicago, 1980.

5.3.2 Women not to sleep with. *Kamasutra* of Vatsyayana, Bombay, 1856, 1.5.29. There are many Sanskrit erotic textbooks (the *Anangaranga*, the *Ratirahasya*, the *Kokashastra*, and so forth), but the *Kamasutra*, from about the third century A.D., is the oldest and by far the best known. In the nineteenth century, Sir Richard Burton (the explorer, who also translated the *Arabian Nights*) produced what has remained the definitive translation, often reprinted. Unfortunately, he does not translate the commentaries, which go into subtle and charming detail. Among the more reputable studies of the Hindu Kama Shastra tradition are R. Schmidt, *Beitrage zur indischen Erotik*, Berlin, 1911, and *Liebe und Ehe im alten Indien*, Berlin, 1904; H. C. Chakladar, *Studies in Vatsyayana's Kamasutra: Social Life in Ancient India*, Calcutta, 1929; S. K. De, *Ancient Indian Erotics and Erotic Literature*, Calcutta, 1959; N. N. Bhattacharyya, *History of Indian Erotic Literature*, New Delhi, 1975; and I. Fiser, *Indian Erotics of the Oldest Period*, Praha, 1966.

5.3.3 Married women to sleep with. *Kamasutra* 1.5.1–21.

5.3.4 Married women who will sleep with you. *Kamasutra* 5.1.52–54.

5.3.5 Married women who will not sleep with you. *Kamasutra* 5.1.8, 17–43.

5.3.6 The karma of marriage. *Markandeya Purana* 66.3–37, 43–69;

67.1–39; 68.1–29; 69.1–41. For an analysis of this myth, see my 'Karma and rebirth'. pp. 7–8.

5.4 Public life: how to test your ministers. *Arthashastra* of Kautilya, edited by R. P. Kangle, with English translation, 3 vols., Bombay, 1969–72, 1.10.1–20. The *Arthashastra* has also been translated by J. J. Meyer, by T. N. Ramaswamy, and by R. Shamasastry. See L. Sternbach's *Bibliography of Kautiliya Arthasastra*, Hoshiarpur, 1973.

5.5.1 How to die and go to hell. *Markandeya Purana* 10.47.87; 12.3–28; 10.88–97; 11.22–32. For discussions of hell, see my 'Karma and rebirth'.

5.5.2 The punishment to fit the crime. *Markandeya Purana* 14.39–96.

5.5.3 How not to go to hell. *Brahmavaivarta Purana*, Poona, 1935, 2.32.1–33.

5.5.4 How to perform a funeral sacrifice. *Hiranyakeshin Grihya Sutra* (in *Hiranyakesa Srauta Sutra and Grihya Sutra*, edited by K. Agase and S. Marulakara, 10 vols., Poona, 1907–32) 20.4.1–26 (2.4.10.1–7, 2.4.11.1–5, 2.4.12.1–11, 2.4.13.1–5). For discussions of the *shraddha* and of ancient Indian funerary practices in general, see W. Caland, *Altindischer Ahnenkult: das Sraddha nach den verschiedene Schuler: mit benutzend handschriftliche quellen dargestellt*, Leiden, 1893; *Die Altindischen Todten- und Bestattungs-gebräuche*, Amsterdam, 1896; reprinted Wiesbaden, 1967; P. Hacker, 'Sraddha', *Wiener Zeitschrift fur die Kunde Sud— und Ostasiens,*, VII, 1963, pp. 151–89; C. G. Kashikar, 'The Pitrmedhasutra of Bharadhvaja vis-à-vis Apastamba and Satyasadha Hiranyakeshin', *Journal of Oriental Research* (Madras), XXVIII, 1958–9, pp. 1–10; D. R. Shastri, *Origin and Development of the Rituals of Ancestor Worship in India*, Calcutta, 1963; M. Winternitz, 'Notes on sraddhas and ancestral worship among the Indo-European nations', *Wiener Zeitschrift fur die Kunde des Morgenlandes*, IV 1890, pp. 199–212.

5.5.5 Who not to invite to the funeral. *Manusmriti* 3.122, 3.149–70.

5.5.6 How to perform a Tantric funeral. *Mahanirvana Tantra*, Calcutta, 1884, 10.67–83.

6 TANTRAS

The most reliable, and perhaps inevitably the least interesting, study of the Hindu Tantras is *Hindu Tantrism*, by S. Gupta, D. J. Hoens, and T. Goudriaan, Leiden, 1979, in the series edited by J. Gonda for E. J. Brill. Sir John Woodroffe published a number of Tantric texts in Sanskrit, many with his own translations, under the pseudonym of Arthur Avalon. These include, among the texts he edited and translated (some in the series Tantrik Texts), the *Anandalahari* Madras, 1961, *Kamakalavilasa*, Madras, 1953, and *Mahanirvanatantra*, Calcutta, London, 1913; also under this name are his essays such as *Principles of Tantra*, Madras, 1914, and *The Serpent Power*, Madras, 1938. Under his own name, he published *Shakti and Shakta*, Madras, 1929.

Other good studies of Tantrism are P. C. Bagchi, *Studies in the Tantras*, Calcutta, 1939; S. Beyer, *The Cult of Tara*, Berkeley, 1973; A. Bharati, *The Tantric Tradition*, London, 1965; K. W. Bolle, *The Persistence of Religion*, Leiden, 1965; G. W. Briggs, *Gorakhnath and the Kanphata Yogis*, Calcutta, 1938; D. Desai, *Erotic Sculpture of India*, New Delhi, 1975; C. G. Diehl, *Instrument and Purpose*, Lund, 1956; E. C. Dimock, *The Place of the Hidden Moon*, Chicago, 1966; M. Eliade, *Yoga: Immortality and Freedom*, New York, 1958; P. H. Pott, *Yoga and Yantra*, Leiden, 1946; P. Rawson, *The Art of Tantra*, London, 1973; D. C. Sircar, *The Sakta Pithas*, Calcutta, 1948; 1973.

6.1.1 The five elements of Tantric ritual. *Mahanirvana Tantra*, Calcutta, 1884, 6.1–20.

6.1.2 A Tantric animal sacrifice.

Mahanirvana Tantra 11.104–43.

    6.1.3 Tantric sins of excess. *Mahanirvana Tantra* 11.104–43.

    6.2.1 Tantric caste law. *Mahanirvana Tantra* 14.180–89.

    6.2.2 Tantric Release. *Mahanirvana Tantra* 14.117–21. Cf. my *Women, Androgynes*, pp. 33–64, 97–130, and 259–82.

7 THE HINDI TRADITION

1. See C. Vaudeville, *Kabir*, I, Oxford, 1974, pp. 36–9.
2. Both the textual recensions of and the scholarship on Kabir are extensive. P. Tivari (ed.), *Kabir Granthavali*, Prayag, 1961, gives weight to collections that highlight the devotional side of Kabir. The couplets from Tivari's edition are given a carefully annotated scholarly translation by Vaudeville, who also provides a valuable introduction (*Kabir*, I). A polished literary translation based on a more yogic tradition of Kabir's verse is given by L. Hess and S. Singh, *The Bijak of Kabir*, San Francisco, 1983.
3. The references to Kabir's couplets cite the chapter and verse of Tivari's collection of couplets; the references to Kabir's longer poems cite the numbers given by Tivari to his collection of lyrics.
4. The sacred shrine in Mecca venerated by Muslim pilgrims.
5. A jurist versed in Islamic law.
6. An epithet of Lord Vishnu.
7. 'The Merciful', an epithet of Allah.
8. The Persian term for the spiritual master of Sufi tradition.
9. The word translated as 'gone bad'(*bigarna*) is one that suggests a transformation for the worse – like the souring of milk. The term here is used ironically for spiritual transformation – which from the limited perspective of the grasping self may well appear as a negative change.
10. The 'true guru', a word that for most

sants does not seem to differ radically in meaning from the simpler term 'guru'.

11. The 'bumble-bee' (*bhrangi*) and 'bug' (*kit*) are common metaphors for the guru and disciple among *sants*. The bumble-bee in this sense becomes a fantastic insect who manages to turn the bug into a creature like himself.
12. Elegant translations together with a literary analysis of the image of the divine child are given by K. E. Bryant, *Poems to the Child God: Structures and Strategies in the Poetry of Sur Das*, Berkeley and Los Angeles, 1978. Fine translations also enliven J. Hawley's substantial religio-historical study of *Krishna, the Butter Thief*, Princeton, 1983.
13. A reference to Vishnu's incarnation as Vamana the dwarf: when granted as much land as he could cover in three steps, Vamana took on cosmic dimensions and in three steps traversed the earth, sky, and heavens.
14. The references to Sur's songs follow the numbering given in *Sursagar*, ed. Jagannathdas 'Ratnakar' and others, Varanasi, 1971.
15. Kanha is a Hindi variant of 'Krishna'.
16. As an epithet of Lord Vishnu, Hari is also a name for Krishna, Vishnu's incarnation.
17. 'The dark one' – a common epithet of Krishna.
18. Krishna's friend Uddhava in these songs is called a black bee (*bhramar*): like a bee he is noisy, annoying, and erratic. In this he contrasts to Krishna the honey-bee, who takes the sweetness from all the flowers of the milkmaids without getting caught by any of them (see Hawley, p. 246). Cf. Kabir's reference to the bee-mind (1, 9:17)
19. *Kanphat* ('split-eared') yogis wear heavy rings through holes pierced through the cartilage of their ears.
20. Translated from *Sri Ramcharitmanas*, Gorakhpur, Uttar Pradesh, 1965, pp. 64–8.
21. Shambhu is an epithet of Shiva.
22. Agastya, born when Mitra and Varuna

– aroused at the sight of Urvashi –
spilled their seed, which fell in a
water-jar and germinated there. For
details see J. Dowson, *A Classical
Dictionary of Hindu Mythology*,
reprinted New Delhi, 1937, pp. 4–6,
339.

23. The *nigamas* here refer to the Vedas,
in contrast to the *agamas* – later texts
incorporating tantric elements and
oriented towards one of the great
Hindu deities, usually Shiva.

24. There is no way to date Paltu from his
corpus alone, but he probably
flourished in the mid-eighteenth
century: one of his disciples records the
date of his own initiation as 1769, by
which time Paltu had probably reached
spiritual maturity and middle age.

25. The texts of Paltu's songs are taken
from *Paltu Sahib ki Bani*, 3 vols.,
Allahabad, 1965–8.

26. *Nam* in this verse and *surat* and *shabda*
in the next are technical terms of yoga.

27. The song makes an extended analogy
between the merchant's shop and the
yogi's body. *Trikuti* and the tenth door
are usually identified as centres in the
head; *ida, pingala*, and *sushumna* are
standard terms for the main channels of
yogic energy in the body.

28. An epithet of Shiva.

29. A reference to the state of conscious
awareness (*turiya*) that transcends the
three states of wakefulness, dreaming,
and dreamless sleep.

30. *Bhaktisagar* (*The Sea of Devotion*),
Lucknow, 1966, is the collected works
of Charandas.

8 THE BENGALI TRADITION

1. This story is taken from the
Manasa-mangala of Ketakadasa
Kshemananda, edited by Shri
Yatindramohan Bhattacharya,
Calcutta, 1943, pp. 403–10.

2. This is a signature line (*bhanita*), which
serves to identify the poet as well as to
reveal the poet's degree of participation
in the world that the poem describes.

3. I translate from the
Chaitanya-charitamrita of Krishnadasa
Kaviraja, with commentary by
Sacchidananda Bhaktivinod Thakur
and Barshobhanabidayita Dasa,
Calcutta, 1958.

4. *Rasa* is a technical term borrowed from
the Indian aesthetic tradition. It refers
to an artistic sentiment, but can
perhaps best be understood here as a
basis of enjoyment. See the following
section for more on the religious
meaning and use of *rasa*.

5. The legendary author of the *Natya
Shastra*, an early treatise on dharma
which is the first that systematically
presents the *rasa* theory.

6. Vraja is the mythical environment in
which Krishna enacted his love affair
with Radha. It is identified by modern
Hindus with a region that lies about
eighty miles south of Delhi.

7. A Sanskrit play written by the famous
theologian and teacher of Krishnadasa
Kaviraja, Rupa Gosvamin.

8. Krishna's three unsatisfied desires are:
(1) the desire to reverse the
subject-object relationship and
experience the emotional position of
Radha, (2) the desire to assume Radha's
identity and thereby taste his own
sweetness, and (3) the desire to
experience the intensity of Radha's
supreme love.

9. Shri Advaita was an exemplary devotee
and elderly leader in the Vaishnava
movement associated with Chaitanya.

10. Shachi was Chaitanya's mother; she
lived in the town of Navadvipa.

11. Ramanada Raya is here vaguely aware
of the two forms of Radha (the one with
trembling lotus eyes) and Krishna (the
one holding the flute) within the body
of Chaitanya. Krishna is the dark blue
cowherd and Radha is the radiantly
golden one.

12. *Bhagavata Purana*, verses 11.2.45 and
10.35.9.

13. The proper names in this verse all
refer to *gopis*, or milkmaids of Vraja in
love with Krishna.

14. Hari and Chaitanya are grammatically equated in this verse, an identity supported by Gaudiya Vaishnava theology.
15. The mythological image invoked here is that of Vishnu as Nayayana resting with his eternal body on the cosmic ocean. Rupa prays that his work may be such a comfortable bed for the Lord to rest on. Punning on the word Sanatana ('eternal'), Rupa also pays respect to his guru Sanatana Gosvamin.
16. In this verse Rupa establishes *bhakti* as a goal superior to *mukti*, the Advaitin goal which I translate as 'liberation'. Following traditional Vaishnava theologians (e.g. Ramanuja), Rupa makes liberation a penultimate goal, merely a step to be accomplished on the way to *bhakti*.
17. The Mimamsakas are pictured as dry ritualists in Rupa's works.
18. This 'ocean' is divided up into four major sections, the four directions, and each section is further divided into several chapters, or 'waves'.
19. The foundational emotions form the basis of *rasa*, referred to here as supreme love, *prema*.
20. The Sanskrit term Rupa uses to define *bhakti* is *anushilana*, which I have translated as 'devoted service'. Jiva Gosvamin's commentary indicates that this term denotes both internal emotions (*bhava*) and external actions (*ceshta*). Intellectual knowledge (*jnana*) and sacrificial action (*karma*), the two other ways (*marga*) recognised by the Hindu tradition, are here made subordinate to *bhakti*.
21. The *Narada Pancaratra* is an old Vaishnava Samhita text.
22. *Bhagavata Purana* 3.29.12–14.
23. 'Supreme Purity' is a translation of *vishuddha sattva*, a technical term denoting that which is beyond the influence of the three elements (*gunas*) which make up the world of illusion.
24. *Bhagavata Purana*, 11.14.19.
25. *Bhagavata Purana* 3.33.6.
26. *Bhagavata Purana* 6.2.17.

27. That is, the first practices listed can purify one of sins committed in this life, but not the deep *vasanas*, the karmic dispositions which accompany the soul in its round of births.
28. *Bhagavata Purana* 4.22.39.
29. *Bhagavata Purana* 5.18.12.
30. *Brahman*, ultimate reality, is the impersonal Absolute, the goal of the Advaitin tradition; and Ishvara is the personal Lord, the goal of *bhakti*.
31. The four goals are personal pleasure (*kama*), wealth (*artha*), duty (*dharma*), and liberation (*moksha*).
32. *Bhagavata Purana* 5.6.18
33. The *Bhavarthadipika* is Shridara Svamin's commentary on the *Bhagavata Purana*. Here again *moksha* is devalued in the face of *bhakti*.
34. *Bhagavata Purana* 11.14.20.
35. *Bhagavata Purana* 7.10.48.
36. That is, 'the destruction of suffering' and 'the bestowal of auspiciousness' are distinguishing characteristics of Sadhana Bhakti; 'the easy accomplishment of liberation' and 'the difficulty of obtainment' are distinguishing characteristics of Bhava Bhakti; and 'the special concentrated joy' and 'the attraction of Shri Krishna' are distinguishing characteristics of Prema Bhakti. Since these are arranged hierarchically, Bhava Bhakti includes the first four, and Prema Bhakti includes all six characteristics.
37. Rupa is here saying that something as important as religion should not be based on something as wavering as argumentative reasoning.
38. From the Sanskrit text in S. K. De, *The Early History of the Vaishnava Faith and Movement in Bengal*, second ed., Calcutta, 1960, pp. 673–5. I have tried only to preserve the meaning of these verses; to appreciate the beauty of Rupa's poetry, one must read the Sanskrit.
39. The path of passion refers to a religious practice called *raganuga sadhana* which aims at sharing in Krishna's playful love through

dramatic technique.

9. THE TAMIL TRADITION

1. Bibliography for Tamil sources
F. Gros., *Le Paripatal*, Pondichéry, 1968.
F. Hardy, *Viraha-Bhakti: the Early History of Krsna Devotion in South India*, Delhi, 1983.
G. L. Hart, III, *The Poems of Ancient Tamil, their Milieu and their Sanskrit Counterparts*, Berkeley, 1975.
G. L. Hart, III, *Poets of the Tamil Anthologies*, Princeton, 1979.
K. Kailasapathy. *Tamil Heroic Poetry*, Oxford, 1968.
V. Narayana Rao and H. Heifetz, *For the Lord of the Animals*, Berkeley, 1987.
A. K. Ramanujan, *The Interior Landscape*, London, 1968.
A. K. Ramanujan, *Speaking of Siva*, Penguin Books, 1973.
A. K. Ramnujan, *Hymns for the Drowning: Poems of Nammalvar*, Princeton, 1981.
A. K. Ramanujan, *Poems of Love and War*, New York, 1985.
D. Shulman, *Tamil Temple Myths: Sacrifice and Divine Marriage in the South Indian Saiva Tradition*, Princeton, 1985.
D. Shulman, *The King and the Clown in South Indian Myth and Poetry*, (Princetown, 1985).
K. V. Zvelebil, *The Smile of Murugan: on Tamil Literature of South India*, Leiden, 1973.
K. V. Zvelebil, *Tamil Literature*, Wiesbaden, 1974.

2. See especially the exquisite translations of A. K. Ramanujan, *The Interior Landscape*, London, 1970, and *Poems of Love and War*, New York, 1985; also G. L. Hart, III, *Poems of the Tamil Anthologies*, Princeton, 1979.
3. In Tiruccirappalli District.
4. Shiva burned with his smile the three flying cities of the demons.
5. When the gods and demons churned the ocean of milk, a terrible poison emerged from the depths; to save the world, Shiva drank the poison, which remained in his neck, colouring it blue-black (hence his name Nilakantha, 'Black-Neck').
6. The Triple City of the demons: see note 4.
7. Shiva holds in his hand the skull of Brahma, whom he decapitated because of the latter's arrogance.
8. Shiva is called disfigured (*vikrta*) because of the three eyes on his face, but the implications of the epithet extend to his nature and temperament – he is deformed, uncanny, weird.
9. South Arcot District.
10. Parvati-Uma, Shiva's wife, takes up the left half of the god's body.
11. This line is patterned after *Tirukkural* 339: 'Death is like a sleep, and birth is like awakening after sleep'.
12. The *makara* is a mythological aquatic animal; one of Shiva's earrings bears its shape.
13. The vowel *a* inheres in the base-form of characters in the Tamil syllabic script, thus suggesting the god's inherent presence in the world.
14. Ravana, 'crushed' when he lifted up Mount Kailasa with Shiva and Parvati seated upon it.
15. Perhaps because of the association with the *mullai* pasture-lands (see line 2 of this poem).
16. Vishnu, who took the form of a dwarf (Vamana) but then stretched out to the limits of the universe when Bali gave him the space that he could cover in three steps.
17. Brahma, seated on the lotus that emerges from Visnu's navel.
18. Shiva appeared to Brahma and Vishnu in the form of a *lingam*, a pillar of fire without beginning or end; Brahma and Vishnu tried to find its top and bottom, respectively, but failed.
19. Tanjore District.
20. The image is taken from a Tamil proverb: 'Does the ass know the scent of the camphor he carries?'

Interpretations of the line vary; the implication seems to be that the devotee struggles through his life unaware of the divine nature he bears.

21. Hara = Shiva.

22. Tiruvarur, Cuntarar's home shrine, is also home to Shiva in his forms of Tyagaraja Vitivitankar, etc.

23. The five senses.

24. Again the senses.

25. Another proverb, referring to the foolish anticipation that the plantain will bear fruit more than once.

26. Uran = Nampi Aruran, the name Cuntarar uses for himself.

27. Tanjore District, Cuntarar's chosen home.

28. The refrain in this *patikam* is a sardonic reworking of a curse (literally, 'go on living, and go away!'). This ironic congratulation is placed by the hagiographic tradition in the context of Cuntarar's return to Tiruvarur from his adventures with his second wife Cankiliyar, in Tiruvorriyur; he is still blind in one eye, and very angry because of this.

29. The question supposedly arises from his partial blindness – the poet is not sure what he is seeing.

30. Perhaps the middle of the road, as if afraid they might lose him?

31. The central shrine (*mulasthana*) of the Tiruvarur temple.

32. See discussion of this passage in my article, 'The anthropology of the avatar in Kampan's *Iramavataram*', in *Gilgul* (*Festschrift* R. J. Z. Werblowsky), Leiden, 1987, pp. 270–87.

33. Sugriva.

34. Sugriva.

35. Hindu cosmology pictures the world as a vast egg, the *brahmanda*.

36. Sita, in fact, *is* an incarnation of Shri/Lakshmi.

37. Heaven, the earth, and the nether world.

38. Brahma.

39. Shiva, who holds his wife Parvati in his left side.

40. Vishnu.

41. Sugriva's brother Valin has usurped the kingdom and driven Sugriva into hiding in the forest; Rama has already promised to help Sugriva to regain his throne.

42. Sita.

43. Sugriva is the son of Surya, the sun god.

44. Rama is Vishnu, who holds Shri on his breast.

45. Women normally break their bangles and other ornaments only on becoming widowed; Sita has performed this highly inauspicious act while Rama is still alive.

46. The 60,000 sons of Sagara dug the ocean's pit in their search for their father's sacrificial horse, stolen by Indra.

47. Bhagiratha, one of Rama's ancestors, performed penance in order to bring the Ganges down to earth.

48. Mandhatr, an ideal king.

49. Shambara, slain by Dasharatha, Rama's father.

50. Dasharatha had promised his wife Kaikeyi two boons; she chose to have her son Bharata crowned king, and to have Rama exiled for fourteen years to the forest. Rama accepted this decree in order to safeguard his father's honour.

51. Rama.

52. Hanuman, Sugriva's minister.

53. = Shri-Sita.

54. A mythical beast known to attack elephants; here, Sugriva.

55. The group consists of Sugriva, his four ministers and commanders, and Rama and Lakshmana (the two lions).

56. Verses 122, 115, and 156 in M. Viraverpillai (ed.), *Tanippatar rirattu*, Madras, 1940.

57. i.e. Shiva. Kalamekam was supposedly a convert from Shrivaishnavism to Shaivism.

58. The ten avatars of Vishnu.

59. The Butter-eater is Krishna-Vishnu, here located at Kannapuram in the vicinity of the great Shaiva temple of Tiruccenkattankuti. In the Tamil tradition, Shiva and Vishnu are

brothers-in-law; the poet suggests that Vishnu of Kannapuram, mortified by his brother-in-law's eccentric behaviour, has locked up his shrine in shame and taken to eating earth (instead of the usual tasty offerings). The baby Krishna had a preference for eating dirt, and Vishnu 'eats' the world at the end of the aeon by absorbing it back into himself. A story suggests that this verse was composed when the poet arrived at Kannapuram and found the temple locked.

60. Tillai is the old Tamil name for Cidambaram.

61. Arjuna struck Shiva, disguised as a Kirata hunter, with his bow; the hunter-saint Kannappar touched him with his unclean leather sandal; Cakkiyanayanar, originally a Buddhist, threw stones at the *lingam*; the Pantiya king struck Shiva with his staff when the latter came to work at building a dam but persistently misbehaved.

62. *Tiruccenturttalapuranam* of Venrimalaikkavirayar, 16.2–18, 22–31.

63. An impure foreigner – perhaps, in this case, a Muslim.

64. The Sanskrit name for Tiruccentur.

65. The Tiricutantirar temple-priests at this shrine.

66. Six-head, i.e. Skanda-Murukan, the main god of this shrine.

67. Skanda-Murukan.

68. According to the Tamil tradition, Murukan was born from six sparks produced from six heads of his father, Shiva (Shankara).

69. Taraka, said in *Kantapuranam* 2.3.24 to have had an elephant's head.

70. *arral* = Shakti, power as embodied in the goddess.

71. Shiva.

72. Skanda-Shanmukha.

73. The god of death, ruler of the southern quarter.

74. Skanda/Murukan.

75. Yama.

76. Skanda/Murukan.

77. Valliyamman, Murukan's wife, born from a deer impregnated by the glance of a sage.

78. Teyvayanai (=Sanskrit Devasena), daughter of Indra and Murukan's high-caste wife, whose Tamil name connects her to the elephant (*yanai*).

79. A Vedic sage, patron of Tamil and the Tamil country.

80. By slaying their husbands – since the Hindu wife removes her ornaments at her husband's death.

81. Parvati, daughter of Himalaya.

82. Murukan's mount is the peacock.

83. Shiva.

84. Each of the cosmic eras is presided over by a Manu, progenitor of the human race.

85. Murukan.

86. Shiva.

87. *Periya Puranam* 1828–1847.

88. In Tanjore District, on the south bank of the Kaveri.

89. The musical hymns of the *Sama Veda*.

90. The reference is to the sacred burnt ash with which Shiva covers his body, and which is seen in Tamil Shaivism as a protective sign of ultimate reality.

91. The three Vedic fires – Ahavaniya, Garhapatya, Dakshinagni.

92. Shiva swallowed the Halahala poison that emerged from the ocean of milk and threatened to destroy the world.

93. *ullurai*, a crucial term for classical Tamil poetics, which uses it to denote the hidden, suggested meaning of a verse.

94. The river Ganges flows through Shiva's matted hair.

95. Shiva.

96. The ritual texts used in South Indian Shaiva temples.

97. These are the two main categories of temple worship in the South – daily (*nitya*) and occasional (*naimittika*) rites.

98. The Tiruvatirai festival sacred to Shiva, in the Tamil month of Markali (December–January).

99. i.e. Shiva; note the use of the title also applied to Shiva's devotees.

100. Ayavanti is the name of the temple in this same village of Cattamankai.

101. The *pancakshara*, Shiva's *mantra*:

namah sivaya, "homage to Shiva'.

102. The sacred texts.

103. In his campaign against the demons of the Triple City, Shiva took the great mountain Meru as his bow.

104. The Brahmin characteristically thinks to himself in elevated Sanskrit phrases; his concern, of course, is that his wife has polluted the *lingam* with her saliva, one of the most impure substances in the South Indian classification.

105. The touch of a spider is said to cause the body to blister.

106. The story of Nilanakkanar concludes with his meeting with the great poet-saint Tirunanacampantar, at whose wedding Nilanakkanar is said to have officiated (and immediately thereafter to have disappeared into the god).

107. These poems were translated jointly by David Shulman and Velcheru Narayana Rao.

108. *Annamacaryula samkirtanalu*, Tirupati, 1982, no. 7.

109. *Venkatacala vihara satakamu*, in *Srivenkatesvara laghukrtulu*, edited by V. P. Shastri, Tirupati, 1981, verses 2, 6–9.

110 The images of the deities' vehicles (*vahana*), on which the processional images are carried through the streets.

111. An honorific Vaishnava title.

112. Capital of the Muslim Sultanate.

113. Telugu *gullam*, from Arabic *ghulam*, a young man; here, a Muslim warrior.

114. Persian *khuda*, God.

115. The ritual texts of the Tirupati temple.

GLOSSARIAL INDEX